Twayne's Theatrical Arts Series

Warren French
EDITOR

Anthony Mann

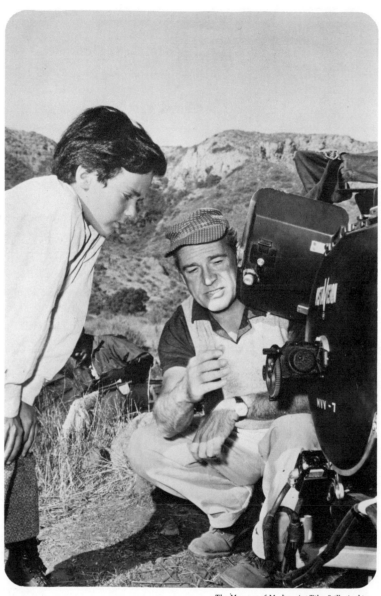

The Museum of Modern Art/Film Stills Archive

Anthony Mann explains the mysteries of the Vista-Vision camera to young
Michael Ray (who plays Betsy Palmer's son) during the location filming of
The Tin Star.

Anthony Mann

JEANINE BASINGER

Wesleyan University

BOSTON

Twayne Publishers

1979

Anthony Mann
is first published in 1979 by Twayne Publishers,
A Division of G. K. Hall & Co.

Copyright © 1979 by G. K. Hall & Co.

Printed on permanent/durable acid-free paper and bound
in the United States of America

First Printing, June 1979

Library of Congress Cataloging in Publication Data

Basinger, Jeanine.
Anthony Mann.

(Twayne's theatrical arts series)
Bibliography: p. 207–208
"Filmography": p. 209–26
Includes index.
1. Mann, Anthony, 1906–1967.
PN1998.A3M321143   791.43'0233'0924   78-27552
ISBN 0-8057-9263-5

Contents

About the Author

JEANINE BASINGER is an Associate Professor at Wesleyan University in Middletown, Connecticut, where she teaches courses on all aspects of American film. Her writings have appeared in many publications, including *American Film*, the *New York Times*, *Bright Lights*, *Film Fan Monthly*, and others. She is the author of three titles in the Pyramid History of the Movies series (*Shirley Temple*, *Gene Kelly*, and *Lana Turner*) as well as various articles in anthologies on film. She dates her interest in film back to her childhood in South Dakota, and her entry into serious film study to the days she spent watching the same films over and over again as an usher in a movie theater. She holds both a bachelor's and a master's degree from South Dakota State University in Brookings, South Dakota.

Editor's Foreword

BEING ABLE to offer readers Jeanine Basinger's *Anthony Mann* is a special satisfaction because one of the particular aims of this series is to honor creative artists who have not previously received adequate consideration. We were pleased to be able to launch this policy with *Abel Gance*, the first book in English about this remarkable pioneer of the "seventh art." We are now happy to provide a comparable tribute to one of our neglected American artists.

Anthony Mann was at the peak of his powers in the 1950s. His succession of distinctive westerns from *Winchester '73* to *Man of the West*, upon which his reputation will principally depend, span the decade. These years from 1950 to 1958 were crucial for a much-shaken Hollywood. The giant studio system that had dominated the industry for three decades was breaking up, imaginative and sometimes desperately ludicrous measures were taken to meet the threat from television, and foreign films on the "art circuit" proved most attractive to serious filmgoers contemptuous of the "boob tube." These years of uncertainty offered, paradoxically, both great advantages and almost overwhelming disadvantages to filmmakers with a personal vision who still saw in the medium the opportunity to carry on the tradition of D. W. Griffith and Orson Welles, despite the crippling reverses these two masters had suffered.

In the power vacuum that existed during this decade when even the persistence of Hollywood as a major filmmaking center was in doubt, a serious, determined artist had an unprecedented opportunity for experimentation and growth if he kept a low profile and worked within modest budgets. A striking number of our strongest-minded *auteurs* began their careers or did their most vital work at this time—Robert Aldrich, Richard Brooks, Blake Edwards, Sam Fuller, Stanley Kubrick, Nicholas Ray, Douglas Sirk. Many perfected their styles, like Mann, making westerns, which could be produced relatively inexpensively and without constant interference on location in natural settings. When the age of the road-show epics arrived in the 1960s, costs spiraled and moneymen again began to exercise restrictive control over temperamental visionaries that drove many of them out of Hollywood. The 1950s present the golden opportunity for a hard-driving artist committed to his vision to work out its presentation through the commercial cinema.

The great drawback during this period, however, was that hardly anyone elsewhere paid much attention then to what Hollywood was doing. While Mann and others were doing their apprentice work, clarifying their visions, and bringing an unfamiliar bitterness to the American screen in *film noir*, audiences overlooked their work, preferring the more sophisticated irony of British black comedies like *Kind Hearts and Coronets* and *The Lady Killers* and the sentimental neorealism of Italian imports like *Shoeshine* and *The Bicycle Thief*.

While Mann was recording his heroes' journeys through the old American West to self-knowledge and salvation, serious audiences were pondering the frustrated journeys of the doomed protagonists in the films of the two men who internationally dominated the decade—Federico Fellini's *La Strada* and *La Dolce Vita*, and Ingmar Bergman's *Wild Strawberries* and *The Magician*. When Hollywood put its new master filmmakers at the service of opulent historical fantasies like *Fall of the Roman Empire* and a retread *King of Kings*, critics turned to speculating on the inscrutable mysteries of minimalist films like *Last Year at Marienbad* and *L'Avventura*. Anthony Mann languished. His relatively early death in 1967 deprived us, as Jeanine Basinger points out, of one whose clarity of vision and dedication to visual narrative should have made him an illuminating spokesman for the conceptions that have come to be appreciated at last in retrospective reviews of his achievement.

The principal concept that Basinger illuminates in this study in a discussion of the neglected film *Side Street* is what she calls "architectural story line," a narrative form built "layer upon layer of incident upon incident, while still taking strange turns and angles." Mann, we can see from this analysis, was bringing to the cinema something of the powerful structural design that Cézanne imposed upon painting as it moved from the evanescent forms of Impressionism to the rigid structuralism of Cubism. Mann imposed an analogous discipline upon the talky formlessness of early sound days and, striving to communicate through the eye rather than the ear, he stripped away competing elements as Mondrian in painting had stripped away representational clichés to free form of surface distractions.

Basinger catalogues and charts in her analysis of his westerns the basic patterns that Mann arrived at. How he communicates these patterns visually she explains lucidly early in the book in her discussion of *film noir*, especially through her analysis of a key episode from *Border Incident* (1949) that shows how Mann used "a specific kind of composition against a specific background to establish meaning" and then moved figures and camera within that frame to redefine meaning until the possibilities of these redefinitions had been exhaustively explored. Then, appropriately adapting Mann's technique to her own medium, she shows how he manipulated his elements within the specific setting of the old West (with its huge cluster of physical and metaphysical implications) until he had defined and redefined to his own satisfaction the variations on the heroic quest—especially in a series of films starring James Stewart as the evolving hero—culminating in the transmutation of man into myth in a prototype of the old West, the medieval Spain of *El Cid*.

What we present here, it must be noted, is only a part of Basinger's work on Anthony Mann. To concentrate attention on the central importance of his western films, we have omitted detailed analyses of many later films and have moved quickly through the early films that provide evidence of the evolution of his vision and techniques. The full story of Anthony Mann's contribution to Gance's "seventh art" demands a larger canvas than an introductory study can supply. We hope, however, that this book may help arouse the interest that will lead to a demand for this further work at the same time that it contributes to the grand design of the mosaic. We hope this series will constitute a sparkling vignette that will call attention to the significance of what was happening in American film at a time when the attention of contemporary cinephiles had wandered elsewhere.

W. F.

The mathematical possibilities of five times five in *The Naked Spur*. James Stewart, Janet Leigh, and Millard Mitchell beside Leigh's dead horse, with Robert Ryan and Ralph Meeker watching.

Preface

I FIRST BECAME interested in Anthony Mann in 1953 when I watched *The Naked Spur* fifteen times in four days. What was initially an entertaining experience became a sobering experience and ultimately an overwhelming experience. The film's impact grew. On the fifteenth go-around, I was as much a set of exposed raw nerves as Jimmy Stewart himself, and my reactions to events were as shaky and psychotic as his. For the first time in which I was clearly aware of it, I did not identify with the female character in the film (Janet Leigh), but instead allied myself with Stewart. I seemed to have no choice in that matter. Why? Furthermore, the audiences that watched the film with me all reacted to the events in the film as a unified group. Of course, it was not unusual for an audience to laugh together, or cry together, or to scream out loud together, but it *was* peculiar to see them ducking their heads, leaning back in their seats, raising their hands to ward off blows, in a kind of one-two-three viewer's ballet. Why did they do this?

I'm still thinking about it. The attempt to figure it out forms the basis of this book on Mann's work. Primarily an auteurist study, the book assumes that there *is* such a thing as a single conscious film artist, that this person is likely to be the director, and that Anthony Mann is such a director, such an artist. Without attempting to downgrade the importance to Mann's career of his collaborators (in particular, screenwriters John C. Higgins, Borden Chase, Phillip Yordan, and cinematographer John Alton) the book defines Mann's films in terms of recurring thematic and formal characteristics as if Mann were the guiding artistic force.

Since auteurism is the most misunderstood of film-study methods, I wish to point out that I do not assume that Mann's work can be fully evaluated without taking into consideration his col-

laborators. Nor do I assume that study of his films ends here. Auteurism is a method, really, not a theory, based on the conviction
that the America cinema is worth studying in depth, and that mas-
terpieces of film can be found in the commercial cinema. It is a
method with which to discover and decipher authors, and thus
prove that film is a mature art. Once the author is established, his
work can be studied from a variety of critical viewpoints—sociological, political, semiological, or whatever. The contribution of auteurism to the understanding of film is that it has stressed an exami-
nation of form (or style) in conjunction with content. Indeed, it
suggests that the defining characteristics of a director's work may be
those which are not most readily apparent to the average viewer
who is steeped in the literary tradition and not trained in film. The
point is not that Mann is a better director than Lloyd Bacon (although he is), but that his work is cinematic and that studying it
helps us understand more about film. I do not quarrel with the idea
of studying film by other methods or theories (although I admit
some of those methods are boring to me personally), but I do quarrel with trying to apply those methods without first understanding
film as film. Looking at a finished film without taking into consideration its nonliterary elements—the "language" of film—is potentially
a wasted effort.

In her book on Barbara Stanwyck's career, Ella Smith says she
thinks authors of film books ought to bare their viewing credentials
to the reader. I agree, and therefore I want to say that not only have
I seen every film directed (or even worked on) by Anthony Mann,
but that I have taught his films for a period of years. To write this
book, I carefully rescreened every film except *Nobody's Darling,
My Best Gal, The Great Flamarion, Two O'Clock Courage, Sing
Your Way Home, Strange Impersonation,* and *Serenade.* All are
minor works which I felt were unimportant enough to be left without further reviewings, and, to be honest, I couldn't stand looking at
any of them again. I hope saying this will convince everyone that not
only am I thorough, but that I am an endearing sort whose errors in
describing action (always a pitfall for film study) can be ascribed to
typesetters' errors!

I regret, however, that space required my cutting copy on Mann's
early films, his incompleted projects, and his minor films, such as
The Glenn Miller Story (one of Mann's best love relationships), *The
Tall Target* (a personal favorite, an exercise in limited space and

controlled time), *Thunder Bay* (in which Mann presents a changing industrial landscape as if it were nature, predating Antonioni's *Red Desert* by several years), *Strategic Air Command* (with its poetic airplanes and use of the entire sky as landscape), and *Serenade* (with Mann vs. Mario Lanza, a Godzilla vs. The Thing situation).

Very little has been written on Anthony Mann in English, but as Spencer Tracy says of Katharine Hepburn in *Pat and Mike:* "There ain't much there, but what there is, is cherce." I want to urge readers to turn in particular to Bob Smith's excellent article on Mann's early period, "Mann in the Dark" (from which I borrowed the title for my own chapter on the *noir* films) and Steve Handzo's detailed analysis of the early westerns, "Through the Devil's Doorway." Both articles appeared in *Bright Lights,* which, I am proud to say, is edited by a former Wesleyan student, Gary Morris. Handzo's description of "Devil's Doorway" covers the film thoroughly, and his analysis of the fight inside the Medicine Bow bar is more detailed than mine. Also, Jim Kitses's structuralist study of Mann's westerns in *Horizons West* is of primary importance, as is the excellent special issue of *Movietone News* devoted to Mann. I am indebted to all these articles, and recommend them to my readers. I hope this book will help to turn people's attention to Mann. I happily await the next books to deal with his work in ways I have not thought of.

Last of all, I want to say that I love the films of Anthony Mann. With the exception of the minor works I named above, I have screened and rescreened his films and have never tired of them. It has been my joy to share them with my students and find that they, too, love them. If this book carried a dedication, it would have to be to the Mann himself, with respect, with gratitude, and with love.

JEANINE BASINGER

* * *

In Memoriam
ANTHONY MANN

Acknowledgments

I WISH TO THANK all those who provided films for reviewing for this book: William K. Everson, Rhonda Bloom, Doug McKinney, Bob Smith, Ron Collier, Kit Parker, Pat Moore, and the University Film Study Center. I also want to thank all the students in my two Wesleyan film classes, Film Noir (Spring 1977) and The Western Film (Spring 1978), who listened and responded to my lectures on Anthony Mann. In particular, I want to thank my teaching assistant, Paul Kaiser, whose thoughts on Anthony Mann—and on film in general—taught me so much.

Thanks, too, to Gary Collins; to Mrs. Peter Arico, who typed my manuscripts; to my kind editor, Warren French; to everyone who provided stills, especially Mary Corliss and Carole Carey at the Museum of Modern Art, and Paula Klaw of Movie Star News; to Wesleyan University for allowing me to teach Mann's films. Also, thanks to everyone who allowed me to quote from their articles, especially Gary Morris. Gary's magazine, *Bright Lights*, has been the champion of Mann's work, and has maintained a standard of excellence throughout its publication. Last of all I thank my daughter, Savannah, and my husband, John. Without John's work in reading and responding, this book would, like one of Mann's epics, have been "years in the making."

J.B.

Chronology

1907   Probable birth date of Anthony Mann, born Anton (or Emil) Bundsmann, in Point Loma (or San Diego), California.

1917   Approximate date of Bundsmann family move to New York City.

1923   Leaves school to seek work in the theater after the death of his father.

1931   Marries first wife, Mildred Kenyon, by whom he has two children, a son and a daughter, Nina and Anthony.

1926–   Sometime during this period, hired as Production Manager
1933   by the Theater Guild, where he would work with David Belasco, Rouben Mamoulian, Chester Erskine.

1933   Directs two productions for the Theater Guild, *The Squall*, in which he plays minor role, and *Thunder on the Left*, by John Ferguson Black, adapted from Christopher Morley's novel.

1936   Directs *Cherokee Night*, produced at the Federal Theater in Harlem by the Acting Theatre Technical Unit and *So Proudly We Hail*, by Joseph M. Viertal, at the 46th St. Theater.

1938   Directs *The Big Blow*, produced by the WPA Federal Theatre. Also directs *New Faces* and *Swing Your Lady*.

Late   Hired by David O. Selznick to come to Hollywood as a talent
1938,   scout. Works for Selznick as scout, and also as casting direc-
early   tor. Directs screen tests for numerous films, including *Gone*
1939   *With the Wind*, *Intermezzo*, and *Rebecca*.

1939   Leaves Selznick to go to Paramount as an Assistant Director. Works with prestige directors, notably Preston Sturges.

1942   Directs first two films, *Dr. Broadway* and *Moonlight in Havana*, the first for Paramount B unit and the latter for Universal-International.

1943   Goes to work for Republic Pictures. *Nobody's Darling.*
1944   *My Best Gal* and *Strangers in the Night.*
1945   *The Great Flamarion.* Moves to RKO-Radio for *Two O'Clock Courage* and *Sing Your Way Home.*
1946   *Strange Impersonation* (Republic) and *The Bamboo Blonde* (RKO).
1947   First critical and commercial success: *Desperate* (RKO). Moves to Producers Releasing Corporation to make *Railroaded.* When PRC unites with England's J. Arthur Rank Organization to form Eagle-Lion, directs *T-Men,* first film to gain widespread attention.
1948   Directs *Raw Deal* for Eagle-Lion, and takes over direction of *He Walked by Night* from Alfred Werker, whose name remains on finished film.
1949   Directs final film for Eagle-Lion, *Reign of Terror.* Writes script for *Follow Me Quietly* in collaboration with Francis Rosewalk. Signs contract with Metro-Goldwyn-Mayer. *Border Incident* and *Side Street.*
1950   Directs first western, *Devil's Doorway,* for MGM, which brings him to attention of James Stewart. Takes over direction of *Winchester '73* with Stewart from Fritz Lang at Universal-International, film to become his first A budget critical and commercial success. *The Furies* (Paramount).
1951   *The Tall Target* (MGM). Assigned to *Quo Vadis* and works twenty-four nights (uncredited) filming the burning-of-Rome sequences.
1952   *Bend of the River* (Universal-International).
1953   *Thunder Bay* (U-I), *The Naked Spur* (MGM).
1954   *The Glenn Miller Story* (U-I).
1955   *The Far Country* (U-I); *Strategic Air Command* (Paramount); and *The Man from Laramie* (Columbia).
1956   Divorces his first wife, Mildred Kenyon. *The Last Frontier* (Columbia) and *Serenade* (Warner Brothers).
1957   Marries Sarita Montiel, star of *Serenade. Men in War* (Security Pictures), and *The Tin Star* (Paramount). Prepares to direct *Night Passage,* but withdraws at the last minute.
1958   *God's Little Acre* (Security-UA) and *Man of the West* (United Artists release).
1960   Begins work on *Spartacus,* but withdraws after quarreling with Kirk Douglas. Directs *Cimarron.* Quits in the middle of

shooting because of conflict with producer Edmund Grainger, though released film retains his name.

1961 *El Cid*.

1963 Marriage to Sarita Montiel is annulled.

1964 *Fall of the Roman Empire*. Marries a Russian-born ballerina of the Sadlers Wells ballet who bears him one son, Nicholas.

1965 *The Heroes of Telemark*.

1967 Begins work on *A Dandy in Aspic*. While on location in Germany, suffers fatal heart attack. Dies April 29.

1968 Release of *A Dandy in Aspic*, bearing Mann's name but completed by actor Laurence Harvey.

1

The Career of Anthony Mann

The Man

IN 1968, Andrew Sarris rang up the curtain on a rediscovery of Hollywood films with the publication of his influential book *The American Cinema: Directors and Directions 1929–1968*. Under the category "The Far Side of Paradise," Sarris included Anthony Mann. Cautioning the reader not to confuse Anthony with "dreary Daniel and Delbert," Sarris defined Mann as someone who "directed action movies with a kind of tough-guy authority that never found favor among the more cultivated critics of the medium." Mann, said Sarris, had been overlooked by the Americans until it was "too late for his career to find a firmer footing than obscure cult interest."[1]

Sarris correctly pointed out that this was true not only for Anthony Mann, but for a startling number of talented directors: Douglas Sirk, Nicholas Ray, Samuel Fuller, and Otto Preminger, among others. The publication of Sarris's book, however, altered the situation for the majority. As the curtain went up, they trotted on stage to bask in a well-deserved limelight that was, although small and scholarly and recipient of not a little scorn from many sources, nevertheless a limelight, warm and comforting after years of neglect.

For Anthony Mann, however, it was another story. Just as the curtain went up, he collapsed and died in the wings. At the relatively young age of sixty, Mann suffered a fatal heart attack while completing location work for his final film, *A Dandy in Aspic*. Articulate and intelligent on the subject of his own work, Mann might have been a major figure of the auteur focus Sarris inspired, but he did not live to participate in the great reevaluation. His untimely

The overwhelming visual beauty of Fall of the Roman Empire. *The funeral-in-the-snow, with Stephen Boyd and Sophia Loren.*

19

death made him of secondary interest as critics and scholars rushed
to interview and praise those who could explain in person their
motives and work habits. Although respected by serious film scholars everywhere, Anthony Mann's name was mostly that—a name
that remained on auteurists' Best American Directors list while attention was turned to Sirk, Preminger, Ray, and Fuller.

By 1978, it looked as if it would always be "too late for his career
to find a firmer footing than obscure cult interest." For almost a
decade Anthony Mann had remained mostly a name. There had
been no complete retrospectives at major museums, no campus film
festivals celebrating his style, and no specials on public television to
celebrate his accomplishment. And if the films were relatively
obscure, the man himself was virtually unknown. Except for minor
interviews in foreign film magazines, Mann had left no oral history.
Whereas film students could readily identify Walsh's eye patch,
Ford's baseball cap, and Hawks's Red River D belt, no one even
knew what Mann looked like. It was too late for an honorary Oscar
or life achievement award, too late for the talk shows, the best-sell-
ing autobiography, or the "told to" biography. In fact, where Anthony Mann was concerned, it was practically too late to accumulate
a biography.

Attempts to research Mann's background bear little fruit. What is
known about him is not only shadowy, but largely contradictory. His
real name is known not to have been Anthony Mann, but the original is variously listed as Emil Bundsmann and Anton Bundsman. It
is certain that he was born in California, but whether the birthplace
is Point Loma or San Diego is in doubt. The date of birth is thought
to be approximately 1907, and his parents are thought to have been
two school teachers, Emil and Bertha Bundsmann.

Although the early years are shadowy, it is clear that the
Bundsmanns encouraged Mann's interest in the theater. When the
family relocated to New York City at the time he was about ten years
old, the young boy was able to attend Broadway plays, the experience of which made him determined to become an actor. After his
father's death, which occurred during his high-school years, Mann
left his formal education behind and sought work in his chosen
profession. He made his Broadway debut as a walk-on, and went on
to become a leading actor in various stock companies. On Broadway,
the name of "Anton Mann" can be found listed in the casts of *The
Dybbuk* (1925) and *The Little Clay Cart* (1926).

Mann did not limit himself to acting. He tried his hand at every role in the theater, including assistant production manager, stage manager, and set designer. His first big break came when he was hired as production manager for the prestigious Theater Guild. It was during his years with the Guild he discovered that his greatest interest was in directing, not acting. He made a minor success as director of such productions as *Thunder on the Left* (1933), *Cherokee Night* (1936), *So Proudly We Hail* (1936), and *The Big Blow* (1938), the latter produced by the WPA Federal Theatre.

Mann's minor Broadway success came to the attention of Hollywood. From that point onward, his professional life is more fully documented. Producer David O. Selznick hired him to come to California to work as a talent scout, work that helped develop his excellent skill at casting. More importantly, it gave him his first taste of directing actors on film, for Selznick assigned him the job of directing new talent in screen tests for various productions, among them *Gone With the Wind*, *Intermezzo*, and *Rebecca*.

In 1939 Mann left Selznick in order to work for Paramount as an assistant director. He worked three years in this capacity, serving many prominent directors, among them Preston Sturges. Finally Mann was asssigned to direct his first film, *Dr. Broadway*, largely through the efforts of his friend MacDonald Carey, who was to star in the low-budget feature for Paramount.

Mann's obituary notices fill in the remainder of the details of his private life. He had been married three times, first to Mildred Kenyon, by whom he had two children, Nina and Anthony. Their twenty-five-year marriage ended in divorce in 1956. The following year, he wed Mexican actress Sarita Montiel, who had starred in his film *Serenade*, based on James M. Cain's novel. Their marriage was annulled in 1963. At the time of his death, Mann was married to a former ballerina, listed in the obituaries as Anna Mann. The couple had one son, Nicholas.

It is a scanty biography, and one which sheds little light on his work. To understand Anthony Mann, it is necessary to look to the films. The best information lies there. In private life, he might easily be confused with "dreary Daniel or Delbert," but in his films— never.

The Films

Anthony Mann came to Hollywood from Broadway. Unlike many who made that transition, he did not think of film as an extension of theater. He wasted no time trying to bend movies into plays. Instead he saw film as an entirely different medium, with special properties of its own. As soon as he was allowed to direct, he set about the task of exploring those properties and playing with them for various kinds of effects and meanings. From the very beginning of his career, he made films that were inherently cinematic.

Mann began by thinking in terms of what *the image said*. He understood that films spoke with pictures as much as, if not more than, with the words of the script. He planned each film as if the story would emerge from the images as clearly as it would from the dialogue. He further understood that films had their own special language, that of editing, camera movement and placement, and composition. The viewer took meaning, consciously or unconsciously, from *all* the elements placed before him in the frame, and from the way they were placed before him. If a filmmaker wanted to control totally the audience's understanding of and response to the film, he would have to consider the meanings of all those elements. If he wanted to speak clearly to a viewer, he would have to organize those elements around a central narrative meaning. Since films were moving pictures, not photographs, this meaning would shift and change.

All understanding of Anthony Mann grows out of this basic fact—in his films, meaning is contained primarily within the frame through composition, and this meaning is in a state of emotional as well as visual flux. He evolved the concept of the total image, one which contained story (content) and presentation of story with the tools of cinema (form) as a unified event.

Mann's career follows a clear progression toward purity and simplification. It is a scholar's dream, easily divided into four main periods of development that will provide the framework for this study: I. Beginnings, 1942–1947; II. Film Noir, 1947–1950; III. Westerns, 1950–1960; IV. Epics, 1960–1965.

Mann spent five years, from 1942 to 1947, learning the fundamentals of his craft in a series of low-budget features for Paramount, RKO, Universal, and Republic. The six films he directed were typical B film projects of two types—musicals and atmospheric thrillers, made with little money, minor stars, and an abbreviated running time of under seventy minutes.[2] Designed to help fill the enormous demand for movies—any kind of movies—from escape-hungry audiences during World War II, they were meant to be made quickly and cheaply.

Mann's experience with well-crafted plays on Broadway alerted him to the fact that the scripts he was assigned were, to put it kindly, lousy. Not only were the characters cardboard, but the storylines were almost abstract in their thin development. The swiftly paced B film counted on an experienced viewing audience to fill in the story gaps for themselves, based on knowledge gleaned from more lavish A productions with similar plots. In addition, Mann was saddled with a small budget and actors who could barely speak lines.

Assessing his chances to turn these liabilities into films good enough to keep him working in the medium, Mann decided it was up to him to create story depth and characterization where none existed. He formed two rules for himself on how to direct a picture: 1) select a clear and simple story; 2) make the story better.

Throughout his career, Mann never wavered from these two ideas. Even after he became a top-name director and could choose his own scripts and actors, he looked for stories that were, in his own words, "simple and pictorial." He always considered himself a storyteller, and he endeavored to present his story to the audience as clearly and directly as possible.

"If you're going to tell a story," Mann said, "instead of telling an intellectual story—which by necessity requires a tremendous number of words—you should pick one that has great pictorial qualities to start with."[3] As often as he could, he avoided making films which contained *overt* moral and political significance. This helped him make his films powerful and direct, but it contributed to his being overlooked as an artist. Although his work contains recurring thematic concerns (some of which are indirectly political and moral, and some of which concern personal morality), his films are genre films which too many critics still do not recognize as capable of depth. Since any film has political and social significance, such interpretations can logically be made for his work. And since many of his characters are caught in moral or psychological dilemmas, viewers can interpret his morality. But his films do not mean to teach us about politics, sociology, or morality. They mean to tell us a story. Mann does not sermonize.

Mann's second idea, after the selection of a simple story, was to make the story better, to deepen what was contained in the scripts he was given. Mann worked on using the tools available to him—lighting, camera angles, composition, editing—to enhance the plot and deepen characterizations.

The first thing he discovered was an obvious fact. It was easier to develop meaning formally in a thriller than in a musical. He could play with shadowy lighting patterns, bizarre camera angles, and sudden camera movements more easily in a film which featured a murder than one which featured a Cuban musical number. After 1947, Mann avoided making musicals as much as he could, since they simply did not suit his style. During these first years, he demonstrated a lack of interest in comedy and a tendency to emphasize the darker side of any story. (This is particularly evident in his first film, *Dr. Broadway*, which was meant to be a comedy-thriller.) He also showed a definite talent for presenting characters with psychiatric problems.

Of the first ten films directed by Mann, the most interesting are *Strangers in the Night, The Great Flamarion,* and *Strange Impersonation,* in addition to his very first full-length feature, *Dr. Broadway.* His musicals are competently directed, but impersonal. They provide no insight into his later work other than that he had mastered his craft.

The four films of interest to the later work show how he improved weak scripts. His visual effects are exactly that, however—effects. Violent swish pans, off-angle compositions, baroque lighting patterns, and unsettling camera movements are used to create scenes of substantial impact. These scenes stand out from the rest of the film partly because they are so visually impressive, but also because they are not fully integrated into the whole. Mann could make lousy scripts better by creating brilliant moments in them, but he couldn't yet make the entire film better. Yet these early works are important, for they show how he was attempting to create specific narrative meaning with form.

At first, the idea of providing depth through form had been a challenge for the intelligent Broadway-ite directing a poor script. By 1947, it had become his choice. Each film Mann directed between 1947 and 1950 shows him playing with technical devices as if they were toys, pushing and stretching his ability to create meaning where none existed. By the end of his period working with *film noir*, this was a clearly established style.

Mann's films between 1947 and 1950 all lie within a body of work known as *film noir*. It was a tradition that stressed the darker side of American life, and thus was perfect for Mann's developing sensibility. It afforded him a wide range of possibilities in using studio work

Film Noir Fascination with Mirrors: (Top) Brenda Marshall and Hillary Brooke in *Strange Impersonation*, (Bottom) John Ireland, reflected in Jane Randolph's mirror, prepares to teach her a lesson in manners in *Railroaded*.

Credit: The Museum of Modern Art/Film Stills Archive

and location shooting. On the one hand, he could photograph realistic locations (lit to look like sound stages) and on the other, sound stages (lit to look as realistic as possible). This chance to work in all types of backgrounds prepared the way for his very specific use of landscape in the western films to come.

By the end of his *film noir* period, Mann had achieved a remarkable technical mastery. His basic unit of expression became composition. Mann forced a viewer to contemplate characters in the space of the frame, and to take from their position and background an understanding of their situation in the narrative. Because the compositions were done with such extreme care, the understanding was not just about the surface level of the story, but also about the internal, psychological state of the character.

Mann was now able to organize all the elements within his frame around a central narrative meaning. He was also able to integrate his scenes of dramatic visual power into the entire film, a marked improvement over the first years.

Between 1947 and 1950, Mann also evolved a set of thematic concerns that would recur in all his work. Where first he stressed violence or psychosis as a means to the end of playing with style, such aberrations became important and useful for their own sake. Mann now not only knew how he wanted to film his stories, but what he wanted his stories to be about. His own personal world on film emerged, the summation of his form and content into the Mann universe.

By 1950, Mann's cinematic world contained a hero who is linked in the narrative to someone else. In *Side Street* and *Desperate* it is a woman he loves. In *T-Men* and *Border Incident*, it is to a fellow government agent. The audience is aligned with the hero, who is established for them as the center of the film. Even though he may be weak, criminal, or psychotic, the audience is set up to identify with him and his situation. The hero's position in the narrative dictates the emotional situation the audience is going to be put through.

The heroes of these films all have something to hide. Either they have committed crimes, are escaping from jail or various captors, or they are in disguise, like the government agents of *T-Men* and *Border Incident*. They are surrounded with crazy, violent characters, and the worlds they inhabit are seedy, brutal, and outside the law. Dialogue is downplayed as a means of explanation for the audience. The stories are simple, dramatic, and certainly pictorial. Whatever

political or moral issues are present are either deemphasized, un-
dermined, or localized in the hero's personal world.

In *film noir*, Mann had found an excellent milieu. By 1950, he was
an accomplished artist, capable of directing a film with pace,
energy, and raw power while making a personal kind of film that
reflected his interest in using style for specific meaning.

In 1950, Mann directed his first western, *Devil's Doorway*. With
his westerns, he found the freedom to simplify and to express in
purely formal terms what most of his predecessors in the genre had
expressed in content. The previously established set of characters
and conventions associated with the genre allowed him the freedom
not to explain in words various kinds of information. Viewers understood and accepted a man who came from nowhere, and a revenge
based upon a conflict never shown.

It is in this decade that Mann's work unifies completely. He finds
a story pattern that fits his needs, and uses all his technical skill to
enhance it. He centered his films around a basic narrative pattern,
involving a recurring set of characters:

THE HERO:	A man with a secret, who by choice or for imposed reasons has (or has had) a conflict with organized society.
THE VILLAIN:	The hero's opposite, but emotionally linked to him through either blood relationship, shared experience, psychological imbalance, or desired goals.
THE OLD MAN:	If a major character, a good or evil patriarch, If a minor character, usually a friend to the hero, or an agent of comic relief.
THE WOMAN OR WOMEN:	Representative of the conscience of the hero, or of his internal state. When two women are used, they often reflect the hero's duality, or his link to the villain, by presenting two opposing sides of his nature.
THE SECONDARY VILLAIN OR VILLAINS:	Used mainly for plot development or nuance.

The hero, the villain, the old man, the women, and the secondary
villains undertake a journey of some sort. It is usually physical,

across space through time, but it is always psychological for the characters (who undergo internal changes) and emotional for both characters *and* audience.

Through the use of this narrative pattern combined with his highly sophisticated mastery of technique, Mann achieved the fusion of three levels of storytelling on film:

1. The literal level (the plot).
2. The psychological level for the hero (which is found in the plot and reflected in the presentation of the landscape of the film). As the hero undergoes an internal change, the landscape he crosses and his relationship to it changes by way of his position in the frame.
3. The emotional level for both hero and audience (which responds to and is dictated by the narrative line, the shifting landscape, and the psychological, internal character development).

In other words, Mann's westerns present a story about a hero who is undergoing a psychological change. The landscape, or background, is aligned with him and used to illustrate his internal change through the device of the journey. This internal change, demonstrated visually by background (and position in frame) and revealed by plot, causes the hero to demonstrate his emotional stress through action. The action, usually culminating in violence, creates an emotional effect on the audience which is like that the hero is undergoing in the narrative. The story, the internal and external life of the hero, and the effect on the audience are all unified.

This remarkable achievement of Mann's is among the greatest in all of film. Because its nature is primarily emotional for the audience, and technical in terms of presentation, it has been totally overlooked by critics and scholars attuned only to intellectual, political, or sociological achievements on film.

With his epic films between 1960 and 1965, Mann stripped away characterization in the conventional sense. Since the people of an epic film (particularly El Cid) are legends, or mythical figures, the need to develop them as ordinary heroes with psychological problems was unnecessary. Their problems were historical, and the personal was sacrificed to the epic. With his final films, Mann almost returned to his original position as a director, in which he enhanced cardboard characters with form. In the final period of his work, his set of recurring thematic concerns (which emerged clearly in the westerns), his basic narrative line, and his formal characteristics underwent no further development. In his final great film, *El Cid*, his simplicity was almost primeval. He removed the last vestiges of literary meaning from his work, and *El Cid* stands as an example of what might be called "pure cinema," yet still functioning within the restrictions of conventional, generic, mass entertainment.

The four periods of Mann's work, Beginnings, *Film Noir*, Westerns, and Epics, account for all his major work except *Men in War* and *God's Little Acre*. These two films are among his best, but do not fit into the categories outlined above. *Men in War* is a Korean war film, and *God's Little Acre* is Mann's only *real* literary adaptation. However, since neither film departs from his explorations of theme and style during the 1950s, they fit easily into the pattern of development described. They vary from the major categories only in their generic traditions.

Films which do not fit into the categories mentioned are all minor works. They are commercial assignments which kept him working and furthered his career. They too reflect his developing style, and any one of them is recognizable as an Anthony Mann film. However, they are minor efforts because they are directed more impersonally than the other films, and, although competently done, it is not through them that Mann's reputation was made or will endure. These films include *The Tall Target* (1951), *Thunder Bay* (1953), *The Glenn Miller Story* (1955), *Strategic Air Command* (1955)—which Mann reportedly did not want to direct but accepted as a favor to his old friend James Stewart—and *Serenade* (1956), with Mario Lanza in a bowdlerization of James M. Cain's novel.

Incompleted Projects

In Hollywood, people worked for a living. It was a day-to-day job for any director, with tempers flaring, projects collapsing, and energies dying. Like anyone else who worked under the studio system, Mann had his share of ups and downs. He was involved in planning projects that were never filmed, or that began shooting and were taken away from him and finished by someone else. Sometimes he inherited projects that had been begun by another man. Mann was a thorough professional, willing to step in—or out—as the case demanded. Compiling an exact list of a director's unsigned films is always difficult, but it is particularly complicated when the subject is dead and cannot be queried.

In 1948, Mann took over direction of *He Walked by Night*, an Eagle-Lion *film noir* starring Richard Basehart and Scott Brady. The name of Alfred Werker, the original director, was retained on the final print, and few people know that Mann directed the majority of the film. In particular, his stamp is on the following sequences which he has identified as his own: all the exteriors involving Richard Basehart; the night battle inside an electric company between Brady and Basehart; the scene in which Basehart extracts a bullet from himself; and the final chase in the flood-control pipes.

For those who wish to argue auteurist theory, *He Walked by Night* makes ready material for discussion. It was written by John C. Higgins, who also collaborated with Mann on *Railroaded, T-Men, Raw Deal,* and *Border Incident.* Furthermore, it was photographed by John Alton, and unmistakably bears his imprint. Without knowing that Mann had anything to do with it, one might ask—who needs a director? Alfred Werker may be a nobody, but Higgins and Alton have done the job. But the difference between a flatly directed scene in which Brady and a wounded cop discuss the case at the wounded man's apartment and the scenes listed above illustrates exactly the importance of a good director.

In 1951, an event of major importance occurred which, had it been fulfilled, might have changed the direction of Mann's career. He was assigned to work on MGM's big-budget production of *Quo Vadis.* He worked twenty-four nights, filming the burning of Rome with the assistant photographer, William V. Skall. Since this is the best-directed sequence in the entire film, it is interesting to speculate what might have happened to Mann's career had he been allowed to direct the entire film (a blockbuster hit). Would he have turned to directing big-budget epics sooner, and thus have never made his westerns?

In 1957, Mann was set to direct *Night Passage,* a Technicolor film to star James Stewart, based on a screenplay about a railroad cop by Borden Chase. Mann assembled the crew for this film, actors as well as technicians, and up until the last minute planned to direct. At the eleventh hour, he withdrew, saying the script was weak and asking that he be replaced. James Neilsen took over, and the final film justifies Mann's judgment. (Mann has said in interviews that he did direct the opening sequence.)

About *Night Passage* Mann has said, "The story was one of such incoherence that I said, 'The audience isn't going to understand any of it.' But Jimmy was very set on that film. He had to play the accordion, and do a bunch of stunts that actors adore. He didn't care about the script at all, and I abandoned the production. The film was a nearly total failure, and Jimmy has always held it against me."[4]

In 1960, just prior to his own epic production of *Cimarron*, Mann worked on another big-name, big-budget production, *Spartacus*. He directed all the scenes taking place in the desert, and all those in the school for gladiators (excepting those with Jean Simmons). These scenes are notably done in Mann's familiar compositional style, and are markedly superior to many in the remainder of the picture.

When asked why he abandoned *Spartacus*, which obviously had such great possibilities and which he had begun shooting with such promise, Mann explained, "Kirk Douglas was the producer of *Spartacus*. He wanted to insist on the message angle. I thought that the message would go over more easily by showing physically all the horror of slavery. A film must be visual. Too much dialogue kills it. From then on, we disagreed. I left."[5] (Stanley Kubrick took over.)

In the winter of 1966, Mann began work on what was to be his final film, a spy-who-came-in-from-the-cold cheat and double cheat story based on a Derek Marlowe novel, *A Dandy in Aspic*. Laurence Harvey, Mia Farrow, and Tom Courtenay costarred. The plot is the sort that enjoyed a brief popularity in the middle to late 1960s. The world of the international spy is used as a metaphor for the lack of values present in the times.

Before a few weeks of shooting were completed, Mann suffered a fatal heart attack, leaving the film to be finished by its star, Laurence Harvey. As a result, the last film to bear Anthony Mann's name was sadly unworthy of his career: cold, confusing, and not up to the standard associated with his best work from the past.

Mann allegedly filmed most of the exteriors done on location in Germany, and certainly a careful viewing of the film reveals the Mann touch in several of those scenes. The opening funeral, various outdoor episodes against a landscape, and a tense confrontation between two top agents in an alleyway all look like his work. But the completed production is unworthy, being marred by the typical self-conscious cinematic tricks that were so popular at that point in film history. Hand-held camera, zoom shots, fancy flashbacks in slow motion, film-within-film sequences, jump cuts, dizzying camera movements, and distorted sound all self-consciously draw attention to a character's inner psychology in ways which the great Anthony Mann in his heyday would not have found necessary.

It is almost tragic to see the purity of Mann's style totally cheapened. Mann has obviously mastered the techniques of the 1960s, but his classic didactic style had more meaning. In one sequence, the spy (Laurence Harvey) sits on a park bench by the Thames, and a zoom to an emerging figure on a distant landscape reveals danger with all the pomp and circumstance of a high-school graduation. Gone is the simplicity of Walter Brennan's death scene in *The Far Country*.

The story of *A Dandy in Aspic* was suitable for Mann. There is the traditional link between hero and villain. And, since the spy is a double agent, he obviously contains within himself the familiar dichotomy of the Mann hero. But either Mann had finished with such matters, had lost his touch, or was too ill to cope.

The poor films made at the end of Mann's career raise the question—what happens to a style like Anthony Mann's in an era in which lack of clear meaning in the story becomes the story itself? When the idea of a film is to leave the audience not knowing where or what loyalties are, Mann's style had to fill in the gaps with the sort of pyrotechnics he once would have eschewed. Even if he had lived, the times were inappropriate for the purity of his style . . . at least in the commercial Hollywood film.

Instead of dwelling on these last years, the chapters which follow discuss in some detail each of Mann's earlier, important films, illustrating how the universe he created evolved. Given the length of his career and the commercial considerations that it necessarily involved, it is notable how clearly this development progressed.

Summary: Anthony Mann

Anthony Mann is a storyteller, but his films are not literary. They are prime examples of film narrative, in which narrative can be defined as image wedded to idea. In the work of some directors, such as John Ford, images dictate the ideas of the film. In others, such as the films of Fritz Lang or Otto Preminger, ideas have dictated the images, as the work is inherently intellectual. In Anthony Mann, image/idea is fused. Which comes first, or means most, is an irrelevant question. With Ford, the viewer translates for himself the myriad of meanings possible from the complex and ambivalent images, whereas with Lang and Preminger he seeks to understand the ideas that have dictated the images. Because of the fusion in Mann's work, the viewer understands all meaning by following the central narrative line.

This means that Mann's work is crystal clear. What it says it is is what it is. Any audience can understand and respond to his stories. But the fact that Mann's work is easy to understand (at the plot level) does not make it simple. It requires the most sophisticated understanding of film-as-film to grasp what he has achieved. The unit of his story is *the total image*.

Obviously, the unit of all film stories is the total image, whether the director knows it or not. Many great directors have known it. And certainly, many great visual storytellers made films before Mann came along. But Anthony Mann's films indicate he believed in the possibility of a high level of communication without words through the specific direction of images and ideas with the tools available to cinema. His work, with its clear progression toward specific visual meaning, becomes almost didactic. He proves the point that there *is* such a thing as *film* narrative. His efforts were directed toward making that narrative flow in a coherent manner in a specific direction.

The wedding of image and idea through the various formal devices of film—editing, composition, etc.—is what makes a brilliant director like John Ford so complex. At the same time, it is what makes a brilliant director like Anthony Mann so perfectly clear. Ford's images reverberate. They not only contribute specific meaning of their own in the storyline, but they also *contain* meaning from other films, Ford's own past films, from history, from Ford's personal life, from the viewer's personal life, from the culture—from everywhere. The viewer sees in them partly what he wants to see. Whatever he is, is what they are. They are ambivalent and contradictory and incredibly beautiful and rich with meaning. They not only reverberate, they accumulate. Each viewing of them is a richer experience than the last. But where Ford builds up, Mann strips down. His images contain only what is linked to the multilayered presentation of story, geography, psychology, and emotion. Mann's images take over the viewer and dominate him. Each successive viewing is an ever more powerful and stark experience.

Anthony Mann liked to quote Ernst Lubitsch's famous remark, "There are 1,000 ways to point a camera, but really only one." Mann pointed his camera in an increasingly specific direction over the years. His ultimate goal was utterly simple. Everything within the frame was to tell the same story as the script, photographed and edited in such a way that the audience would live out the action through the moving pictures, experiencing the same emotional climate that the actors were performing in the story. Utterly simple—like $E = mc^2$.

2

Mann on the Mark

My first films were shot under conditions that I'd rather not talk about. After all, what do you want, with a budget of 50 or 60 thousand dollars, actors who can't be made to say lines, and non-existent sets?

—ANTHONY MANN[1]

IT IS INTERESTING to note that, in 1942, Mann's first year as a director, he made one each of the two types of films that would dominate the first five years of his work—an atmospheric thriller *(Dr. Broadway)* and a low-budget musical *(Moonlight in Havana)*. *Dr. Broadway* demonstrates Mann's developing sensibility and can be linked to his later work. *Moonlight in Havana*, on the other hand, is competently done, but impersonal. Thus the two films illustrate the tendency Mann would follow in those five apprentice years. His interest would be mainly in stories which allowed him to play with atmosphere.

Dr. Broadway, Mann's first film, is practically a textbook example of how an initial film, seen in retrospect, reflects an auteurist director's main thematic and formal concerns. Considering the small budget he had to work with, it is a notably stylish debut. Based on a story by Borden Chase (who would later become an important Mann collaborator), *Dr. Broadway* tells a Runyonesque tale about a medic, played by MacDonald Carey, who works the Broadway beat, associating with a colorful collection of supposedly lovable bookies, chippies, and small-time chiselers.

The significant thing about *Dr. Broadway* is that, in his first movie, Mann skillfully employed four formal devices that would later become primary to his work: swish pans,[2] backgrounds for specific meaning, benign objects used violently, and compositions.

Swish pans: Dr. Broadway's opening sequence swiftly establishes the dark-night urban milieu the title character inhabits. A series of

MacDonald Carey and Jean Phillips in a precarious position   35
from Dr. Broadway. *Mann's first film illustrates his typical use
of film noir lighting and bizarre composition.*

rapid wipes shows first the fire department, then the police department, and finally a rapacious set of newspapermen arriving at the
scene of a disaster. They find a rapt crowd staring up at the top of a
Manhattan hotel. A sudden, abrupt swish pan upward and to the left
focuses in on a young woman standing on a ledge outside one of the
hotel windows. In a bizarre composition that stresses the precari-
ousness of her position (while still revealing the crowd below), she is
seen framed beside a gigantic neon letter "S" from the hotel sign. A
subjective shot from her point of view looks down on the crowd. The
angle reveals the hard white searchlights coldly watching her, as
well as the city street (wet and shiny in the inky darkness of the
night) with its voyeuristic crowd, waiting for her to fall. ("The dame
won't jump," one of its members later complains. "She's a real nut
sundae.")

This use of the swish pan is to become one of Mann's most typical
formal characteristics. The suddenness of its motion has an unsettling effect on the viewer, and the blurred image flashing by offers
no explanation of what is happening. The swift shifting from the
crowd below to the girl above changes the viewer's perspective.
From being one of the eager crowd, wanting to know what is going
on, the viewer is switched to the position of the frightened girl,
looking down, through a rapid and violent movement.

Backgrounds for specific narrative meaning: In a key scene from
Dr. Broadway, MacDonald Carey enters a large night club to meet
the man his testimony sent up the river (Eduardo Ciannelli). Carey,
as well as all the patrons of the club, believe Ciannelli is waiting to
kill him. Carey walks into the club, and a long tracking shot follows
him to the gangster's table. As the customers notice him walking by,
they begin to get up out of their seats and back off, disappearing out
of the frame. When it becomes apparent the two men are going to
talk in civilized fashion, the people slowly filter back into the frame
and reseat themselves.

It is a simple example of an idea Mann would later develop
further. The background action in the frame, seen in depth behind
the leading figures, was used to define the emotional and narrative
status of the hero in the scene. At first, Carey himself is uncertain
what is going to happen. The patrons reflect this sense of danger by
disappearing. As Carey realizes the man has summoned him to
bargain, his situation returns to normal, and the night club takes up
its regular evening ritual. Thus the space of the night club and the

characters in it are used to define both what is happening in the storyline and, more significantly, what Carey is feeling inside as he goes to meet the man he fears. The emotional significance of the narrative line is demonstrated through background action.

Obviously, Carey and Ciannelli are having a discussion which also reveals this information to the audience. But by matching background action to the *meaning* of the dialogue—and linking it to the internal feelings of the character—Mann sought to unify all meaning within the frame. In his later career, he would master this technique to such an extent that specific dialogue would become unnecessary.

Benign objects used violently: Dr. Broadway is supposed to be a comedy-thriller, but Mann instinctively stressed the noncomic elements. His greatest care went into scenes that illustrate the dangerous side of the doctor's world. Perhaps his penchant for using innocent items for torture and death grew out of this first assignment, an alleged comedy, in which, surrounded by benign objects, he was forced to transfer them into instruments of death and destruction in order to make the film interesting.

An example takes place when Ciannelli, the gangster, is fried to death under the doctor's ultraviolet lamp. An object that is supposed to make him healthier kills him when it is used by evil people for evil purposes. It's the first such instance in a Mann film, but it won't be the last. Steam baths, chafing dishes, stuffed animals, farm machinery, scissors, boot spurs—many objects that were to be used for innocent or good purposes are turned into killers' aids in Mann's films over the years.

Composition: The scene in the night club described above demonstrated how Mann used backgrounds to reflect the internal emotional state of a character. The audience, however, could remain detached from this emotion. Mann's desire to involve the audience is shown by his masterful use of composition and lighting in a later scene.

When the film's love interest (Jean Phillips) follows a murder suspect, she is led through a stage door and into deep darkness. She is seen walking through the door and into the dark, toward the audience in the frame. As she progresses slowly forward, the audience realizes that the shoulder and profile of a man can be seen at frame right. He awaits her, but because of the darkness, she cannot yet see him.

With this one composition—no cuts, no camera movement— Mann places the audience in the same emotional position as the character. The viewer's eyes have to search the frame for danger— and find it—in the same way the character has to search the space as she moves in the story. The revelation of the danger to the audience before the character finds it does not lessen the tension. On the contrary, it makes it worse as the audience waits for the inevitable. It would, of course, have been possible for Mann to stage the scene so that the captor would jump out at her and startle the audience as it startles her. The effect would have been sudden, but, in the long run, less subtle than forcing an audience to search cautiously, as the character does, and then find what is already waiting there. The involvement for the audience would not only be briefer, but would not be as closely matched to the character's emotional state.

The significance of the scene is that Mann contains the story, the character, and the emotional effect on the audience in one composition inside the frame. In order to achieve this effect, he elects composition over cuts or camera movements, a choice that would ultimately become his primary formal characteristic.

With *Dr. Broadway,* Mann established himself as capable of directing B budget projects—and making them better than they had any right to be. As Robert Smith observes in his article on Mann's early films, *Dr. Broadway*'s "dramatically lit, big standing sets and Mann's adroit pacing give the film an expensive look not accounted for by the budget."[3]

Mann's second film, *Moonlight in Havana,* was less impressive, little more than a routine cheapie, starring the queen of the B musicals, Jane Frazee, and Allan Jones. Frazee is a singer and Jones a baseball player suspended for bad behavior. In order to earn a living, he is forced to take a job singing with Frazee's troupe of players on their way to Havana. Naturally, the two fall in love.

The difference between the A budget musical and the B was largely a matter of plot development. In an expensive musical, it was considered necessary to provide an adequate story around which to organize the musical numbers and to provide impetus for their performance. The plot might be a fluffy angel cake, but it was well made. The music was the frosting. In a B musical, the songs and dances were the cake and the plot was the frosting, since the short running time made it impossible to develop both. *Moonlight in Havana* had nine musical numbers in sixty-three minutes, leaving

Mann no time to be creative with swish pans and compositions. To his credit, he did the best he could. The script is a melange of feeble jokes ("You're so dry, Martinez"), overworked gags (including Jack Norton as a shipboard drunk), and undeveloped characters. The musical numbers themselves are uninspired, with the possible exception of a satire on the Veloz and Yolanda style of ballroom dancing that was popular in 1940s musicals. It is hilariously danced by a couple called Grace and Nicco who should be awarded a good-conduct medal for the help they give the audience.

The threadbare material of both films provides very little insight into Mann's later works other than the remarkable stylistic explorations described for *Dr. Broadway*. Yet if one knows the characteristic concerns that emerge later, it is possible to establish certain rudimentary connections between *Dr. Broadway* and other films.

The idea of a hero who is linked emotionally to a villain is primitively present. Ciannelli believes Carey is the only man he can trust and makes him responsible for presenting a large sum of money to his daughter. Thus, the two men are linked by guilt and responsibility. When Ciannelli is murdered, Carey spends the rest of the film searching for the daughter and risking his life on the mission. This idea of an emotional connection between a good and a bad man was to become one of Mann's dominant themes. Later, however, the good/bad would be less clear-cut, with the hero taking on more of the characteristics of the villain.

In addition, *Dr. Broadway* presents a set of urban characters and situations which Mann would later use less sympathetically. The lovable Broadway types that surround Carey, and that are played for laughs, would later materialize in their more realistic and seedy forms. The charmingly Runyonesque setting would become totally violent.

Though *Dr. Broadway* and *Moonlight in Havana* were hardly *Citizen Kane*, Mann had started his career with two effectively directed, inexpensive films that made money. His next project—and his only film released in 1943—might have killed a lesser talent. Fortunately, nobody remembers it.

Nobody's Darling was a Republic film, starring Mary Lee, Louis Calhern, and Gladys George. Its storyline was one that had been used before, most notably by Universal for Deanna Durbin. It concerned an ugly duckling who brags about her famous theatrical parents to her schoolmates. Her parents have little time for her, taken up as they are in their divorce proceedings. When she runs away, everyone shapes up—the parents, the schoolmates, and the little girl herself, who suddenly becomes a swan. *Nobody's Darling* (appropriately named) in no way reflects Mann's later works, and justly remains a forgotten film.

Mann's next film, also for Republic, was *My Best Gal* (1944), starring Jane Withers and Jimmy Lydon. It was a variation on the familiar plot in which a group of talented youngsters decide to put on a musical show. Like *Moonlight in Havana* and *Nobody's Darling*, it was another minor exercise that sheds no light on Mann.

It was with *Strangers in the Night* (also 1944) that Mann took his first real step forward in developing the formal promise he had shown with *Dr. Broadway*. A relatively lavish production for its studio (Republic), *Strangers in the Night* marks the first time Mann would make the bad character in the film (in this case, a villainess) its most interesting person. The story is like some incredible mutation, part *Laura*, part *Rebecca*, part *Who's Afraid of Virginia Woolf?*, and part *The Old Dark House*. It has a grab-bag plot about a crazed older woman (Helene Thimig) who pretends she has a beautiful daughter, Rosemary. On behalf of this imaginary creature, she writes letters to a marine on Guadalcanal (William Terry). When Terry is wounded and sent home, he comes to visit the girl he has fallen in love with via the army post office. When he meets the town's lady doctor (Virginia Grey), he finds she is the one he really cares about. The stress is too much for Thimig, who wants someone besides herself to believe in the fake daughter. She murders her faithful companion (Edith Barrett) and tries to do in the lovers.

Where some B films suffer from not enough plot, *Strangers in the Night* suffers from too much. In order to set up this complicated story, and then resolve it, the characters are forced to keep up a steady barrage of conversation for the fifty-six minutes of running time. At this point, Mann is not yet expert enough to find ways of compensating for this talk, or omitting it altogether and telling what it said via other means.

What the film does have, however, is expressive photography that greatly enhances the story and helps to develop the craziness of the main character. The cinematographer (Reggie Lanning) and Mann have together worked up a visual story that uses deep focus, daring camera angles, exaggerated close-ups, and deeply shadowed environments. The collaborators miss almost no opportunity to use

Virginia Grey, Helene Thimig, and the portrait of "Rosemary" from *Strangers in the Night*, shortly after "Rosemary" has answered Thimig's plea for help.

photography to improve the quality of the film, particularly in a
scene in which the crazed villainess and her almost equally dotty
companion conduct a birthday toast to "Rosemary's" portrait.
Thimig insists the lamps be turned out, and the candles lit. The
firelight casts a flickering light over the faces of the two women, and
the lack of direct illumination engulfs the large, handsomely ap-
pointed room in ominous shadows. The portrait itself has a shadow
across it, and the entire scene has an eerie, demented quality,
achieved entirely from the lighting. Thimig's face as she talks to
"Rosemary" is lit so that it stands out with the too-bright look of the
insane.

Mann has done the best he can under the circumstances, and the
end result is quite a nice little film, hampered by a wooden hero and
too much talk. The psychological aberration of Thimig preshadows
those of Mann's later heroes and heroines. Thimig's character fills a
vacuum in the film, and she becomes hero, heroine, villain, and
villainess. This is an almost accidental accomplishment, of course,
but one that will become a characteristic of Mann's work, as the
leading character will almost always be one who is unbalanced emotionally.

Thimig's character, who lurks behind doors and peeps out windows while thumping around with a crutch and a bad leg, is bla-
tantly overdrawn. Yet, Mann and Lanning manage to help the actress (who is not inept) bring off her best moment in the film. When
she reveals the truth about Rosemary, the camera makes a slow,
unsteady track toward her, and the shot ends with an intense
close-up of her crazed face. When she speaks her best dramatic line
to the hero, "You were loving *me*, Johnny . . .," the effect is powerful. Unfortunately, this power is dissipated by an ending that is
unintentionally funny. When Thimig's crimes are found out, she
begs the portrait of Rosemary: "Help me, help me," and it falls
down and bops her to death. *Strangers in the Night* is obviously a
minor film, but an important one visually. There is nothing better in
Mann's career between *Dr. Broadway* and the first films of the *noir*
period, *Desperate, Railroaded,* and *T-Men.*

Two O'Clock Courage and *Sing Your Way Home* were both made
in 1945 for RKO. *Two O'Clock Courage* was a remake of a 1936
comedy-thriller, *Two In The Dark* (which starred Walter Abel,
Margot Grahame, and Gail Patrick). The original, directed by Ben
Stoloff, opted for comedy, as is indicated by its slate of character
actors, Eric Blore, Erik Rhodes, and Alan Hale. The remake, as

might be guessed with Mann directing, stressed the mystery in a plot about an amnesiac accused of murder (Tom Conway). Conway tries to find out who-the-heck he is with the help of Ann Rutherford.

Sing Your Way Home, with Jack Haley, Nancy McGuire, and Anne Jeffreys, is a mixture of music, comedy, and wartime spy melodrama. Like *Moonlight in Havana,* it justified its existence with a long string of back-to-back musical numbers that kept the seventy-two minutes of running time nicely padded out.

The Great Flamarion (also 1945) provided more opportunity for Mann's developing style. It contains the prototype of what would become the Mann hero—a character whose present is shaped by a scar (or secret) from his past. As Robert Smith describes it:

The all-bad girl format, the mirror image of the equally popular innocent-wife-driven-insane-by-diabolical-husband, becomes the basis for a sporadically effective and generally entertaining melodrama. The resources of Republic provide for a number of extensive tracking shots into a theater and around the perimeter of an orchestra pit. Characters are framed with precision and incisiveness in the course of these tracks, establishing more complex relationships than the screenplay indicates. The plotting of Mary Beth Hughes vis-à-vis Erich Von Stroheim and other of her victims takes on the conventional, as well as unexpectedly subversive and humorous connotations, again provided almost wholly by Mann's choice of camera placement and angle. Hughes sizing up her next victim in a portentous low-angle shot or scheming in two-shot is undercuttingly amusing as is the devastating image of pretentious Erich dancing around a hotel room on the wings of love. The many shots accentuating the kinkiness of Stroheim, such as the close-up shaving of his head, provide for additional amusement at the expense of the screenplay's more lofty aspirations. The big set-pieces, Dan Duryea's and Hughes' deaths and the opening sequence, are far more seriously approached and very well calculated in terms of camera movement, elaborate cutting (generally on one-shots) and angling. (Smith, p. 12)

In 1946, Mann directed two films, *Strange Impersonation* and *Bamboo Blonde.* The latter is another minor musical, this time starring the famous "bamboo blonde" of the 1940s, singer Frances Langford. Exploiting democracy for all it's worth in order to appeal to the wartime audience, *Bamboo Blonde* celebrates enthusiastically the charms of the sort of girl who "has ideals and spunk." (She's also the sort of girl who threatens, "I don't like ul-ti-mah-tums.")

Bamboo Blonde is nothing more than a cut-rate *Pin-Up Girl.* Yet it has energy and appeal, and the sense of truth about the era that is often found in a B film. Since there was little money to work with, some B films fell back on clothes and furniture that were realistic. Instead of a "decorated" look to the sets and a designer-created dream world of fashion, the films presented ordinary stuff like ordinary people wore and used. *Bamboo Blonde* has a touch of this honesty, and is rather refreshing to look at today. In addition, its compositions are carefully set up, and a mobile camera enhances the action.

Robert Smith comments on the other 1946 release:

Strange Impersonation (1946) is surely one of the cheapest films ever made by an important artist (always excepting Edgar G. Ulmer, of course), and the most impoverished film of Mann's career . . . . The story of a woman research scientist who tries her own experimental anesthetic with horrifying and surreal results, the film points the way to what would be Mann's forte during this period: a nightmare landscape of pain, trapped characters and vicious, unscrupulous villains. The overstated and coincidence-prone material and silly screenplay and performances frequently bog down the film, but often *Strange Impersonation* is reflective of Mann's *noir* preoccupations. A down-and-out alcoholic who robs the heroine and leads to the "strange impersonation" and the milieu of neon-lit streets, punk hustlers, and double-dealing "friends" are realized by the director with economy (enforced) and conviction. The clever ending which reveals that it was all a dream is a disappointment, dissipating the nightmare just as it was becoming consistently oppressive. A rather conventional lighting scheme, primarily white with little in the way of textured high contrast black/white patterning is another flaw of the film, probably due to the very short shooting schedule. (Smith, p. 12)

The significance of these early films is that because of low budgets, weak performances, and undeveloped scripts, Mann instinctively turned to form for meaning. Despite the use of urban scenes and characters, various psychological aberrations, and crude examples of hero/villain relationships, it is stretching a point to connect these films to the fuller works in terms of their content. They can, however, be connected to later films in their formal experimentation.

Between 1942 and the end of 1946, Mann completed ten films. He had mastered his craft and was ready for more. In 1947 he directed his first films that might be said to reflect totally the Mann style. It was the beginning of a period of work in the *film noir* tradition, and his first real fame as a low-budget filmmaker.

3

Mann in the Dark

1947 . . . is important for me . . . it marks my first critical and commercial success.

—ANTHONY MANN[1]

IN 1947, Mann made three films, two for a company newly formed by a merger of Poverty Row's Producers Releasing Corporation (PRC), and England's powerful J. Arthur Rank organization. In a move to upgrade the image of PRC, the old name was changed to Eagle-Lion International, and a brave new motto was adopted—"Sic Pro Optima."

The independence of Eagle-Lion afforded Mann the opportunity to keep on making inexpensive films, but to make them under a less studio-dominated atmosphere than he had found at Paramount, Universal, RKO, or even Republic. If anything, there was even more freedom at Eagle-Lion than in the B units of those studios, and formal experiments were actively encouraged. The work for Eagle-Lion gave Mann three important things besides this freedom: slightly larger budgets to work with, better scripts well suited to his emerging style, and, most importantly, cinematographer John Alton as a collaborator.

John Alton's influence in Mann's work cannot be overemphasized. One of the greatest of American cinematographers, Alton knew how to achieve the effects Mann wanted, and also how to create new effects of his own. After Mann teamed up with Alton at Eagle-Lion, his work took on a new subtlety of light and shadow. In fairness to earlier collaborators, it should be pointed out that Mann's work *had* photographic subtlety earlier. Most notably, Reggie Lanning's contributions to *Strangers in the Night* stand out. And, *Desperate*, the only 1947 film *not* made for Eagle-Lion (it is an RKO

release), was photographed by the talented George Diskant, himself
a notable contributor to the works of Nicholas Ray and others. *Railroaded*, shot by Guy Roe, is also well done, but it is with *T-Men* and
the list of Mann-Alton films which follow that Mann reaches his full
visual maturity.

Film Noir

The films Mann directed between 1947 and 1950 fall within the
tradition known as *film noir*. They are as much a definition of that
tradition as they are a result of it, so that describing *film noir* and
Mann's *film noir* is somewhat of a repetitive business. Nevertheless,
a basic definition of *film noir* is important to the understanding of
Mann's contribution to it.

Film noir is usually defined not as a genre, but as a mood, charac-
terized largely by a postwar feeling of alienation and disillusionment
that permeated such familiar genres as gangster films, women's
films, detective films, and melodramas of all types. It appeared even
in westerns (*Pursued*, 1947; *The Halliday Brand*, 1957) and musicals
(*Love Me or Leave Me*, 1955; *Pete Kelly's Blues*, 1955). Although it
was present throughout the early 1940s (and also in the Depression
era), it reached a peak in the period immediately following World
War II and continued its subversive invasion of popular entertainment throughout the 1950s.[2]

While *film noir*, because it is a mood or style, is best defined
visually, it does have its own set of recurring motifs and attitudes.
Whereas earlier movies often depicted America as a rural place,
pastoral and secure, *film noir* switched the view to an urban world,
decidedly dangerous and insecure. The older, simpler values disap-
peared, and the world was pictured as corrupt and treacherous.
Modern man was presented as trapped in an unfriendly environment, with the hero usually on the run down the mean streets of a
darkly lit, hostile city.

These films took up the subjects of paranoia, violence, fate, betrayal, corruption, materialism, murder, suicide, lust, greed, revenge, hatred, and torture. In other words, they afforded Mann
with perfect material for his developing sensibility. They were set in
crummy hotels, run-down beaneries, dirty locker rooms, cheap
massage parlors, steam baths, and back-room hideouts of the criminal and downtrodden. These dreary places were often contrasted
with expense account restaurants, ritzy night clubs, Park Avenue

apartments, and the playgrounds of the rich and spoiled. This juxtaposition of the world of the haves to the world of the have-nots provided much of the conflict found in *film noir,* as those that didn't have tried to wrench power and money from those that did. The icons of *film noir* include guns, liquor, fast cars, faster women, and money, always money. It is a darkly lit, dismal world almost totally without hope. The endings usually find the hero dead.

Technically, *film noir* stands out as a gold mine for film study. Since it *is* a style, it features the dramatic use of all formal elements, most notably:

> —Night photography on location.
> —Extreme contrasts between black and white.
> —Low-key lighting, featuring entrapping shadows
>   that hold characters prisoner in the frame.
> —Bizarre camera angles to suggest a world gone
>   mad, and to disorient a viewer.
> —Wide-angle lens and deep focus composition,
>   to create distortions and depth of image.

Mann's Use of *Film Noir*

Film noir afforded Mann a milieu rich with possibilities for the development of his own personal sense of a hero at odds with himself and the world. By the end of 1949, Mann's "universe" (in auteurist terms) had emerged thematically as well as formally, as he used *all* the themes and techniques outlined above.

At the same time, he continued to hone his technique into increasingly specific narrative meaning. It is in this three-year period that Mann's use of light reduction, space, editing, camera movement, and composition crystalizes into the recognizable Mann imprint.

Reduction of Light: By removing lighting from above and letting it fall on characters and objects from behind, Mann and Alton presented a deeply darkened world, heavily accentuated by lengthy shadows. An image illuminated this way was unreal, full of danger and destruction. Its message was one of primal fear and lack of safety and clarity. The effect on the viewer was one of seeing a nightmare world, full of menacing shadows that held heaven-knows-what. It also dehumanized actors, and deemphasized the traditional Hollywood use of decor for pretty effects.

Noir films use a minimum of illumination. Thus the entire frame reflects the status of the hero in his world. He has very little sunshine (quite literally) in his life. Furthermore, he seldom knows the total picture about what is happening to him. He trusts where he shouldn't trust, and misuses those who might help or sustain him. The pinpoints of light in his dim world come from hastily lit matches, flashlights probing the dark night, hazy street lamps over patches of wet pavement, and flickering, menacing candles.

Extreme contrasts between black and white images provide the visual correlative of later thematic developments of hero/villain in Mann's films. In *film noir*, the contrasts are actually physical, and starkly presented. The characters themselves are neither black nor white, however, in moral terms. They are neither good nor bad, just human.

If one single characteristic object had to be chosen to represent typical *film noir* lighting patterns, it would have to be the use of those splintered phenomena of the 1940s, Venetian blinds. Every well-appointed window had them, but only in *film noir* did they seem so menacing as they fractured objects and faces, cutting and slicing up rooms, hiding killers, turning cozy bedrooms into prisons with bars, and generally spreading a prairie of planes of light and dark over the frame.

Space: Spatial distortions of all types were used by Mann in his *noir* years. He also perfected an idea he had developed earlier in which he used space to define an area one way for the viewer, and then suddenly, unexpectedly redefine it. A room which seemed comfortable or cozy would become a trap. Or, conversely, a room which seemed tight and cramped would open up and become safe. These definitions and redefinitions of interiors were closely related to both narrative and character development. Mann used them for scenes of entrapment and escape, and also to reflect the emotions the hero was undergoing. By breaking down the viewer's realistic sense of space, and reassembling it on his own terms, Mann also put the audience in a state of emotional insecurity, not unlike that of the characters in the film.

Although this skill was practiced mostly on interior space, Mann also explored its possibilities on an entire outdoor location. The idea of externalizing an internal conflict for a character by placing him in an actual outdoor location—and modulating the space around him—would become one of the most important aspects of Mann's western films.

Editing: In Mann's later films, editing would become secondary to composition in importance. In the *noir* films, his editing patterns were used to emphasize jarring juxtapositions. Night to day, and day to night . . . safety to danger and danger to safety. The relationship he was establishing to space (through definition and redefinition) was carried on partly through editing, not just composition alone, during this period of his career. He often cut back and forth between an intense close-up and a long shot, thus alienating the audience and creating in them the same sense of helplessness and confusion as the characters. In *Side Street,* as Farley Granger drives the canyons of Manhattan, attempting to escape the police, the audience alternates its view between close-ups of his perspiring and worried face to high-angle shots from above which show his little car pursued relentlessly by the police. This pattern of alternation shows us he's foolish to try, we're foolish to care, etc., but also involves the viewer in his plight.

Camera Movement: Since movement of the camera generally suggests to a viewer a sense of freedom, or joy, Mann's *noir* films rely on it little. He does use movement, carefully and deliberately, of two main types:

1. Short tracks, either forward or backwards. Sudden short tracks in the middle of a take, or swift backward movements, stress the treachery inherent in the noir world. The viewer feels unsettled watching them and is plunged into a new situation vis-à-vis his relationship to the narrative.
2. Long backward tracks. Used in front of a running man, allowing the audience to see his desperate face, as well as what is pursuing him. Such takes not only involve the audience directly in the runner's motion, but also in his horror.

It is important to note that long fluid tracks *do* occur in the *noir* films, which are not as totally consistent as the westerns. When such movements are used, they provide release, not joy, and the release comes when characters break free of their traps or pursuers. (This release is usually temporary.)

Composition: From the beginning of his career, Mann had explored meaning through composition. Between 1947 and 1950, he featured an unbalanced, unsettling kind of composition. Low ceilings and tight framing helped further a sense of claustrophobia that was appropriate to the subjects of the films.

Throughout these years, Mann practices presenting the main

Mann's use of the wide-angle lens for depth, and an increased sense of distance and
alienation between characters. Marsha Hunt and Dennis O'Keefe in *Raw Deal*.

events of the narrative within one shot as often as possible. His
desire to concentrate the dramatic meaning within-the-frame
(rather than through cuts) naturally led him to use depth of field, so
that all objects could be seen at the same time. This desire was
greatly helped by the development of the wide-angle lens in the
1940s. Wide-angle lenses enlarged the depth of field of the image,
and distorted the size of objects within it. Depth of field gives
background objects a sharp focus, so that all objects within the frame
have equal emphasis within it. Such a world viewed is a rigid world,
an unchanging, unheeding world, perfect for the ideas of *film noir*.

Mann used wide-angle lenses to stress the inhumanity of dangerous objects, such as the discing machine which kills George Murphy
in *Border Incident*. The lenses made it possible to place such objects
in clear, rigid focus in the forward frame, while still preserving the
visual clarity of the action deeper in the frame, behind the object.
Mann also used depth of field or deep focus to allow objects to
assume more power than people, by thrusting them forward into the
frame, allowing them to dominate and overtake the human images

behind them. It was a standard metaphor of *film noir* for illustrating
the indifference of the modern materialistic world to the individual
hero.

Michael Stern comments on Mann's use of wide-angle lenses:

Mann's work in the *film noir* . . . tended to stretch the boundaries of studio
filmmaking. Mann's consistent use of wide angle lenses in order to distort
depth for dramatic "readings" of shots may be seen as an attempt to broaden
the horizons of the 1.33:1 screen ratio.[3]

Stern sees Mann's use of wide-angle photography as foreshadowing
CinemaScope.

At the same time that Mann was achieving the technical control
outlined above, he was also shaping his personal set of themes and
concerns. In his first five years, he found his penchant for the darker
elements of any story, and *film noir* provided him with the perfect
milieu in which to continue this predeliction.

Mann now began to develop the morally complex relationships
between hero and villain, man and woman, and hero to his world
that he would make clear in his western films. While it is true that
these relationships may be found more clearly in his technique than
in his plots (he was still deepening the script with his own form), it is
also obvious that Mann is concerned with a particular set of values in
these years. In addition, Mann's work reflects *noir* preoccupations
with the alienated and corrupt world of urban America in the following ways:

Paranoia: Mann's *noir* characters learn not to trust anyone. A
hand on his arm makes a character jump. And why not? It's just
when he sits down to relax in the steam room that . . . . The heroes
of these films are either men on the run from the law, or from the
underworld, or are lawmen in disguise as criminals and thus in a
precarious position in their world. There is no safety anywhere, and
no one who can be counted on. Even in *Reign of Terror*, a period
film, the action is set in a fundamentally paranoid era, that of postrevolutionary France.

Violence: Mann's films are among the most relentlessly violent for
this period of any in American cinema. Murders and beatings take
place frequently and with graphic details, sparing an audience
nothing.

Fate: The hand of fate chokes the *noir* hero, and the Mann films
are no exceptions to the tradition. In every film, one of the most

sympathetic characters, if not the hero himself, is killed. The stories
concern men trapped in situations they cannot control and can
barely understand. In this regard, they represent a modern sensibility, presenting a world in which an individual feels overwhelmed
by forces bigger than he is.

To reflect the fatalistic structure of the story, many *noir* films
employ the narrative device of the flashback. Mann's desire for a
simple, straightforward story—and for a "now" emotional effect—
caused him to eschew the flashback, although he found its equivalent in various types of narration. In *Side Street,* the story is narrated from a fatalistic vantage point. The film appears to begin in the
present tense, in that no character in the film "tells" what happened
in a conscious fade from present and return to past. Yet the narrator
knows what the total story is before he begins telling it. Thus, the
narration contributes to the fatalistic, entrapping sense of time the
story presents.

Raw Deal is narrated in a hopeless, oh-my-god-look-what-is-
happening-but-I-am-powerless-to-stop-it tone of voice which comments on action that is occurring at that moment. Its effect on the
listener is one of providing a sense of helplessness and impending
doom. *T-Men* and *Border Incident* are both introduced by a narrator, an omniscient force that provides the semidocumentary aura
of the two films. As the films move back and forth from this realistic
approach to a more intensely personal story, the sense of events that
are larger than the characters can control (and which they cannot
fully understand) is maintained for the audience. Mann's heroes
were never free of the secrets from their past, and all lived under
the clouds of their previous mistakes and passions.

Lust and Greed: Motivations are not noble in *film noir.* Those who
don't have are willing to kill to get. Those who have, kill to keep.
Women are used as sexual objects, and the few good women in the
films (who act as foils to the bad) are as helpless as the entrapped
heroes. True love is an illusion, snatched on the run, and not strong
enough to overcome the forces of evil that surround the leading
characters.

The Urban World: Every film Mann made between 1947 and 1950
takes place in the modern urban world, with the exception of *Reign
of Terror,* in which, ironically, the 1794 Paris setting is treated as if
it were a modern city.

The *Noir* Films

Mann's seven films in the *noir* tradition saw the emergence of his fully defined universe. His world became not just a formal entity that improved a weak story, but a fully integrated set of techniques, characters, and ideas.

Desperate (1947) attempts to contrast two worlds, that of a young couple drawn into the evil world of *film noir* against their wills, and the underworld itself, personified by a blimpish Raymond Burr. The young couple (Steve Brody and Audrey Long) are trapped in a hopeless situation in which both the law and a gang of criminals are chasing them. There is no shelter anywhere. Their "desperate" flight on foot is emphasized dramatically by showing them photographed from low angle, small and vulnerable against a dark and cloudy sky. Unfortunately, Mann is so much more effective at presenting the underworld than he is at presenting the world of normal folk, that the film is slightly off balance. The scenes in which the young couple are shown living their healthy, normal life are flat. On the other hand, the scenes involving the criminals are exciting enough to make *Desperate* worthy of mention by Don Miller in his list of top B films as one which "exceeds most expectations."[4]

The best scene in the film takes place when Burr's henchmen administer a violent beating to Brody. A swinging light bulb throws a pattern of chaotic, ever-changing light over the proceedings, representing the erratic, out-of-control situation the hero finds himself in. The beating is intercut by low-angle shots of Burr watching. Seen from below, he is like an evil monster, huge and misshapen in the swinging light.

Railroaded (1947) is more unified than *Desperate* and points toward the coherence of Mann's later works. It is perhaps his first really unified film, presenting the story of a young woman (Sheila Ryan) and her attempts to clear her brother's name of a murder charge.

Like *Desperate*, *Railroaded* attempts to contrast two worlds, that of a healthy young couple (a cop and a girl) and an underworld duo (a lush and a killer). Also like *Desperate*, *Railroaded* is much better when dealing with the criminal than the ordinary. Here, the villain, played by John Ireland, inadvertently becomes the hero by virtue of being the only fully drawn, well-acted character. He is photographed in shadows, a technique which associates his nature with darkness and evil, and he is frequently seen from a low-angle shot from below his waist. The result is that he seems ominous, unstable, and appears to loom over the proceedings. He is often found forward in the frame in close-up, so that he dominates the action and events of the film, and seems to control everything that is happening by his presence. Thus, he has power in the film, and since Ireland is the only person who is even remotely acquainted with acting technique (with the possible exception of Jane Randolph), he becomes the most colorful and exciting character. In this sense, he is a forerunner to the charming villains played by Robert Ryan in *Naked Spur* and Arthur Kennedy in *Bend of the River*. If there were a strong hero to balance him, the film might provide Mann's first complex hero-villain relationship. Without such a hero, Ireland takes on the importance of hero-villain in one character, although he is totally unsympathetic. If he never becomes sympathetic, however, he at least involves the spectator, so that a moral complexity exists in the audience's minds, as they find themselves much more interested in the villain than in the hero!

Everything about *Railroaded* is cheap: the sets, the costumes, the actors, and the very situation itself. The people of the film have a low-class urgency, and they seldom have anything decent to say to one another. "Just when you ought to keep your head clear, you start pickling it," whines Ireland to his alcoholic girl friend (Randolph). When he wants to court the leading lady (Sheila Ryan), he buys her a drink in a flea-bag night club and says sociably, "Did you ever hunt gophers?" Even the innocent young brother of Ryan, who is falsely accused of robbery and murder, snaps back when the police ask him what he did with the money: "I bought beer with the first $1,000 and spent the rest on bubble gum."

Railroaded is an exercise in demonstrating what can be done with nothing. It is masterfully directed, and the lighting is particularly effective. Characters have been developed with small bits of stage business—Randolph drinks, Ireland wears perfume, the owner of the night club quotes Oscar Wilde, and Sheila Ryan (the poor man's Ann Sheridan) becomes a trifle more interested in Ireland than she really ought to be.

Railroaded is held together by its overall lighting pattern, which is consistent and atmospheric even in scenes which do not call for visual pyrotechnics, such as the police chief's office and the department's science laboratory. In fact, *Railroaded* is something of a stylistic tour de force, with a beginning and ending that lifts it above the ordinary.

The opening scenes take place in a beauty parlor in which bets are taken in the back room. Randolph, one of the beauticians, signals two men who are waiting in the shadows of the alley. With her help, they enter and undertake a robbery of the bookie funds. With considerable dramatic power and storytelling economy, Mann directs a wordless scene in which everything goes wrong as stylishly as possible. A co-worker of Randolph's is threatened by one of the masked bandits. As his double-barreled gun moves forward in the frame, growing larger and larger, the two barrels ultimately filling the image, an intense close-up shows the woman's mouth splitting open into a hideous scream. His gun flashes, literally on fire in the blackness, alerting a policeman. All is chaos, as a gun battle erupts in which the dead cop falls, crashing through the shop window.

The finale takes place in a deserted and darkened night club, the "Club Bombay," a typical noirish setting. Ireland waits in the darkness, hidden, for Sheila Ryan to enter. The entire space is lit only by a street lamp outside, and the broken patterns of light fall across tables on which upended chairs sit for the night. Ireland confronts Ryan, accusing her of betrayal, and ultimately shoots her, his gun once again blazing out like fire in the darkness, its smoke filling the frame afterwards. Ryan, hit realistically, staggers and falls, just as the policeman-hero (Hugh Beaumont) bursts in. Ireland and Beaumont then engage in a shoot-out in the darkness, crawling on their hands and knees amidst the tables and their burdens of junglelike chair-legs. Not knowing which man is which, the viewer is forced to search the darkness, unable to see exactly where they are in relation to one another. Bullets zing back and forth, until Ireland runs frame forward and dies, literally falling *on* the viewer. This final shoot-out preshadows the western films with its spatial complexity, emotional involvement for the audience, linking of two men in the frame, and its sense of the characters hiding amidst their "landscape," with the tables and chairs of the club standing in for the rocks and trees of the westerns to come.

Railroaded is an important film because it is consistent, particularly in its masterful lighting scheme. It is the last film in which Mann would have to work with literally nothing in the way of money, actors, and story. Released by PRC just as it merged with J.

Arthur Rank, his next film, *T-Men*, would be the first with the newly formed Eagle-Lion, and his first real critical and commercial success.

With *T-Men* (1947) everything fell into place. The relationship between form and content that Mann was developing seemed to cohere for the first time. His control of all formal elements was refined and perfected, and his ability to wed the big moments of formal excitement with the overall narrative was in full bloom. Furthermore, a more fully developed script presented him with characters that are well written and fully drawn. The two treasury agents, Dennis O'Keefe and Alfred Ryder, are distinctly different types who provide subtle contrast to one another.

Even the minor characters are depicted with more depth than in Mann's prior films. When Ryder sacrifices his life to save the mission, the totally visual depiction of O'Keefe's anguish as he stands helplessly by—as well as Ryder's mute indication that "this is the way it has to be"—has real poignance of the sort not associated with the B film.

"We're going to take you inside . . . ," says a narrator at the beginning of *T-Men*, referring to the plot device of beginning the film as a semidocumentary report of a typical treasury agent case and then moving inside to a tense personal drama. This kind of story redefinition matches Mann's tendency to define the space of a set and then redefine it. (Actually, the story line was a composite of several major cases cracked by the T-Men.)

The opening of the film clearly illustrates this definition/redefinition. At first, the official seal of the Treasury Department is seen, and a department spokesman pompously describes the activities of the six branches of the department ("six fingers that makes a fist—it hits fair, but it hits hard"). But when his narration says, "The case started in Los Angeles . . . ," the mood shifts totally into the dark-nights/wet-streets world of *film noir*. A tiny figure walks through a hostile urban landscape, is met, and is ruthlessly murdered. The plot concerns two undercover treasury agents who are after a gang of clever counterfeiters. Working back and forth between distanced narration (the documentary half of the film) and the intense, brooding *film noir* style, the story unfolds with a wealth of fascinating details combined with brutal violence.

The composition of the images stresses the alienation of the two agents, adrift in a hostile environment, attempting to make contacts and connections that may cost them their lives. They are photo-

The first John Alton–Anthony Mann collaboration, *T-Men*, illustrates Mann's emerging style: (Top) lighting which cuts, entraps, and shadows (Bottom) composition which reinforces helplessness, as Charles McGraw (right) locks Wallace Ford inside the steam room in *T-Men*'s famous murder scene.

The Museum of Modern Art/Film Stills Archive

graphed in dark and shadowy urban spaces which depict the dangers they face and their precarious status. Since characters are often passing information to one another in secret during the film, bizarre camera angles and unique compositions stress conspiratorial relationships.

O'Keefe's search through a series of low-class steam baths for a criminal about whom he knows only that he chews Chinese health herbs is a gruesome event. A montage of phone-book numbers, yellow-page ads, neon signs, half-naked bodies steaming in sordid rooms, menacing silhouettes, and sweat-streaked faces surrounded with foglike steam is a glimpse of hell. It is like a tour through one of the levels of Dante's Inferno.

Mann exploits depth of composition to indicate relationships in a key scene in a night club. Wallace Ford, the steam-bath enthusiast, sits in the foreground at a table. Seen in depth across the enormous space of the club, O'Keefe is clearly in view in a phone booth, with the rest of the space of the room reflected on the glass of the booth door. Later, this vantage point is reversed, and the audience is placed inside the phone booth with O'Keefe, looking across the enormous room to see Ford at his table. The effect of this reversal is an unsettling one. The balance of safety seems to become unclear as point of view shifts radically.

When the two agents decide to "work" on Ford's insecurity about his position in the mob, they trap him in a chair in a seedy hotel room. They stand over him in a menacing fashion, with the room lamps focused down on him like spotlights for police grilling. As shadows fall across him, slicing him into pieces, their images are reflected in the mirror on top of the bureau. Their menacing reality combined with their false images (they are tricking him) as they hover over him is a scene of classic *noir* paranoia.

Ford's death later is the single most gruesome scene in the film. As he sits steaming himself in one of the clubs he frequents, his killer's shadow falls ominously across his face. When Ford tries to run, he is blocked, and locked in the steam room. Calmly, the killer stands outside, turning the steam up as far as it will go. The composition presents the killer's profile at frame right, standing his ground until he knows it's over, with Ford's anguished face in the window of the steam-room door. Ford tries to get out by beating on the door with his fists. He then picks up a stool and tries to smash the glass in the door. The audience, along with the killer, sits outside while

Ford desperately pounds and bangs the stool against the glass, over and over again, in a scene that seems to last for two days.

The finale is a grand-slam chase on board a ship at night. A maze of ladders, iron pipes, gangways, planks, and sealed doors confuses the audience as to where the chased and the chaser are in relationship to one another at any given point. In a kind of poetic justice, the man who killed Ford in the steam bath is himself shut out from safety and left banging on a sealed door, begging to be let in to hide as the agents close in on him. These two scenes have a visual power that illustrates the ambivalent "let me in" and "let me out" feelings of modern society and its alienated souls.

T-Men is Mann's first fully mature film. While telling a story that is suspenseful and exciting, Mann depicts depth of feeling between the major characters without losing any of the potential drama and brutality. At the same time, the visual pyrotechnics, such as the steam-bath murder and the final chase, are more fluidly integrated into the overall narrative structure than ever before. At this point in his career, it was clear that Mann had not only mastered his technique, but now knew how to relate it to his content for a more unified and coherent whole.

Like *T-Men*, *Raw Deal* (1948) is a fully realized project. In describing the action, it is striking to note how many visually exciting episodes are contained within its meager running time of seventy-eight minutes—a prison break, an exciting car chase, a tense fight inside a taxidermist's shop, a shoot-out in foggy city streets, and a huge fire to list only parts of the action. Its atmospheric, even poetic, photography by John Alton marks the film as a mature effort, proving that the Mann/Alton collaboration on *T-Men* was not a one-shot achievement.

Raw Deal is important in that it plays with the interaction of four characters of some depth and complexity: Joe, a prison inmate (Dennis O'Keefe); Pat, his moll, (Claire Trevor); Ann, a girl who worked with Joe's lawyer on his case (Marsha Hunt); and Rick, a crime king (Raymond Burr): Although similar interaction was present in the main relationship of *T-Men*, Mann first creates in *Raw Deal* four major characters who are bad/good opposites in a morally complex way. Through his baroque use of lighting, camera angles, fatalistic narration, etc., each character is deepened, and the relationships of one to another are similarly further complicated.

As the film opens, Joe is in prison, sent up because he agreed to take a rap for Rick, with the understanding that Rick would get him out and pay him $50,000 for the favor. Rick sets up a prison escape for Joe which is, in fact, designed for his capture. With Pat's help, however, Joe escapes and contacts Ann, forcing her to aid them. While the three of them successfully outmaneuver the police, Joe and Ann fall in love. When Ann is taken hostage by Rick, Joe passes up his chance for a boat to Panama in order to rescue her, managing to kill Rick but not without being shot himself first. Joe dies in the streets at the end of the film. Within the framework of this plot, Mann creates a series of individual portraits.

"I want to breathe," says Joe in prison, "that's why I want out of this place. . . . All I want is a breath of fresh air." Like the typical heroes of *film noir*, he spends the entire running time of the film searching for that breath of fresh air. And, like those heroes, he never finds it, and remains unable to escape from the trap in which he lives.

Ironically, Joe is as much in prison after his escape as before. This idea is emphasized by his always being photographed in cramped places. He is seen on the floor of the back seat of the escape car driven by Pat and later wedged into the front seat of Ann's car with the two women. Inside rooms, he is lit by a pattern of entrapping shadows, such as those of the Venetian blinds in Ann's bedroom. When rooms are photographed to show their full size, Joe is placed inside the frame so that he appears out of place, a bull in a China shop. Even out of doors, among the pine trees of the forest, he appears to be in prison, the trees surrounding him like guards, photographed to look like cell doors, or so that their shadows fall across him like prison bars. Outside in the forest, he draws a deep breath and says, "There's that breath of fresh air I've been wanting." "Is it?" asks Ann, sarcastically, and moments later he is forced to hide as a mounted policeman appears to question the two women.

Wherever he goes, Joe is trapped by his fate. The audience's first view of him shows him in prison. He is seen behind the visitors' screen, endistanced and hopelessly cut off from others. A complicated shot sets up the relationship of Ann and Joe in their first conversation together. Ann sits opposite Joe, across a space which is elongated and emphasized by the composition. (It is an example of Mann's use of wide-angle lenses.) The visitors' screen splits the viewing screen in half, furthering their alienation and distance from one another. In deep focus, at the back of the frame sit two prison guards, ever watching and listening. In one shot, Mann has composed within the frame a complex statement of their entire relationship and the forces which inevitably separate them.

Joe is a tough guy who explains himself to Ann by telling her he was a Corkscrew Alley juvenile delinquent who barely had enough to eat. She points out that she read in his file in the lawyer's office that he had at the age of twelve earned a medal for saving the lives of several people in a fire. "Whatever happened to that boy?" she wants to know. Joe is cynical. "He pawned the medal because he was hungry."

It was a period in films in which interest emerged in juvenile delinquents, and society was blamed for their having gone wrong. Mann always eschewed such sentiment, and *Raw Deal* makes its token gesture toward sociology with Joe's having been a childhood hero—and then Mann promptly undercuts the idea. Marsha Hunt is seen as an overly idealistic do-gooder, who must reevaluate her understanding of what a man like Joe really stands for. She herself ends up shooting someone. There is no happy ending in which Joe sees the light and gives himself up to the police. He returns to rescue Ann from Rick because it is his fate to love her, to rescue her, and to die for it. As Pat looks down on Joe's dead body, lying on the wet city pavement, she intones, "In my heart, I know this is right for Joe. This is what he wanted."

"I got my breath of fresh air," he tells Ann, just before dying in her arms. Like Henry Fonda at the end of *You Only Live Once* ("free . . . free . . . ") and so many other heroes of *film noir*, Joe finds his breath of fresh air only on the other side of the grave.

Pat (Claire Trevor) and Ann (Marsha Hunt) represent an early example of Mann's tendency to link two characters as narrative opposites, with the relationship being complicated morally since both characters have each other's strengths and weaknesses. Pat and Ann represent a rehearsal for the portrayal of relationships in the westerns that will follow in the next decade, an early example of Mann's using two women to reflect the two sides of a hero's nature as he does later in *The Far Country, Serenade,* and *Cimarron.*

Pat, well played by Claire Trevor, is one of the most interesting women characters to be found in Mann's career. It is her voice, flat and fatalistic, without any real hope or joy in it, that speaks the present tense narration of the film. "This is the day," she says on the sound track at the beginning of the film, "this is the last day I'll have to drive up to these walls." She has come to tell Joe that his escape is set, and that they will be reunited at last. Yet her voice seems to indicate that this is a hopeless deal, and she knows it. She goes through the motions of trying for happiness because she doesn't know what else to do. It's her fate.

Pat is the classic female victim. She too comes from Corkscrew Alley, and the film indicates she has spent her life being kicked around by men. Certainly she can and will take anything from Joe, the man she loves to the point of obsession. Her condition is passive. She *receives* insult and injury because that's the view she has of herself. This situation is well illustrated when Pat sits inside the getaway car awaiting Joe's escape from prison. A car drives past her while she sits at the driver's wheel. It is an ordinary every-day occurrence, but Alton has photographed it so that the lights of the car passing cut harshly across her face, nearly blinding her, revealing her fear and panic. The hot white car lights literally cut her to pieces as she sits in the darkness, finally wiping her out altogether as she raises her arm to protect herself, as if to ward off a blow. She is obliterated by the light. This treatment of an ordinary event—the passing of a car—as if it were a brutal assault on Pat's person illustrates her position in life. "Waiting—waiting—all my life it seems I've been waiting for Joe," her voice intones dully on the track.

The helplessness of Pat's situation reaches its climax visually when she and Joe await the departure of the boat which will take them to freedom in Panama. As they enter the tight, controlled space of the cabin, it is clearly seen as just another prison cell. "Nice snug little place," Joe says ironically, trying to convince himself. Inside the cramped cabin, they are both trapped. Even though the small space is tiny, they are seen as totally separate from one another. Each is photographed individually within the frame, and the few two-shots illustrate the distance between them, even in the tight cabin. Joe stands alone, looking out the window at the San Francisco bridge. He is as much behind bars as ever. Cheerlessly, he begins to talk about their future. "Maybe we can make a better life for ourselves. . . . " He says they will marry at sea, live like normal people. As she listens to the words she has waited all her life to hear, Pat is seen in intense close-up to frame left, a large clock on her right. Time is ticking away and she knows she must tell him Ann is Rick's prisoner. The engines of the boat start up, and her face is seen reflected on the clock's face. The clock takes over her world. Her image is tiny, and the face of the clock huge. The narration,

Pat's internal voice, begins talking over Joe's gloomy attempt to be optimistic about their future. "All my life I've waited for those words . . . the lyrics are his, but the music is Ann's." She knows it's hopeless, and gives up. She tells Joe about Ann and he runs out.

Ann is the opposite of Pat. She is not a rich girl, but she is idealistic. Any attempt at using sociology to explain and excuse Joe's life is snatched away from the audience by way of Ann's telling him off in one of their scenes together. She says she was poor, too . . . it's no excuse. Ann and Pat are the opposite of the usual femme-fatale/decent-girl characterizations of *film noir*. Usually it is the decent girl who might have saved the hero, and the femme fatale who draws him into a life of crime. Pat, the moll, tries to save Joe by getting him away from Rick and off to Panama. Ann, however unwittingly, is the cause of his downfall.

Ann and Pat are linked visually by Mann from the very beginning of the film. By setting up this formal connection between them, Mann enriches the film considerably. Both women visit Joe in prison, sit opposite him in the same position, and are photographed in close-up during their conversations with him. In each close-up, light is reflected off their eyes in an identical set-up. They are often side by side in the frame, and their alternating positions to Joe are stressed. Ann takes Pat's place in Joe's affection, but Joe sends her back to her own world, reclaiming Pat. This is beautifully realized in a scene in which Joe and Ann drive up to meet Pat on a flat stretch of deserted road along the coastal highway. Joe stops his car at frame right, a goodly distance from Pat in her car at frame left. A long shot stresses the distance between the two cars, the isolation of all three characters, the hopeless, fatalistic sense of their situation, and the relationship of the two women vis-à-vis Joe. After Joe pushes Ann out of the car, another long shot shows the two women walking silently past one another as they change positions. Pat's voice on the track says, "I suppose I should feel some kind of victory, but I don't. Walking past her this way. . . . She, too, is just a dame in love with Joe." The image of the two women passing without speaking, set against the loneliness of the barren highway, is the equivalent of a bleak modern poem. Years before the alienated European films of the 1960s, Mann captured the same feeling in a cheapie for Eagle-Lion.

In forming her relationship with Joe, Ann undergoes a moral change. After idealizing him as a former child hero gone wrong (a possible rehabilitation project for a good woman), she learns that the

Sex and violence in *Raw Deal:* (Top) the great cinematographer John Alton sets up a scene between Dennis O'Keefe and Marsha Hunt (bottom) the fight in the taxidermist's shop, John Ireland (left) and Marsha Hunt (right).

situation is more hopeless—in *film noir* terms, more pre-determined—than that. She has to reform her understanding of him along newer, more realistic lines. Her learning is illustrated in a powerful scene inside a taxidermist's shop. Joe enters the back room, thinking he is to meet Rick and receive his $50,000. Instead, one of Rick's henchmen is waiting, and a brutal fight breaks out. It is the classic Mann fight, involving the tools of the taxidermist's trade—sharp knives, brutal clubs, stuffed animals (the villain is temporarily impaled on a deer's antler). The two men are enmeshed in gigantic fishnets which are hung about the room, and Joe loses his gun in the scuffle. The taxidermist (appropriately named Grimshaw) joins the fight against Joe, and Ann watches in terror. Ultimately, she takes up Joe's gun and fires at the villain. Intense close-ups showing both her relief and her horror follow this action, and she bursts out of the nightmarish shop, as if she is desperate for that same breath of fresh air that Joe has been longing for. She runs out into the night, trying to break free of her action.

Pat and Ann are both losers, both victims. Ann is captured and tortured by Rick, and Pat lives a life of total torture in loving Joe. They are inevitably linked by their fates, by their love of Joe. Mann explores every possible visual device of linking the two women in the frame, and thus in the narrative in *Raw Deal*. This idea of linking two characters in a complex moral relationship, to be explored and depicted visually, would become an important aspect of his western films.

One of the best examples of Mann's developing ability to deepen characters through style is illustrated by the character of Rick in *Raw Deal* (Raymond Burr). There is literally nothing to go on in the script, but by enhancing Rick formally, Mann creates a memorable villain.

Rick is a kingpin of crime. He is thus photographed as if he were bigger than life, from a low angle. Given the bulk of Raymond Burr's person, this low-angle photography makes Rick literally loom over the viewer, filling the frame to bursting point. He seems bigger than the frame itself, and the sense of an all-powerful menace is clearly demonstrated.

Settings are carefully designed to further identify Rick's inner character, a device that would be carried even further in the western films. Rick's satiny, overdecorated apartment suggests weird tastes and hidden perversions. In particular, his unwillingness to face Joe ("I don't want to see his face" and "I don't want him to see me" are repeated several times) is developed into a full-scale visual motif.

Rick is a villain who can't stand the light of day. He lives in eternal night inside his apartment. He is related to the Mabuselike type of villain who manipulates the hero from inside his domain, sending out minions to do his killing for him. The implication is that of a very sick being living in hiding, the under-the-rock type of villain. Rick's light is always artificial, and in particular, it is usually not electric light, but fire.

Rick's instrument of torture is also fire. When he says he will make Ann talk—that there are ways of making her talk—he ominously strikes his cigarette lighter, watching the flame leap up. His apartment is filled with candles, and candlelight is his major source of illumination. In a hideous moment, he seizes up a chafing dish full of flaming brandy and heaves it into the face of his mistress (actually, straight into the camera and thus straight at the viewer), burning her horribly. (She bothered him when he was playing cards.)

When Joe is advancing toward Rick's apartment, Rick turns out all the lights, and extinguishes his candles. He demonstrates his feeling of insecurity and imminent danger by dousing the lights. Later, when he thinks Joe has been killed, he sighs with relief and relights the candles.

It is inevitable that Rick will be burned himself, that flames will engulf him. During the struggle in which both he and Joe are shot, his candles fall to the floor and the curtains catch fire. As the apartment is consumed, Rick falls backwards out of the window, surrounded by flames. By use of a striking optical, Burr makes a long fall backwards, looking up at the audience, his face twisted in horror.

Without Mann and Alton's mastery of form, Rick would be a dull villain, dependent on Burr's girth for his originality. By enhancing his evil through camera angles, decor, and the fire motif, a character was deepened—created, really—where none existed before.

Raw Deal proved that *T-Men* was no accident. The depth of field image, the complex compositions, the swift pacing, the skillful use of lighting patterns with Venetian blinds, etc., all mark it as a mini-masterpiece of form. It also points ahead to the western films not only in terms of the use of background, the linked characters, but also in its remarkable final shoot-out in the streets. Joe approaches Rick's apartment down mean city streets, surrounded by fog in dark of night.

Raw Deal's influence on other directors would be felt later—in Hitchcock's use of a taxidermist's shop in his remake of *The Man Who Knew Too Much* and in the scene in Fritz Lang's *The Big Heat* in which Lee Marvin would throw burning hot coffee in the face of his mistress.

Border Incident (1949) follows the pattern Mann established with such success in *T-Men*. It moves back and forth between semidocumentary and violent fictional narrative. Like *T-Men*, the entire film is a sort of redefinition of the original narrative "space." After establishing itself as a documentary about the Immigration Office's problems with Mexican wetbacks illegally entering the country, it switches to a violent story about the agents involved in the cases and the innocent Mexican victims of immigration swindlers.

An opening narration discusses the need for a vast army of workers to work the farmlands of Imperial Valley, in California. The dependence on cheap Mexican labor is illustrated by a shot from the air of tiny, insignificant figures—hundreds of them—working in the fields below. The impersonality of this shot is almost immediately undercut by the presentation of a desperate scene in which some of the illegal entrants who have worked in those same fields are robbed of the money they made when they attempt to sneak back across the border.

Three men are seen running across a night landscape. The sound of their desperate, panting breath fills the sound track. Suddenly, a signal light is seen from atop a high mountain in the distance. The light is first seen from the distance, and then suddenly in blinding close-up, and then from distance again. This close-far device has an unsettling effect on the audience, and a world of fear and danger is established. The scene is played out wordlessly with intense compositions stressing entrapment, fear, and alienation. The three men are met, brutally knifed, and thrown into quicksand with a businesslike efficiency that leaves an audience limp.

As in *T-Men*, two agents are sent out on the case. One is a representative of the Mexican government (Ricardo Montalban), and one represents the United States (George Murphy). It is decided that the Mexican will attempt to impersonate a wetback himself and discover the illegal network that smuggles workers in, only to kill them and steal back their wages when their work is finished.

The compositions of *Border Incident* are among the best in any Mann film. Composition is its raison d'être, as lighting was for *Railroaded*. Over and over again, dark scenes, partially lit with abstract, menacing patterns, present off-angle close-ups, compositions which stress entrapment. An arhythmic pattern of editing is established which alternates intense close-ups with long shots. The constant shifting of in-close/far-out space leaves a viewer insecure, a perfect equivalent for the situation the story presents.

Objects are placed forward in the frame to dominate space and overwhelm human beings, who seem always to be at the mercy of things and events. Pieces of things, as well as parts of people, intrude into the frame, throwing meaning and security off balance. A disembodied hand will enter the frame with a gun, or a cigarette, blotting out the image of the character previously seen alone in the frame, making it visually clear that there is no security anywhere. The space one occupies can be taken over, or lost, at any minute.

Bodies are packed horizontally in the back of a truck like sardines, as the wetbacks are transported across the border. One image shows an incomprehensible number of actors inside the frame, establishing the quantity of the cheap labor they represent. A cut changes the composition so that the next image shows the agent alone in the frame, alienated from the other workers, facing his danger without help.

Border Incident establishes clearly an overall formal pattern which Mann would later employ to its fullest artistic degree in his westerns:

1. Utilize a specific kind of composition against a specific background to establish meaning.
2. Move figures within that composition to readjust meaning.
3. Move camera if necessary to readjust (or redefine) meaning.
4. Cut when the possibilities of these redefinitions and readjustments have been thoroughly explored and/or exhausted.

One key scene in *Border Incident* illustrates this pattern. George Murphy is being held prisoner atop a small water tower on Howard DaSilva's ranch. Montalban must reach him in order to share valuable information. As Montalban stealthily climbs up the side of the water tower, Arthur Hunnicutt (Murphy's guard) hears a sound and starts to climb the stairs to check. Montalban reaches Murphy, and a complex image is presented in which Montalban is outside the tower's screen door in the darkness, and Murphy is behind it, inside,

seen in depth, striking a match for light. As they talk, the scene cuts
to Hunnicutt again, starting up the stairs. In the next cut, all three
men are seen in one single composition. The prisoner, the pursuer,
and the pursued are all contained within the frame simultaneously
in a complicated set-up: Montalban outside, Murphy inside, behind
the screen, and Hunnicutt moving up the side on the stairs. The
audience's view of this scene is such that it seems impossible that
Hunnicutt will not discover Montalban, trapped as he is on the level
outside Murphy's door.

Suddenly, unexpectedly, Montalban climbs to a higher level on a
stairway that the audience has not previously been able to see.
Momentary relief occurs. But Hunnicutt continues on to this second
level! Montalban is forced to progress to the rooftop and out onto a
tree limb to keep himself hidden. Relief again. But Hunnicutt decides to walk around the upper level of the tower, checking the roof
and the entire area. Montalban moves down the tree and drops to
the ground, silently stealing away. A long shot now shows the audience the entire spatial area of the water tower, with its total number
of levels and hiding places. In a series of images that are almost
indescribably complicated spatially, Mann has defined and
redefined an area so that a viewer feels safe, and then unsafe, in a
series of events. In this scene, the audience is forced to undergo the
relationship to the space, and thus to the narrative, that the hero is
undergoing. It is one of the first examples of Mann's total control of
such a scene, a method of definition and redefinition that would
become a prime characteristic of his later work.

The chief villain, Howard DaSilva plays with an air pistol in his
game room, shooting clay pigeons at a distance of twenty feet. There
is no reality to killing Mexicans to DaSilva—they are the equivalent of his clay pigeons. He even refers to them as "Mexican straw
dolls." The vantage point of the pigeons to the shooter, and the
shooter's viewpoint of them by way of mirrors as well as normal
distance is played with in a scene in which Murphy and DaSilva
negotiate for phony immigration cards. The use of the pistol is a
metaphor for their negotiations, as each man aims, shoots, and succeeds. They are evenly matched.

The space of DaSilva's game room is defined and redefined in
Murphy's final struggle with his captors before his death. As he first
overcomes DaSilva and races for the door, the space seems to open
up and provide escape, but at the point of his recapture it closes
down around him again.

It is practically a generic axiom that the likable minority figure in movies such as *Border Incident* must be killed in some horrible way, allowing the WASP figure to rescue the situation and pontificate on the sacrifice. In countless films, blacks, Orientals, and Mexicans have served as fodder for the audience's need for violence. In *Border Incident*, clues anticipating the gruesome demise of Ricardo Montalban are built into the narrative.

Montalban, however, survives. In a generic upset, it is good old George Murphy who is killed off, and with a considerable share of the running time of the film remaining. It was twelve years prior to Hitchcock's daring murder of Janet Leigh in the middle of *Psycho*. The murder of George Murphy—a brutal and graphic murder—is equally shocking and unexpected. Murphy was certainly as big a star as Montalban at the time. And as the American agent in the case, he clearly was playing the hero. Yet he not only is mercilessly tortured, but also wiped out with a brutality that is almost unmatched in American film. If one scene were chosen to illustrate the violence of *film noir*, Murphy's death in *Border Incident* would surely be the best choice.

His death scene takes place at night in an open, newly plowed field. Sitting in the field is a Caterpillar tractor pulling a disc. (After a field is plowed, a discing machine is used to break up, or churn, the new furrows.) The vicious blades of this machine are established early in the sequence through an intense close-up. Murphy is brought out into the field to be shot, but he fights, runs, and attempts to escape. One of the villains jumps into the machine, and begins to drive toward him.

The machine moves forward slowly, relentlessly, getting bigger and bigger in the frame, its lights cutting through the black night with an eerie omniscience. Murphy, shot and beaten, has fallen into the dirt. He lies helpless in front of the onslaught. His face is filthy, covered with the fresh soil, his eyes and mouth filled with it. He appears totally helpless, and the fresh soil almost looks like baby pablum on his face. As he sees the machine's advance, he tries desperately to crawl, his hands digging uselessly in the soft earth.

A cutting pattern is established that moves back and forth from the machine—to Murphy in the dirt—then to Montalban and his Mexican friend who watch helplessly from afar. These two figures, who have run forward to help but who realize it is hopeless, are stand-ins for the audience. Like the viewers, these characters must sit helplessly, mirroring the tension and anxiety the viewer feels.

Murphy's face grows larger and larger in the frame as the close-up intensifies. His face is twisted with fear and pain. His mouth drops open, and his face screws up. The machine, however, marches on. Underneath it, the audience is keenly aware of the cutters chewing up the earth. Finally, a hideous rhythm is played out in the cutting—machine, Murphy, machine, Murphy, machine, Murphy —over and over again in a seemingly endless agony of waiting. Throughout this, the viewer hopes and believes that Murphy will be rescued at the last minute. But he is not.

Prior to Murphy's death, Montalban and his Mexican ally (James Mitchell) commandeer a truck and careen down the highway, hoping to save him. The villain from whom they take over driving the truck (while it speeds along the highway) has been thrown out. But as they turn around in the road, he jumps up on the running board, making an attempt to strangle Montalban through the window. Montalban rolls up the truck's window, smashing the villain's hands. For minutes, he dangles outside the window, his twisted hands flapping inside the truck, his face equally twisted in pain. He dangles while the truck races along, and Montalban, ignoring him, lays his plans with Mitchell. A viewer cannot help but sympathize with the tortured villain, particularly when, in desperation, he bangs his head on the truck window, a la Wallace Ford in the steam-bath murder of *T-Men*. Both audience and character are helplessly trapped.

The maximum paranoia of the *noir* world is clearly illustrated when Montalban races up to a house by the side of the road to phone the immigration authorities for help. A woman comes to the door and says he *can* use her phone. She listens as he calls the authorities, leaves the room briefly, and reappears with a loaded gun. She is the wife of one of the villains! Since she has not been seen in the film before, the effect on the viewer is as shocking as it is to Montalban. No safety anywhere!

Mann's films in this period all ended with a dramatic action sequence—the shoot-out in the night club in *Railroaded*, the shipboard chase in *T-Men*, the shoot-out and final struggle of *Raw Deal*. *Border Incident* was no exception, as it culminated in an intense sequence in which Montalban, Mitchell, and the other wetbacks are taken to an abandoned quarry to be robbed and shot. Their bodies are to be sunk in quicksand to hide all traces of the perfidy. The herding of the Mexicans through the rocks toward the quarry suggests the movements through rocky terrains that would appear

in the films of the next decade. The horrible hand-to-hand struggles
of the Mexicans against their assailants, and the inevitable fall into
the quicksand, are all obvious rehearsals for the western struggles
amidst hostile terrain.

Border Incident hits a peak of emotional intensity, beginning with
Montalban's climb to the water tower, and onward through the theft
of the truck, Murphy's murder, the capture of Montalban, and the
quicksand climax. One dramatic moment is piled on top of another
in such a way that the audience is never allowed to relax. At the
same time, the main storyline is never sacrificed to these effects,
and the film stands as minor masterpiece of tension and dramatic
clarity. It is one of Mann's most powerful works of his early period,
and reflects his emerging status not only as a capable director but as
a name Hollywood *recognized* as a capable director. To make *Border
Incident*, Mann had been invited over to the prestigious Metro-
Goldwyn-Mayer studios. (He had wisely persuaded John Alton to
accompany him.) Mann was soon to finish his work in the B picture,
and become a full-fledged Hollywood director of class A projects.

First, however, came *Reign of Terror* (1949), truly a formal exercise. It represents a total triumph of form over content—or,
perhaps, form over lack of content. Given a script which has little
depth, but plenty of excitement, Mann responds accordingly. It is as
if he were saying, "Ok, ok, I know how to fill in the gaps left by a
poor script. . . . I've just spent five years doing it." He uses every
stylistic device he had learned, and uses them well. *Reign of Terror*
is pure fun, a "look, ma, no hands" tour de force of directorial skill.
No opportunity is missed. Shadows, bizarre camera angles, low
ceilings, slick wet cobblestone streets barely illuminated, rooms lit
only by candles, offbeat compositions, intense close-ups, gently
lifting and descending cameras—all the Mann touches are present.

Set in Paris in the postrevolutionary period, *Reign of Terror*
shows how Mann adapted his *film noir* techniques to a period picture. An intense but still documentarian narrator intones, "Paris,
July 26, 1794 . . .anarchy, misery, murder, arson. . . ." In other
words, perfect Mann subjects. These words are matched to a montage of fanatic revolutionists, their faces set in distorted close-ups
against raging flames. This opening sets the tone of baroque horror
which is to follow, and indicates the exaggeration that will be put to
good use. The script itself has an almost campy quality, in which the
dialogue might be interpreted as an early spoof of the genre. "Don't
call me Max," barks an irritable Maximilian Robespierre, and "What

this country needs is an elegant slow death," suggests Robert Cummings, the hero, who is pretending to be a killer from Strasbourg.

It is the familiar *film noir* world of urban Los Angeles or New York translated into Paris, 1794. For instance, one scene shows a horse-drawn carriage racing down a cobblestone street, late at night. Inside ride Robert Cummings and Arnold Moss, hero and villain, respectively. Suddenly, a blazing torch is thrown through the window. The composition and lighting create an almost three-dimensional effect, so that the viewer literally feels that the torch has been thrown at him. A hideous face appears at the carriage window, but Moss blows a hole in the head right before the audience's eyes. It is another example of Mann's use of a character, seen in depth outside a window, who is apparently in forward motion but is really trapped and ultimately doomed. He had used this effect in the truck sequence in *Border Incident,* and, without the forward motion, in the steam-bath murder in *T-Men.*

The plot concerns the in-group squabbling among the leading figures of the post-Louis XVI period. It has been modernized somewhat with the threat of a dictator and an ominous black list (as in the McCarthy era during which the film was released). But no real political issues are present, and Mann, as usual, has deemphasized everything but the love, speed, and thrills of the main story. *Reign of Terror* moves at a dizzying pace, creating a tension that never stops. It's almost a game. There's capture and escape, recapture and reescape, played at a breakneck pace until the final conclusion.

Reign of Terror is a minor film but it is interesting because it is Mann's first period piece. It also proves his skill yet again, and provides another of his fascinating villains (Arnold Moss), who is much more fun than the hero (Robert Cummings).

Side Street (1949)—twelve years before *West Side Story*—begins with a circular aerial shot over the typical Manhattan landscape associated with films. Seen from above, the streets are narrow pathways, entrapping and confining, and the movement of the camera makes the credits float and almost swim before the viewer's eyes. It is a visual equivalent of the situation of the leading character, Farley Granger, whose world is one he can neither control nor see fully, trapped as he is in one of the small canyons below.

As *Side Street* begins, a narrator refers to "New York City—an architectural jungle." The words are the key to the film, in which the compositions stress the sense of space as divided, elongated, enclosed. The storyline itself is architectural, as it builds layer upon layer of incident upon incident, while still taking strange turns and angles.

The film tells how an innocent young man (Granger), saddled with debts and rapidly dying dreams, becomes involved in crime through his own weakness. When the film opens, Granger is seen out of doors, walking the streets of Manhattan in his job of postman. He is reasonably happy and is openly framed and lit by natural light. He seems normal and ordinary, and his world looks safe. Although he dreams of better things, trips and fancy homes and furs for his wife, he feels that someday his ship will come in and these things will be his. His frustration surfaces, however, when he is faced with temptation in the form of easy money left within his grasp at one of his stops. If he takes the money, he won't have to wait for that ship . . . and who would know . . . . He makes the theft. His fate is sealed.

As the film progresses, he plunges vertiginously into the *noir* world and his physical self becomes a *noir* presence. Innocence and safety desert him. Granger changes physically before the audience's eyes. His flawless young face is scratched and scarred. His hand is cut from his using it to break glass. He looks tougher. The lighting casts shadows on him, and he is always placed in a vulnerable position in the frame. The urban landscape, the lighting pattern, the overall decor, and the editing emphasize his progression through a private hell.

The use of Farley Granger contributes greatly to the idea of innocence corrupted. Mann's days as casting director and talent scout for Selznick had taught him how to select the right actor for the role, and in Granger he found the perfect hero for *Side Street*. Granger is one of those minor film actors who in some way reflect an era more clearly than its larger stars. He was a handsome young man who, in another day, would have been assigned exclusively to playing the boy next door. Although he did have his share of such roles in *Small Town Girl* and *Story of Three Loves* (both 1953), for example, he was more often and more effectively used in films in which the plot hinges on some inherent weakness in his character. Alfred Hitchcock and Nicholas Ray both used this weakness, although to different ends, in *Strangers on a Train* (1951) and *They Live by Night* (1947). Farley Granger is a minor axiom of the 1950s. Like the decade itself, he looks good on the surface, but there's rot underneath where it counts.

Mann's use of Granger compares interestingly to Ray's in *They Live by Night*. There is no lyricism in Mann's hero as there is in Ray's, no sense of doomed beauty and a repressive society as a shaping force. Granger in *Side Street* is clearly surrounded by a materialistic society that tempts him, but it is his own weakness that brings him down. He is the typical Mann hero—one whose internal moral struggle brings about his violent or antisocial behavior, and thus his doom. Ray's hero has been hurt by an unheeding world, and contains love and poetry in his soul. Had society been different, he would have been different. Mann's hero carries his problems within himself, whereas Ray's hero has problems that press down on him from without.

Both *Side Street* and *They Live by Night* pair Granger with Cathy O'Donnell. Where Ray used the two lovers in balanced harmony, Mann uses O'Donnell in his own traditional way—to depict the better, more positive side of the morally complex hero. In *Side Street*, the love story is important, but downplayed to the more violent action. Mann generally had less interest in the woman's role than in the man's. He was capable of portraying mature relationships between men and women of an honest and intensely sexual nature, as he indicated in *Raw Deal* and proved later in *Naked Spur, The Glenn Miller Story, Strategic Air Command, El Cid,* and others. Although his women are always interesting characters, his main preoccupation was in portraying the role of the hero at odds with his community or his world.

Granger and O'Donnell are trapped. Although their love is genuine, their situation is hopeless. Thus, their scenes together are usually shot in extreme close-up. The tightness of the frame around them suggests that this tiny world of their love is all they have. It both sustains them and traps them.

When his child is born, Granger, a hunted man, breaks into the maternity ward to visit his wife. It is a classic example of *noir* madness—a father has to commit a criminal act to see his newborn child. The ward, symbol of motherhood, sanity, and order, is treated as if it were an insane asylum. It is photographed to look ominous, menacing. It is a nightmare world of elongated corridors, ghostlike beds with white curtains drawn like shrouds, and dark, threatening shadows everywhere. The technical set-up would be more appropriate for a murder scene. Instead it's a scene which concerns issues usually associated with life and hope, not death. There is no better sequence in any film to illustrate the paranoia of the *film noir* world.

Border Incident. X marks the victim. Arnold Moss (left) and Alfonso Bedoya (right) trap George Murphy in a sleazy hotel room.

Side Street. Farley Granger's beaten face (right) reflects his journey from nice-guy to criminal, as James Craig (left) holds him prisoner in the back of a New York taxi cab.

Side Street reflects the improvement brought to Mann's films by his move to MGM. As in *Border Incident*, he has better sets, locations, costumes, and equipment to work with. In addition, Mann had the Metro depth in character players to choose from, or at least the Metro money behind him in hiring. *Side Street* not only has a strong screenplay which presents fully drawn characters, but it has the actors to play them. In particular, Jean Hagen creates a vivid portrait as an alcoholic singer who is constantly used by men. ("He hit me once when I recited Robert Burns. . . . He had no manners at all.")

The final chase of the film is the visual highpoint. The cars are seen from above in high, wide aerial shots in which the streets become long corridors. Although the cars scurry and rush through them like little bugs, the viewpoint clearly indicates it's no use. The effort is futile. Their drivers are trapped in the lanes, and cannot get out of them. Their fates are predetermined. (The occasional use of narration stresses this sense of determinism throughout the film.)

The tall urban buildings loom over the cars, dwarfing them, dominating the action. Since the story is about a young man who wanted things he couldn't have—things that were all around him in the city stores—these buildings stuffed with goods seem to mock him. Ironically, the money he stole has brought him no pleasure. His wife doesn't even take a private room at the hospital, as he had instructed her.

Despite its excellent compositions and characteristic redefinition of space (particularly when Granger first returns to his bedroom in his own home), *Side Street* is not as flashy in technique as *T-Men* and *Border Incident*. It is more restrained, which fits its love theme. It is still, however, a typical *noir* in its presentation of a weak and flawed hero ("He's only human, and no stronger than most of us"). And in its constant overhead shots it emphasizes the no-way-out, fatalistic themes of *noir* films. Its overall paranoia is extreme. Certainly, its falsely optimistic ending ("He's gonna be all right") convinces no one.

Side Street has been overlooked by Mann devotees. It is not as beautiful to look at as *Raw Deal* or as totally exciting as *Border Incident*. Nor does it contain overwhelming emotional effects, such as the steam-bath murder in *T-Men*. But it is probably Mann's most important film in the *noir* period because the urban landscape, the lighting, the overall decor, the compositions, and the editing are all unified around the character's narrative and psychological progression. It is a minor variation of and rehearsal for the psychological journeys across hostile terrain that Mann's western heroes of the next decade would undergo. What *Side Street* lacks is the complete ability to create an emotional effect in the audience that is like that the hero is acting out for them. Watching *Side Street* is a somewhat more detached experience than watching *T-Men* or *Border Incident*. But in its clarity and in its presentation of a hero descending into a private hell, it is the *film noir* equivalent to Mann's final great western, *Man of the West*.

4

Mann of the West

I was under contract to Metro and had just made my first film for Nicholas Nayfack.[1] Nicholas called me and asked, "Would you like to make a western? I've a scenario here that seems interesting." In fact, that "interesting" scenario was the best script I've ever read! I prepared the film with the greatest care. . . .

—ANTHONY MANN[2]

MANN'S "GREATEST CARE" included the valuable insurance of asking for—and getting—both Robert Taylor (a leading Metro star) to play the hero, and John Alton to do the photography. The resulting film, *Devil's Doorway* (1950), marked the beginning for Mann of a decade of work in the genre. Between 1950 and 1960, he would direct ten major western films,[3] his most commercially and critically successful body of work. He had found the format that could give him the depth and complexity he had been searching for in his *noir* period. As Jean-Luc Godard wrote, Mann's westerns presented "both beautiful landscapes and the explanation of this beauty, both mystery of firearms and the secret of this mystery, both art and the theory of art."[4]

The Mann Westerns—Content

As stated in the preface, the Mann western exists on three levels: the literal, narrative line which corresponds to the presentation of the landscape, or geography of the film; the internal, psychological state for the hero, which is expressed through the narrative, and thus also through landscape and position in the frame; and the emotional state for both hero and the audience, which is controlled by the shifting landscape, narrative line, and character development.

Even the titles of the films reflect this layered meaning. *Bend of*

"The Man With A secret"—James Stewart, Mann's ambivalent and nearly psychotic hero of the old west.

the River defines the locale of the major conflict of the film, but it also defines the major emotional development of the hero, who is at a turning place in his life. *The Far Country* is set in the upper regions of the icy north, and its hero is a man who lives emotionally distant from other people. *The Last Frontier* is set both historically and physically at the closing of the American frontier and at the last outpost of civilization. Its hero, a free-spirited trapper, faces his last emotional frontier during the film, and accepts the limits of civilization into his personal life.

Comparing Mann's westerns to those of other masters, such as John Ford and Raoul Walsh, one finds a marked difference emerging. Ford carried on an ambivalent romance with the genre, using it to express both a poetic vision of the American past and his own shifting set of beliefs over the years. Walsh used the genre more straightforwardly, for purposes of narrative and adventure, to reflect his major concerns of time and space. Mann might be said to have modernized the genre, incorporating into it an increased violence and using it to express man's vision of self, the conflicts of his inner psychology.

Mann's westerns center around the basic narrative pattern that was described earlier. His recurring set of characters include: the hero (a man with a secret), the villain (linked to the hero), and the old man, the women, and the secondary villains. These characters undertake a journey which is simultaneously physical, psychological, and emotional. This journey provides the background for a strong narrative line. In his excellent book, *Horizons West*, Jim Kitses has defined some of the themes and issues of that narrative: contrasts between two worlds and two characters; the revenge hero; the hero's complex relationship to the villain; the community, which for Mann is the family; the closing of the frontier; the tension between wilderness and civilization; extreme men who are pushed by forces inside them to overextend themselves emotionally. Mann heroes are defined by Kitses as "over-reachers," and a clear statement is made by Kitses that "the genre was never to be quite the same for his work within it."[5]

Kitses's observations are both correct and perceptive, and they stand as the introduction to Mann's work. Mann's western films will be treated here as having a narrative pattern which incorporates the issues indicated by Kitses in his major work on Mann in English. Defining the basic narrative of the westerns and indicating how

Mann elected to present that narrative formally is the idea behind this chapter, which will confine itself to an auteurist presentation of the recurring thematic and formal concerns of the director. The implications of Mann's narrative—the effect of the closing of the frontier, the problem of community or family in the modern world—lie outside the format of this book, as explained in my preface. The importance of the years Mann spent making westerns lies in his fully maturing as an artist and evolving a coherent narrative pattern with a set of characters that suited his main thematic goals.

Mann's work during the decade also shows the evolution of a set of formal characteristics. Primarily a simplification and stripping-down of his *film noir* style, the westerns were far less stylistically baroque than the films of the *noir* years. Despite their increased austerity, they are equally intense. The shift in style comes from Mann's having learned to do more with less. Upon the release of *Man of the West,* Jean-Luc Godard observed, "The art of Anthony Mann seems to be evolving toward a purely theoretical schematism of mise en scene."[6]

The western scripts afforded Mann the opportunity to tone down his formal experimentation, as there was no longer any need to provide depth where none existed, as in so many of the *noir* stories. In his westerns, Mann was served by a group of screenwriters whose work contained what he needed and wanted to express visually and formally. Borden Chase, who wrote *Winchester '73* (with Robert L. Richards), *Bend of the River,* and *The Far Country,* along with Philip Yordan (coauthor of *The Man from Laramie* and *The Last Frontier),* Dudley Nichols *(Tin Star),* and Reginald Rose *(Man of the West),* provided Mann with the taut, spare scripts about powerful events that suited his desire for purity and clarity in film.

Since all the formal elements of a Mann western are unified around a central narrative meaning, a discussion of these elements is inevitably redundant. Mann's composition, editing, camera movement, lighting, and use of space all serve the same ends. In considering them and defining them, it is important to remember their single overall purpose, and to realize that repetition is necessary.

Taken separately, the Mann formal characteristics of the western years can be defined as follows:

Use of Landscape: The landscape both frames and embodies action. A character's position in the narrative (as well as his psychological state) is to be read from his relationship to the land-scape. As events occur which change a character's position in the story, the space he occupies is altered accordingly. Not only does the background change, but the character's position in the frame changes, also. These changes demonstrate both the character's out-ward emotional and his inner psychological states. Yet it cannot be said that all there is to a Mann western is a direct matching of character to landscape: rocks = bad man, trees = good man. Ten-sion is created by the constant shifting and revising of backgrounds, so that although a character is defined by his landscape, that land-scape is not static. Thus, the logical story form for a Mann western is that of a journey, which enables a changing terrain to unfold natur-ally.

Mann's landscapes are not those about which one says, "How beautiful!" Without their characters, his western spaces look ordi-nary, even meaningless. It is the character placed *within* the land-scape that brings meaning—and relevance—to the settings he chooses.

Composition: By 1950, composition is clearly the basic unit of Mann's style. Obviously, in the western films, it is through the use of the landscape that this characteristic is demonstrated. As indi-cated above, the hero's position in the narrative may be read via his compositional position within the frame.

Editing: Since Mann's work is based primarily on composition, not editing, cuts occur when the compositional possibilities of a scene have been exhausted. The cut either transfers the same un-folding compositional relationship onto the next scene, or releases it (and thus redefines it) through a violent explosion of cuts.

Relationships are usually established within a shot, rather than across a cut. Cuts are dependent on the requirements of the events unfolding within the frame. Thus, no logical rhythm of shots is developed. Cutting tends to be arhythmical. Shots are not linked together in a smooth, ordered pattern, nor are they linked together in a disordered pattern (which would form an order of its own). Sometimes they are, sometimes they aren't. There is no particular predictability or rhythm to the editing patterns of the Mann west-ern.

Camera Movement: Whether the movement of the camera is functional or dramatic, it serves the same purpose, which is the presentation of the characters in a unified physical, psychological, and emotional world. Oftentimes, the movement functions to follow the hero through space, or to follow the main action. At other times, it is used dramatically, to reveal sudden dangers that were present in the landscape which the hero, and thus the audience, did not know. The main device for this is the swish pan to frame right or left. By rapidly moving the camera through space with the swish pan, Mann illustrates both the violent nature of his world as well as the potential for treachery it contains. This sudden revelation of the larger world visually redefines the narrative situation and the character's position in it (and thus, the audience's relation to it).

The camera is often moved slowly up, or slowly down (with cranes or booms), to provide a larger perspective on the landscape. This method of showing what is above or below the hero's world with camera movement is also a type of redefinition of space.

Lighting: The use of natural sunlight for outdoor sequences creates scenes of great beauty which provide dramatic contrast when violent action takes place in the dappled sunlight of forests. Thus, lighting enhances the paradoxes in the story—hero/villain, good/bad, action/repose, safety/danger—and the sense of contrast and conflict. Interior lighting of sets in the western films often follows that of the *noir* period.

Use of Space: In his westerns, Mann's use of space expanded to include the entire outdoor western landscape, in a variety of geographical locations. As Mann perfected his style, he mastered the use of the entire world as personal space. The westerns use this real space (with outdoor location), but also artificial space (with sets).

The important thing is that, as the hero's relationship to his space shifts, through narrative development, the viewer's look at the space also changes. Thus, the audience is in a position similar to that of the characters. The films thus affect the audience as they affect the characters. The remarkable thing about the Mann western is that physical space becomes the equivalent of psychological space.

To repeat, all formal elements in Mann's westerns serve the same purpose. Mann's importance as an artist is linked to the fact that, because of this, the audience undergoes the same emotional experience as the characters.

Development of the Mann Western

Just as he carefully explored the possibilities of the *film noir*, Mann explored the possibilities of the western. The ten films he

Transition Westerns, still under the film noir influence: (Top) Robert Taylor as Lance Poole in the barroom brawl of *Devil's Doorway*. (Bottom) Barbara Stanwyck, the western femme fatale of *The Furies*, preparing to mete out justice (of sorts) to Walter Juston and Judith Anderson.

made in the genre (always excepting *Cimarron*) can be organized
into a pattern of growth and development in the following way:

1. *Transition: Devil's Doorway, The Furies* (both in 1950).
2. *Exploration and Resolution: Winchester '73* (1950).
3. *Definition:* Four films which form the core of the work, *Bend of the
   River* (1952); *The Naked Spur* (1953); *The Far Country* (1955), and *The
   Man from Laramie* (1955).
4. *Inversion and Abstraction: The Last Frontier* (1955) and *The Tin Star*
   (1957).
5. *Culmination: Man of the West* (1960).

Transition: *Devil's Doorway* and *The Furies*

"I think the result was more powerful than *Broken Arrow*, more
dramatic, too," Mann said, describing his first western, *Devil's
Doorway*.[7]

Both that film and *The Furies* represent the translation of Mann's
film noir style to the western genre. They are primarily stories of
fate in which things that can go wrong, do go wrong—with a ven-
geance. The prominence of women in both stories, in particular the
femme fatale of *The Furies*, links them to the *noir* tradition, in which
women are motivational figures. The power of the women clearly
marks both films as outside the Mann western tradition, in which
the woman is not only a minor figure but has little definition without
the hero, whose better inner self she often represents.

Devil's Doorway is the story of Lance Poole (Robert Taylor), an
Indian who has received the Congressional Medal of Honor for
service to his country during the Civil War. When he returns home
to Wyoming, he expects to resume his peaceful life, ranching with
his tribe in Sweet Meadows, the fertile land he owns. However, the
ordered world he fought for is now threatened by change and
growth. A shyster lawyer from the east (Louis Calhern) hates Indians, and for the first time Lance is subjected to overt Indian
prejudice. The lawyer stirs up a group of sheepherders who want to
graze their stock in Sweet Meadows, and trouble erupts. When
government legislation is passed that says all Indian lands may now
be homesteaded by whites, Lance tries to retain his land legally
with the help of a female lawyer (Paula Raymond), herself a victim of
male prejudice. Their efforts are futile, and Lance and his braves
make a valiant last stand at the ranch. When the cause is totally lost,

Lance, wearing his cavalry uniform and Medal of Honor, marches out to salute the soldiers who have driven him from his home. After his ironic salute, he falls dead.

Devil's Doorway is an extremely dark film, as befits its subject matter. Most scenes take place at night or inside darkened rooms or bars, which is untypical of the western genre, but is obviously a prime characteristic of *film noir*. John Alton's night photography on location is a dominant factor in the formal success of *Devil's Doorway*. Together, Mann and Alton continued the depth of field, angular composition, and intense close-ups they had used for baroque effects in the 1940s films. The influence of the *noir* tradition is exemplified by a scene in which Lance rides into Medicine Bow to deposit money in his bank account (earned by sale of his cattle). As Lance rides into town, a large herd of sheep fills the street, blocking his pathway, as overhead, storm clouds gather. This single image tells the entire plot. When Lance and another Indian dismount, the town marshal gloomily hints, "People resent a rich Indian."

Lance and his companion enter the bar. A sign reading "No liquor for Indians" is immediately seen, and lightning and thunder crash ominously. The length of the bar is established in a depth of field shot, with the shyster lawyer (Calhern) and a friend at one end, and Lance and his friend at the other.

The depth of the image in this scene illustrates Mann and Alton's total mastery of form for storytelling. In one composition, all the plot conflicts are stated. In the foreground, the villain and his cohort dominate the space, the correlative of their situation in the storyline. At the back of the frame, Lance and his friend are seen at the bar, standing near the door. In between these two opposing forces sit the townspeople at their tables, watching for the confrontation, but neutral in their own position. Outside the door of the bar can be seen the sunny streets of the town where Lance, the war hero, was previously welcomed home. The interior of the bar is dark, in perfect lighting contrast to the sunshine seen in deep focus.

An arhythmical pattern of editing is established which alternates between shots showing the length of the bar with the good and bad forces at opposite ends, and then intense close-ups of the two opposing groups. As conversation unfolds, lightning and thunder continue. Onlookers in the bar, sensing the approaching violence (well counterpointed by the noise of the weather) rise from their chairs and move back. The lawyer's companion shoots the drinking glasses off the bar in front of the two Indians. Achieving no reaction, he then shoots off Lance's hat, and fires at his boots.

In a scene characteristic of *film noir,* Lance attacks suddenly, into the camera, violently invading the space which has been so carefully established in prior shots. The length of the bar between the two groups is shortened by this violent action. Space is redefined, as the situation changes.

A brutal fight takes place, in which close-ups of those watching alternate with intense close-ups of the fighters themselves. Longer shots establish the entire space of the barroom and the relationships of all participants in the scene to the space. During this action, thunder is heard continuously, and lightning (the only real illumination) cuts the darkness. The only other sound besides the thunder is the grunting, gasping, thumping sound of the fight. Without the western clothes, it could easily be a scene from *T-Men* or *Raw Deal.*

The story of *Devil's Doorway* presents an outsider (another hold-over from the *noir* years) at odds with his society. Two victims of discrimination are linked in the storyline, a woman and an Indian. This linking of two important characters might be said to represent a rudimentary rehearsal for later pairings of hero and villain in a complex moral relationship. Here, of course, both sides are morally superior to others in the film, are of the opposite sex, and are on the same side.

Both characters are well developed and acted with dignity by Taylor and Raymond. The scene of their initial meeting illustrates their positions in the community clearly. Lance is naturally surprised when a woman answers his inquiry for "A. Masters, Attorney."

"I don't blame you for being surprised," she says. "Most people are when they discover 'A. Masters' is a woman." Her feeble attempt to hide her sex by using her first initial instead of her full name is equivalent to Lance's having joined the cavalry to fight for "his" country. Each has made an attempt to act as if he/she belongs in a situation where he/she is really an outsider. In their first meeting, Masters is unaware that Lance has been forced to hire her himself only because he is an Indian, and cannot get another lawyer. They are linked by their alienation from the established community.

Their relationship is one in which they must overcome their own small prejudices. Lance is suspicious about whether or not she really *is* an effective lawyer. She is worried about his being an Indian. (On her first visit to Lance at his ranch, she takes her mother with her. Mom comes prepared with a shotgun.) They are forced to learn about each other and to accept each other. The learning process is one for the audience, too, and the unfolding mutual respect deepens the story. Masters learns to respect Lance in a scene of simple dignity in which she asks him the necessary questions with which to file his land claim. In filling in his war record, she asks, "Any decorations?" and he replies, "Congressional Medal of Honor." "Any major battles?" and he replies, "Mechanicsville, Antietam, Gettysburg." "Well, you've had your share," she observes, suddenly struck by the unfairness of his having to fight for his own land through the law courts. The real battle, the final one, is yet to come.

There is a hint of a romance between Lance and Masters, or at least a yearning of their two alienated spirits. In one scene, they almost kiss, their two profiles seen in intense close-up, at opposite (opposing) sides of the frame. "One hundred years from now it might have worked," he says cryptically, referring both to their legal battle and to their relationship, and she weeps. At the film's end, Masters says, "It would be too bad if we ever forgot," referring to Lance's desperate, foolhardy battle for his rights.

Devil's Doorway was not a critical or commercial success. Its reception was greatly harmed by the release of Delmer Daves's *Broken Arrow*, starring James Stewart as a western scout who tries to make peace with Cochise. Most critics saw Mann's film as a low-budget black-and-white rip-off of Daves. This was unfortunate, because *Devil's Doorway* is a far superior film. *Broken Arrow* is self-conscious and talky, but its overt moralizing was taken seriously by the same critics who dismissed *Devil's Doorway*. It was not Mann's style to film screenplays which discussed and presented concepts laid over a story. Rather, he presented stories with ideas and concepts built into them, and the depth of his films is still overlooked on this basis.

A key to the relative honesty of the two films might be their attitudes toward sexual relationships between Indians and whites. In *Broken Arrow*, Stewart marries an appropriately beautiful Indian maiden, Debra Paget, who is killed by whites. This clichéd idea of white-man-loves-Pocahontas is a staple of the old-fashioned western story, and does nothing to further the truth about the plight of the Indians. On the contrary, the sight of Paget in her beautifully designed suede moccasins and color-coordinated beads is enough to send any white man scampering to the reservation. No love is allowed in *Devil's Doorway*, a far more truthful situation, and although white-man-can-love-red-woman, white woman still cannot love red man without shame and ostracism.

Fortunately, *Devil's Doorway* has gained in reputation since its release. It is not only an honest portrait of the plight of the Indian, but it also has an interesting portrait of a preliberation woman. It is in every way a modern film. In Mann's career, it stands out as a major step forward, carrying over his *noir* sensibility, both formally and thematically, into a new genre.

This is also true of *The Furies*. *The Furies* sought an epic tone with its opening title card: "This is a story of the 1870s. . .in the New Mexico territory. . .when men created kingdoms out of land and cattle. . .and ruled their empires like feudal lords. Such a man was T. C. Jeffords. . .who wrote this flaming page in the history of the great Southwest."

T. C. Jeffords (Walter Huston) is one of Mann's patriarchal figures who is both good and bad contained in one character. Jeffords not only owns everything surrounding his huge ranch, but he has the audacity to pay off creditors and workers with his own currency, called "T.C.'s." He spoils and adores his only daughter, Vance (Barbara Stanwyck). The film's main plot focuses on their ultimate clash, when Vance falls in love and shifts her loyalty away from her father and onto her lover.

The Jeffords family has been described by Steve Handzo, writing in *Bright Lights*, as "a further variation on the House of Atreus Goes West."[8] There is the strong, domineering father who loves his daughter too much. The daughter is a chip off the old blockhouse, tough and domineering. (Presented with an expensive necklace as her father's gift, she spits at him, "Pearls! Fit for dove-faced little women. I told you anything but pearls!" It turns out to be a joke. The pearls are for her brother's dove-faced little bride. Diamonds, as hard and bright as her character, await her.) The brother is jealous of his father's love for his sister, who herself has an Electra complex. "You won't have it easy finding a man," Jeffords warns her, "I've spoiled you." When she does find a man (Wendell Corey), she finds one who hates her father, having been involved in a land feud with him for many years. Needless to say, her father returns the hatred full force.

Despite its western setting, *The Furies* is typical *film noir*. Fate, madness, and hunger for power and money are its primary concerns. Much of the action takes place at night, linking it, like *Devil's Doorway*, to the *noir* tradition. A noirish duality is set up between the father and the lover, and the daughter and the stepmother Jeffords later marries (Judith Anderson). This duality is expressed usually by casting of lookalike actors. The father and the lover, Huston and Corey, not only look alike facially, but are almost identical in height, carriage, and body type. Stanwyck and Anderson bear a startling resemblance. Even their voices are similar, and both actresses are able to play sympathetic or unsympathetic roles with ease. The characters they play—who shift back and forth from sympathetic to unsympathetic (Stanwyck), and unsympathetic to sympathetic (Anderson)—require actresses of their range. The four characters are linked in complicated relationships. Father loves stepmother because stepmother looks like daughter, and daughter loves lover because he looks like father. Furthermore, these characters not only *look* alike. They *act* alike. They are linked together emotionally by their similar natures as well as their mutual desires. These connections and relationships are stressed by having them together in two-shots, or in groups of four within the frame. Their "reflection" of each other in terms of character is stressed by using mirrors. Thus, when Stanwyck faces a mirror, the audience does not see her reflection, but that of Anderson, who is present in the frame only in the mirror. Mirrors are also used in typical noir fashion to suggest the duality inside each major character.

All the devices Mann learned in the 1940s films are brought to bear—depth of field, shadowed lighting, menacing and overpowering interiors, bizarre camera angles, diffusions, silhouettes. (Victor Milner earned an Oscar nomination for his excellent cinematography.) When Stanwyck viciously hurls a pair of scissors into the face of Anderson, horribly disfiguring her, it is pure *film noir*.

However, although *The Furies* clearly belongs to the *noir* tradition, it also begins Mann's exploration of characteristics that will mark his use of the western genre. Figures are seen starkly posed against the big sky, allied with a sense of nature, using background for definition. The landscape itself is used for psychological meaning to a certain degree, particularly in two scenes which are used later, more fully developed, in *The Naked Spur*—one in which a fiery attack takes place on a group of Mexican land-squatters, and one in which rocks are rained down on Stanwyck when she goes to visit the Mexicans.

The Furies is meant to be the translation of Greek tragedy into the west. The silhouettes of the leading characters which are used repeatedly act as stand-ins for the masks of Greek drama. The characters themselves are archetypes—THE father, THE jealous brother, THE spoiled daughter, THE stepmother, etc. Above all, it is a story of fate, and the fall of a house of proud people who lack humility. Too late, a daughter realizes she loves her father and has brought about his destruction. The father, having lost everything but proved his manhood in a struggle with a bull, hears the cowboys singing a song about his legend. "There'll never be another like me," he says, dying in his daughter's arms.

Thematically, the familial quarrel, a staple of the Mann western, takes place here between father and daughter, instead of father and son. The typical link between hero and villain that would emerge in later films is superimposed upon the relationship between the father and the daughter's lover. *The Furies* loses the focus of its main conflict because the film can't seem to make up its mind whether it is about Jeffords or about his daughter. Mann's later westerns always clearly define a hero, who is allied with the landscape and also with the audience's emotional reaction. That alignment is not clearly present here. The opening sections of the film establish Stanwyck as the central figure, but later a shift to Huston takes place. This reflects Mann's primary interest in strong male figures, and his general lack of interest in a female protagonist.

In comparing both *Devil's Doorway* and *The Furies* to the basic Mann western, certain differences emerge. If Mann's traditional hero is a man with a secret, the hero of *Devil's Doorway* does not have a secret. However, he has its equivalent psychological burden in that he is an Indian, an outcast of society. Thus, like the heroes of the more typical westerns, he carries his problem inside him, and it alienates him from the rest of his community. The problem, or "secret," must be dealt with for him to continue living (or, in this case, die). This type of secret is a *guilty* secret a la *film noir*, as it prevents the hero from living in a more ordered or optimistic society.

As stated earlier, the hero of *The Furies* is unclear. Jeffords contains within him the bad/good dichotomy of the typical Mann western hero. But Jeffords is too old to be the hero, and much of the film does not focus on him. Certainly the daughter's lover (Corey) is not the hero, as he is too weak, too opportunistic, and absent for too much of the running time. There is a minor character, a Mexican played by Gilbert Roland, who has heroic characteristics, but he is secondary in the plot.

The logical hero of *The Furies* is Vance, the character played by Barbara Stanwyck. She is by instinct the son of the family, not the daughter. It is she who conflicts with the old man, defies him, and brings him down. She has her own guilty secret, in that she loves her father too well. Her secret would be in the *noir* tradition, in that it is a psychological secret.

Both *Devil's Doorway* and *The Furies* contain rudimentary examples of the hero, villain, old man, women, secondary-villain scheme. Other than those already discussed, there are the old men in *Devil's Doorway:* a good old man, Lance's father; a bad old man, the villain Louis Calhern; and a bad-good old man, the town marshal played by Edgar Buchanan, who is sympathetic to Lance but has to carry out his duty and ends up unintentionally destructive. Buchanan is a potential force for reason, and is played somewhat for comic relief. Thus, he is a miniature embodiment of all the old-man characters who will provide humor in the films to come (the Millard Mitchell and Walter Brennan characters).

Secondary characters abound in both films. *The Furies* has an entire subplot involving Mexican squatters. *Devil's Doorway* has a group of sheepherders headed by a father-son combination, in which Marshall Thompson plays a good man drawn into the conflict by forces stronger than himself. To the degree that he represents the leader of the good side of the group, he is the equivalent of Lance Poole.

These well-developed secondary groups represent the physical presence of the sense of community that later heroes would be alienated from, although in the films to follow the communities might not actually be present. *Bend of the River* and *Far Country* would physically maintain the groups; *Naked Spur* would not. The complicated subplots of *Devil's Doorway* and *The Furies* would be weeded out of the Mann storyline as his work progressed and was clarified. The implications of those plots would remain, but would be contained within the characters as motivations for their obsessions.

A great deal of effort can be expended finding further differences between these two transitional films and the later westerns. The *key* difference, however, lies in the lack of physical journey in either film. Although it might be said that *Devil's Doorway* represents a social or historical journey for Lance Poole, and that *The Furies* represents a psychological journey for Barbara Stanwyck, these are not the geographical movements of the later films.

The terrain in both movies is the terrain of *film noir*. *Devil's Doorway* and *The Furies* are clearly transitional films between Mann's *noir* period and his fullest use of the western genre.

Exploration and Resolution: *Winchester '73*

As for *Winchester '73*, that was one of my biggest successes. And it's also my favorite western. The gun which passed from hand to hand allowed me to embrace a whole epoch, a whole atmosphere. I really believe that it contains all the ingredients of the western, and that it summarizes them.

—ANTHONY MANN[9]

This film is Mann's first real western. Although it was made after *Devil's Doorway* and before *The Furies*, it represents a complete breaking-away from *film noir*. *Devil's Doorway* and *The Furies* clearly were rehearsals in which he purged himself of his last baroque *noir* tendencies. Beginning with *Winchester '73*, a new simplicity and clarity entered his work, bringing with it the psychological intensity of the *noir* period, but realized in a more direct visual manner.

Fritz Lang had been set to direct *Winchester '73*, but withdrew at the last moment. Mann was hired to replace him, partly at the suggestion of James Stewart, who had been favorably impressed with *Devil's Doorway*. A scenario had been prepared from Stuart N. Lake's book by Robert Richards, but Mann disliked it when he read it. At his insistence, Borden Chase was hired to do a rewrite, and Mann and Chase worked hand in hand on the project, a relationship which would later be repeated.

Winchester '73, which lays the groundwork for the James Stewart/Anthony Mann collaboration, fits the classic pattern of the Mann Western through these characters:

THE HERO:	Stewart is a man with a secret. He hunts another man in order to kill him. Unbeknownst to the audience, that man is really his brother.

THE VILLAIN: The chief villain is the blood-rela-
                                tion, the evil brother who shot their
                                kind father in the back (Stephen
                                McNally).

THE OLD MAN: Prior to the beginning of the film,
                                there was a kind old man, the true
                                father figure, whose death is the
                                motivation for the action. During
                                the running time of the film, there is
                                a kindly old man (Millard Mitchell)
                                who sustains and befriends the
                                hero. He alone knows the hero's
                                secret. A positive force, he functions
                                also as somewhat of a comic relief.

THE WOMAN: The woman is an outcast of society
                                in the tradition of Dallas from John
                                Ford's classic film, *Stagecoach*. Like
                                Dallas, she is a saloon girl, leaving
                                town as the film opens. Also like
                                Dallas, she hopes for a better life,
                                proves her courage, and will love
                                and sustain the hero (Shelley Win-
                                ters).

SECOND VILLAIN: There is a strong second villain.
                                Since it is an important part of the
                                plot structure to keep the secret that
                                McNally is really Stewart's brother,
                                the second villain provides a charac-
                                ter who can deploy audience inter-
                                est in the villain until the final re-
                                velation. The second villain (Dan
                                Duryea) is an unregenerate outlaw,
                                brutal and cruel.

Mann himself clearly understood the success of, as he put it, the "externalization" of the conflict of the film into the physical form of a rifle that could be passed from hand to hand . . . and thus from episode to episode. By following this method, Mann was able to both sum up an era of western filmmaking and revitalize it at the same time. In *Winchester '73*, the hero undertakes a journey which might rightly be said to cover the entire history of the western genre.

Winchester '73 contains all of the following familiar situations of the western film within its ninety-two-minute running time:

—A rifle-shooting contest, with the hero and villain evenly matched.
—A runaway horse, with a helpless woman trapped in the carriage.
—An Indian attack on the cavalry.
—A shoot-out in the streets.
—A final confrontation between hero and villain that takes place out of doors on a rocky landscape.
—A revenge theme.
—A last stand.
—A poker game.
—Outlaws meeting at an isolated way station.
—A group of ruthless outlaws holding an innocent farm family hostage.
—A bank robbery.
—A saloon fight.
—An Indian uprising.

These basic plot situations involve familiar western characters and sets: saloon girl, cowardly easterner, grizzled cavalry officer, Wyatt Earp, crooked gambler, noble Indian savage, etc., and western town with main street, saloon, bank, isolated out-station, outlaw hide-out, campfire, settlers farm, stagecoach, etc.

The symbol of the rifle is present in all episodes as a motivational force. Even the love relationship is worked out through the metaphor of guns. When Shelley Winters is trapped with Stewart and the cavalry, surrounded by Indians, he gives her a gun. "I know how to use it," she says, and when he hesitates, she tells him, "And I understand about the last one." She accepts the idea that she must kill herself rather than fall into the hands of the Indians. Later, after they have successfully withstood the Indian attack, she returns the gun to Stewart, but asks to have the last bullet, the one she was meant to use on herself. "If you want it . . ." he says, looking at her carefully. "I want it," she replies, looking him straight in the eye.

The meaning is definitely sexual. The bullet was the symbol of his protection of her, his concern, but also of her own independence and courage in the moment of crisis. It represents her ability to choose for herself—and she chooses him. When she takes the bullet from him, she is both accepting his offer and making one herself. They are united through the dominant metaphor of the gun.

All conflicts, all love, all motivation, are developed through the rifle. It is the rifle the brothers are fighting over . . . the rifle that

The fight for possession of the *Winchester '73*, with James Stewart in physical and emotional agony.

the chief villain wants for himself . . . the rifle that the Indian chief steals . . . a unification of plot motivation through a visual metaphor is solidly built . . . the foundation of the Mann western.

In *Winchester '73*, Anthony Mann found the right actor to play his hero. As Ford had Wayne, Walsh had Flynn, Preminger had Dana Andrews, and Sirk had Rock Hudson, Mann had James Stewart. Others, of course, had Stewart, too. There was the Capra Stewart and the Hitchcock Stewart as well as the Mann Stewart, and the three bear a direct linear relationship (Capra to Mann to Hitchcock). But the use of Stewart as an icon was never better than in the Anthony Mann westerns, in which an inherent and inexplicable psychosis seemed to dominate and motivate his characters.

The basis for the Stewart/Mann character is laid in *Winchester '73*, in which the hero is hell-bent on revenge. The reason why the film is pointed to as the beginning of the modern western is illustrated in the scene in which Stewart first sees his brother (Stephen McNally). Both have come into Dodge City to try to win the Winchester in a shooting contest. Because it is the Fourth of July celebration, the town marshall (a fatherly old Wyatt Earp, played by a fatherly old Will Geer) makes each man who enters town turn in his weapons for the duration of the event. As a result, when Stewart enters the saloon for a friendly drink and spots his brother, neither man is wearing a gun. Yet both men jump, crouch, and draw with a demoniacal frenzy, only to realize that their shaking hands are empty.

This scene has a shocking effect. For the first time, the devoted viewer of the western is forced to confront a subversive fact: that his noble hero of the west, that man who rides tall in the saddle off into the sunset, may be a flipping maniac. Furthermore, the violence of the pantomimed behavior of drawing to shoot forces a viewer to reevaluate the ritual. Where once one gloried in the action and accepted it as not only necessary, but right, suddenly a new awareness arises. The action itself is called into question. By removing the weapons, Mann makes an audience see the implications of the action. Suddenly it becomes all too evident that a man who solves his problems by shooting them may not be a hero at all. Stripped of the violent glory of the gunfight, the "reach and draw" scene is laid bare as a psychotic event. From *Winchester '73* onward, the idea of the western hero as a man besieged by personal problems—violent and even psychotic—becomes increasingly prevalent in American films.

In *Winchester '73*, Mann created his first western based along the formal lines he would follow from then on. Compositions, camera angles, and background supply meaning, particularly in such scenes as when the two brothers accidentally run across each other in the saloon, and a shootout in a bar near the end of the film.

With *Winchester '73* Mann left *film noir* behind. It was almost as if he had used the film to conduct his own education in the possibilities of the western. By exploring each story cliché, and conquering it (by incorporating it fluidly into an overall structure), he made himself the master of the genre. At the same time, his remarkable use of violence and inner psychology released the film from the earlier, more generalized conflicts found in the western tradition, such as those of sheepmen vs. ranchers, or railroaders vs. settlers. Man against brother and/or man against self became the foundation of the Anthony Mann western. Thus he modernized and reshaped the form, at the same time that he practiced and mastered it.

Definition: Four Key Films, *Bend of the River* (1952), *The Naked Spur* (1953), *The Far Country* (1955), and *The Man From Laramie* (1955)

Jean-Luc Godard has said that "with Anthony Mann, one rediscovers the western, as one discovers arithmetic in an elementary math class."[10] Having mastered and reshaped the genre to his own ends with *Winchester '73*, Mann went on to make four more outstanding westerns starring James Stewart, two of which were written by Borden Chase (*Bend of the River* and *The Far Country*). These four films constitute the core of Mann's work in the western genre. All were photographed in the standard ratio, with the exception of *The Man from Laramie*, which was made in CinemaScope. Each film clearly illustrates the Mann formal style, as well as the basic pattern of his familiar storyline.

The set of characters defined for the Mann western appear in each film in the following way:

The Hero (All played by James Stewart, the man with the secret)	*The Villain*

Bend of the River

The leader of a peaceful wagon train of settlers, who has, however, a guilty past as a murderous Missouri border raider.	Another former border raider (Arthur Kennedy) to whom the hero is linked by shared experience in the past. They save each other's lives in turn.

The Naked Spur

A bounty hunter, searching for a former acquaintance for the reward. He allows people to believe he is a sheriff. Also the woman he once loved made a fool of him by stealing his ranch and selling it.	A wily outlaw who knows all the hero's secrets (Robert Ryan).

The Far Country

A wagon-train leader who takes supplies into the far country and sells cattle and prospects for gold. A woman once made a fool of him, turning him against society.	A powerful judge, who uses his powers corruptly to rob settlers, suppliers, and prospectors alike (John McIntyre).

The Man from Laramie

An incognito army officer, secretly hunting a man who sold guns to the Indians who murdered his brother. He seeks revenge.	A southwestern ranch hand who sold the guns to the Indians (Arthur Kennedy).

The Old Man	The Women

Bend of the River

A good patriarch, the leader of the wagon train (Jay C. Flippen). He believes a bad man can never reform, but changes his mind about the hero.

Two sisters in the wagon train, one of whom (Julia Adams) the hero loves. She falls in love, however, with the villain, but later sees the error of her ways and changes as the hero did when he reformed.

The Naked Spur

A comic-relief character (Millard Mitchell). The villain (Ryan) might be said also be to an example of the evil patriarch.

A young girl befriended by the villain after the death of her father, one of Ryan's outlaw friends (Janet Leigh). Despite her outlaw life, she has good instincts and will shelter and sustain the hero.

The Far Country

A comic-relief character (Walter Brennan), who is also the hero's only real friend.

Two opposite types provide a minor variation on the usual hero/villain link—a bad-girl saloon owner who dies for the hero she truly loves (Ruth Roman) and a good gold prospector (Corinne Calvet).

The Man from Laramie

A good/bad patriarch, who has one bad son (Alex Cord) and one "adopted" (Kennedy) with the potential to be good. (A second old man[Wallace Ford] is a minor figure who aids the hero.)

A good woman who will love and sustain the hero, though also loved by the villain (Cathy O'Donnell), and a good matriarch, a match for the good side of the patriarch (Aline MacMahon).

The Second Villain	The Surface Level Plot–Journey and Geographical Terrain Crossed

Bend of the River

A young gambler (Rock Hudson), who is first on the side of evil, but who reforms and prepares to court the second sister (Lori Nelson).*	A wagon train carrying supplies by river and then overland into the North country—the apple-growing Columbia River country of Oregon, green and fruitful.

The Naked Spur

A brutal womanizer, a former cavalry officer, dishonorably discharged for having raped an Indian princess; unregenerately bad (Ralph Meeker).	The hero's attempt to bring the villain back to justice in Kansas through the Rocky Mountains of Colorado, particularly the "naked spur" rocks.

The Far Country

A vaguely defined group of cohorts of the evil judge. As a group, they represent an evil *society*.	A trek into "the far country" to set up a mining claim and become rich from working it in Oregon Territory, the icy, snowy northernmost sections close to Canada (today Washington state).

The Man from Laramie

The bad son (Alex Nichol) of the patriarch, who also helped sell guns to the Indians. His cohorts form a minor group of villains, one of whom (Jack Elam) tries to kill the hero.	The search to find a gun-runner from the Southwest in the hot, dry, arid salt flats that resemble the passions of the hero (filmed in New Mexico).

*The gambler's changing life style carries out the overall pattern of character development seen in the hero, the girl he loves, and the patriarchal wagon-train leader.

Bend of the River

Bend of the River is the story of a wagon-train leader (James Stewart) who is guiding a group of peaceful settlers to the Oregon Territory. Led by Jay C. Flippen, they plan to become prosperous ranchers, growing fruit trees and building communities. Stewart hopes to join them, to settle down. Behind Stewart lies a life as a murderous Missouri border raider, and he hopes to start completely anew. Along the trail, he saves the life of another former raider (Arthur Kennedy), and the two men ultimately come into conflict.

Bend of the River is a film about changing direction. It's about following a path, such as a river, and then reaching a point at which it becomes necessary to turn, to change. Almost every character in the film changes direction at some point, and the entire plot structure is based on the idea of duality, or the potential for change (either to good or bad) in all of mankind.

Four of the major characters change a bad, rigid side of themselves for the better. Stewart has reformed prior to the film's start, but must work the evil past out of himself. In one of the dramatic high points of the film, the old self emerges and takes control. When his life is threatened, Stewart accepts a knife thrown to him by Kennedy, and, with face twisted and distorted, jumps a man, intending to kill him quickly and efficiently. A scream from the woman he loves stops him. Later, this evil power which has been graphically demonstrated for the audience is channeled into his determination to stop Kennedy once and for all. In a demented, fiercely delivered speech, Stewart tells Kennedy he will follow him and recapture the settlers' supplies. "You'll be seein' me. Every time you bed down for the night, you'll look back in the darkness and wonder if I'm there. And some night I will be. You'll be seein' me."

Jay C. Flippen, the old patriarch of the film, does not believe that any man can ever change for the better. He is deeply prejudiced against men like Stewart, but learns he is wrong. The romantic leading lady, played by Julia Adams, finds herself attracted to the glamorous villain and his way of life. "I like it here," she says of the gold-mining boom town. "It's exciting." But she learns that her basic nature is a more settled one, and rejects Kennedy when the dual side of his own nature is revealed. Even a minor figure (Rock Hudson) changes from a gambling con man into a settler and potential husband for the younger sister.

The shifting from good to bad (or vice versa) is also carried out in large groups of people. An idle bunch of wharf rats, available for hire but not basically bad, become a murderous bunch of thieves when gold is discovered. Similarly, the peaceful miners turn into thugs trying to capture the settlers' supplies. The entire community of Portland, Oregon, changes. A friendly, happy place when the settlers first arrive, the town changes almost overnight after the gold strike. It becomes a rowdy, greedy, and evil society, led by the former hail-fellow-well-met who sold the settlers their supplies. His character represents another major shift in type.

The opening section of *Bend of the River* contains an unusual amount of joking comedy. The laughs these jokes stimulate are a release of audience tension not unlike that which will later be generated through violence. In this regard, the entire film has its duality. At first, it provides relief through comedy, and later through violence. The entire film changes direction!

The character played by James Stewart in all the four core films is in every case not only a man with a secret, but a man who seeks to clarify his relationship with society. Either he's out and he wants in, as in *Bend of the River*, or he's out and he wants to stay out, as in *Far Country* and *The Naked Spur*, or he's voluntarily taken himself out to solve a problem, as in *The Man from Laramie*. Whatever his status, however, all four films end with his being clearly reintegrated into society, which is seen as a positive and necessary thing.

In *Bend of the River*, Stewart plays a man who has learned his lesson. For too long he has lived on the outside of ordered society as an outlaw, and he knows he wants to be an accepted part of a group like the settlers. During the journey of the film, he confronts his old self in the form of Arthur Kennedy. At first, the two men share an easy camaraderie based on their mutual understanding of each other and of the dangers the wagon train faces. Their cryptic conversation shortly after they meet illustrates their shared experience, and the basic link between them. When an innocent female comments on what a pretty bird song she has just heard, the two men, knowing the sound to be Indian signals, speak to each other: Stewart: "Sort of a special kind of bird—." Kennedy: "Red-winged orioles."

The two men demonstrate their equality and their mutual talents in a scene in which they go out alone from the wagon train, into the dark of night, to overcome and kill five Indians. A masterpiece in tension, the scene shows what kind of a past life each man has led and how each knows what the other can do. The camera follows as

James Stewart reveals the truth about himself in *Bend of the River*.

Hero and villain, two linked characters equal in the frame. Arthur Kennedy and James Stewart in *Bend of the River*.

two men crawl through the underbrush. Not one word of dialogue is spoken after the initial counting of the enemy. The audience and the hero both have a limited-eye view of the scene, and a similar knowledge that there is danger everywhere, ready at any moment to pounce. Suddenly, two feathers rise in the foreground of the frame. As Stewart crawls by, the feathered Indians rise higher in the frame, filling and dominating the space. Suddenly, they attack Stewart, overcoming his image. With vicious efficiency, Kennedy kills one of the two, alerting Stewart. From then on, the two former border raiders kill each Indian, one by one, working together as a team, confident in their mutual skills.

The hero's identification with his landscape is established during this sequence. Stewart crawls through water (a rushing stream) and out into the landscape on his belly. He mingles literally with earth and water, an obvious and fundamental identification of a hero with a landscape. As the Indians die, Stewart explores the landscape to resolve danger. In the rest of the film, he will explore landscape to resolve psychological tension.

The link between Kennedy and Stewart is stressed over and over again, through framing, composition, and editing. They are clearly parallel figures. They occupy similar space within the frame, or are photographed in balanced shots of matching medium close-ups. Cutting links them as equals in scene after scene.

The introduction of Kennedy's character with swish pan links them in violence, and also formally establishes the tone of the landscape, which is treacherous and full of unexpected dangers. As Stewart rides ahead of the wagon train to scout the seemingly peaceful territory, a sudden swish pan to the right reveals a close-up of Arthur Kennedy with his head in a noose. A cut returns the viewer to an equal medium close-up of Stewart, who instinctively touches the scarf around his own neck. (The scarf hides a rope-burn scar from a near-hanging in his own checkered past.) The use of the swish pan is the formal equivalent of the situation—sudden, unexpected danger revealed in an otherwise benign landscape. It not only links the hero and the villain through a sudden, violent motion, but, with the return cut to Stewart, helps to explain his own character to the audience.

Arthur Kennedy is Stewart's other self in the deeper meaning of the film. Both men have a dual nature. Although Stewart is the hero, the good man, he is also potentially destructive and violent, and has a somewhat sour nature. Certainly he has no glamour, in the sexual sense. Kennedy, on the other hand, is the villain, but is a joking, obviously attractive man. The girl Stewart loves is attracted to Kennedy from the beginning, and so is the audience. He is more at ease in the world than Stewart, and thus is more likable, more pleasant. His own other self—the evil side—is, of course, revealed later in the film when he steals the settlers' supplies to sell them for money. It is his willingness to allow innocent women and children to starve to death in the Oregon winter that galvanizes Stewart into action.

The link between the hero and the villain is specifically acknowledged through the dialogue. As the two men ride side by side, Kennedy observes to Stewart (whose character name is Glyn McClintock): "McClintock of the border. A rancher. I don't get it. What are you running away from?" Stewart: "A man named Glyn McClintock." Kennedy: "What happens when he catches up with you?" Stewart: "He died on the Missouri border." Kennedy: "No. He'll catch up with you one day." The irony is that he has, of course, already caught up with him, in the form of Kennedy.

Ultimately, Stewart frees himself of his "other self." He fights and destroys Kennedy in a conflict which takes place in water and light, two purifying elements. The two men struggle inside a supply wagon, and then fall outward in a violent movement into the rushing river. After a prolonged fight in the water underneath the bright sunlight of the day, Stewart emerges triumphant as Kennedy's body is borne off downstream. The evil self is washed away in a violent purification rite.

The Naked Spur

The Naked Spur is a masterful achievement. It is formally an almost mathematical film in the precise way it motivates and changes five main characters and their relationships. It is one of the most mature and intelligent films ever made, yet at the same time it has the vitality of the most straightforward storytelling westerns.

The story is simplicity itself. James Stewart, in his third Mann western, searches for outlaw Robert Ryan to bring him to justice for the reward money. Unable to capture Ryan alone, he reluctantly accepts the help of an old prospector (Millard Mitchell) and a dishonorably discharged calvaryman (Ralph Meeker). Ryan is captured and is found to be harboring a pal's young daughter (Janet Leigh).

While the three men attempt to bring Ryan back to Kansas to justice, he attempts to break down their loyalties to each other in order
to divide them and escape himself.

The Naked Spur is such a tightly composed, intense film that
(except for the Indian raiding party) it consists of only these five
characters. The possibilities of interaction among them are worked
and reworked so that the combinations of various alliances among
the characters more than equal five times five.

As Ryan keeps up a steady barrage of talk intended to confuse,
alienate, and separate the three men who are taking him and the girl
in, their shifting positions in the narrative are clearly reflected formally. As they trust and mistrust, they are depicted through separate shots of each individual, or compositions involving two in con-
spiracy, or three in alienation, or all five in uneasy alignment.
"Money splits better two ways then three," Ryan hints to the greedy
prospector. "Do me, Lina," he instructs Leigh, getting her to rub
his back in front of the lecherous Meeker. "He don't care what he do
to women," he warns the gentlemanly Stewart about Meeker. It is a
variation on a theme that never becomes tiresome, with the tension
never letting up.

Perhaps the most interesting villain in all the Mann westerns is
Ben Vandergroat (Robert Ryan). Something of a cracker-barrel
philosopher ("Choosin' a way to die, what's the difference? Choosin'
a way to live—that's the hard part."), he has the easy style and
grace, the sense of humor, the camaraderie, and the knowledge of
life that separate the Mann villain from the Mann hero. Just as
Arthur Kennedy in *Bend of the River* is initially more likable than
Stewart, the charming and relaxed Ryan is also not a villain you love
to hate.

Ryan talks about his miserable childhood, nearly winning the
audience's total sympathy. As he explains about a pa that tied him
up, a ma that caught the fever and died, and the killing in a saloon
that orphaned him, he does it with just the right touch of ironic
self-humor. With his disordered background, Ben is almost a joke
on the sociological westerns that became popular in the 1950s, in
which the poor outlaw was revealed to be nothing more than a
misguided juvenile delinquent. (If only he could have played on the
local basketball team at the Y, all those stagecoaches would have
gone unrobbed!) But Robert Ryan's character is no textbook punk.
He is evil, through and through. His apparent ease is later revealed

to come from a moral vacuum, rather than grace under pressure. He hideously shows his callous nature by casually shooting at the feet of the dead old prospector. When Janet Leigh is horrified, he remarks, "Day after tomorrow it'll be just like a story you once heard." Everything in his life is like the stories he spins out as they ride—distanced, meaningless.

In comparison with Ryan's relaxed nature, Stewart's character lives a tortured existence. Nothing is easy for him. From the very first glimpse the audience has of him, Stewart's face reflects a desperation—a determination that is twisted, unbalanced. This near-psychopathic nature is illustrated during the attack by the Indian raiding party. Stewart viciously kills one of the Indians, stabbing him repeatedly, long after it would be necessary for death. His violent action demonstrates his border-line hysteria, the obsession by which he is driven. After this battle, while the others sleep around the campfire that night, Stewart rises up suddenly from the bottom of the frame, screaming, wild-eyed, deep in a nightmare. His action, moving up into the frame from beneath, cuts into the space of the peaceful campfire in typical Mann style.

Stewart's initial capture of Ryan is carried out only through the help of Meeker and Mitchell. Stewart tries to scale the high rocks but falls back, his hands burned from the rope. Meeker does it easily, laughing down on him. In comparison, Stewart seems blocked from functioning well physically. It is as if the good in him slows him down in some way he cannot understand, holding him back from bounty-hunting. At the same time, the evil in him keeps him off-balance, out of control. He hangs on in his environment as best he can. Meeker, a thoroughly evil person, easily scales the rocks, comfortable in his own lousiness.

Stewart's pain and lack of ease in his environment is furthered in a scene in which he falls from his horse. Having been severely wounded in the leg, he has difficulty riding, and Ryan has deliberately loosened his saddle strap. As the two men ride along a narrow trail on a high mountain ledge, Ryan distracts Stewart with conversation. Watching him droop from pain and lack of sleep, Ryan takes his chance and nudges his horse hard up against Stewart's. Stewart falls, goes over the edge, and rolls to a stop below, his fall fortuitously broken by a tree trunk. Stewart's face comes awake in shock, shown in intense close-up and emphasized by an abrupt cut. Desperately, he begins a torturous climb back up toward the others. He slips back, but starts over, his face crazed. No one speaks. No one helps. It is the essence of the dilemma of the Mann hero. Alone, unaided, he must come to grips with himself, and that problem is illustrated through a physical ordeal.

The revelation of danger through the use of swish pans takes place in *The Naked Spur* immediately. The first image of the film is a landscape behind the credits—peaceful western landscape, with trees, mountains, wildflowers. It appears calm, safe. A sudden swish pan blurs and then focuses in on the side of a horse and a man's riding boot with a vicious-looking naked spur. Only an abstracted portion of the man's total body is seen. As the words *The Naked Spur* appear on the screen, the horse moves forward and the entire man comes into view from the rear. It is James Stewart riding in the frame with his back to the audience, sneaking up on Millard Mitchell. "Don't move. Turn around" are the first words of the film. The audience is plunged into sudden, violent action, shaken out of the peaceful first image by the use of the dramatic swishpan.

The attack of the Indian raiding party, who are searching for Meeker to avenge themselves for his rape of an Indian princess, is a scene of particular chaos and brutality. One minute the small group is riding in the sunlight amongst the trees. The next, the audience is plunged into a chaotic battle, through a series of alienating cuts. Suddenly, as suddenly as it seemed to begin, it is over, and the viewer is back in the sunlight again, looking around at the carnage, wondering what happened. Stewart sits among the bodies, wounded, looking bewildered. What he has undergone in the action of the film has been undergone by the viewing audience. A sudden, unexpected burst of violence, different in form from what has preceded it, hits the viewer, leaving him bewildered like Stewart and, in a sense, wounded.

When the five characters take shelter in a cave during a heavy rain, Stewart and Leigh play a love scene. The other, more human side of Stewart is revealed. He even makes a feeble joke. Hearing the rain fall on their tin cups, he points out that one of the cups is off-key—Meeker's. He makes a wry smile, the first seen on his face since the film started.

The space of the cave during this scene is intimate, with warm, golden lighting in contrast to the grayness outside. A tight frame around the two lovers reveals their emotional intensity, as well as their shared intimacy. When Ryan uses their absorption in each other to make his escape attempt, the space is suddenly, violently altered. A second entrance to the cave, at the back, is revealed. The entire spatial organization of the scene is shifted, to incorporate the narrative change. From the closed intimacy of the love scene, the frame and its composed elements are altered to the scene of an attempted escape. The space of the cave is suddenly seen as larger and quite different from before.

All five of the characters are shown together in the frame in the cave's space, confronting each other with a complete mutual hatred and distrust. For the first time, they are all totally alienated from each and every one of the others. A scene of impending violence is slowly played out. Ryan has stolen a gun, and Stewart challenges him, trembling with rage, "Come on, draw." But Ryan is too smart. "If you're goin' to murder me, Howie, don't try to make it look like somethin' else." "Kill him!" cries the Meeker character, and when Stewart hesitates, he goes for the gun, only to be stopped by Millard.

The intense relationships among the five characters build and erupt in two scenes of violence near the end. In the first, Stewart and Meeker finally fight it out. Beside a rushing blue river, amidst the green trees, they conduct a desperate and violent fist fight. Typically, the other three look on, making no move. Stewart wins, and staggers into the water to cleanse himself. As in *Bend of the River*, water is used as a visual agent of purification.

The finale of the film finds Stewart struggling to reclaim Ryan's dead body out of the rushing river. Without it, he cannot hope to claim the reward money. Meeker loses his own life in the attempt to bring the body to shore, and Leigh begs Stewart to let it go, to free himself of the obsession, to purify himself of his villainous tendencies. When he finally agrees, it is clear they will make a new life together in California.

The Naked Spur begins and ends with a struggle atop rocks, where the villain hides and waits. This attack on a bad man's lair is tantamount to the storming of a fort, or citadel, and is almost a rehearsal for the big battle scenes of the epic films, *El Cid* and *Fall of the Roman Empire*. In each scene, the villain is in a precarious position but can shove rocks down on those who try to capture him, turning the landscape into an instrument of destruction and treachery. (Many more times in Mann's films will the landscape rain down destruction on hapless characters.) The hero is below, and

must scale the heights to win the day, the girl, and his own self-re-
spect. Thus, the rock formations represent the positions of the
characters in the story.

In the first struggle set up this way, Stewart cannot function
alone. He requires help. In the final struggle, he climbs the rocks
himself. Using the "naked spur" from his boot, he laboriously chips
out places for his hands to grip the edge of the solid rock as he
climbs. (These high rocks on the location used for the setting are in
reality known as "the naked spur.") Far below him thunders the
roaring water. Above him waits Ryan, ready to kill. Stewart is in the
position of the Mann hero, suspended between two physical dangers, having to make his own way to solid ground. Complicated
set-ups reveal a maplike view of the space: Ryan on the mountain
top, waiting, the river rushing below, and Stewart torturously chipping his way up the cliff at a dangerous height . . . pursued and
pursuer in one image. Stewart reaches the top, tossing his spur into
Ryan's face, a la Stanwyck tossing the scissors at Anderson in *The
Furies*. In his own eyes, and in the eyes of the audience, Stewart has
overcome and endured. He has earned the right to a better life, as
his physical triumph marks the beginning of his ability to come to
terms with himself.

The Far Country

Where *Winchester '73* explored and defined the traditional western, *The Far Country* explores and defines the Anthony Mann western. Although it follows the pattern of the three other core films, it
has a self-conscious, artificial quality. It is as if Mann, understanding
his own game, decided to abstract it, treat it almost as a joke—while
still preserving its broad outlines. His respect for the basic narrative
makes *The Far Country* function at the entertainment level, yet the
film has an odd quality that leaves a viewer slightly bemused. It is
best understood in relation to the other Mann westerns.

It is in the use of space that *The Far Country* differs from *Bend in
the River, The Naked Spur,* and *The Man from Laramie.* The frame
is treated as a two-dimensional area, whereas Mann's tendency in
his other westerns (and in most of his other films) was to provide an
enormous depth of field, so much so that the frame seemed to be
opening and receding in the center of the screen. There is no such
sense of space in *The Far Country*.

Instead of natural settings, *The Far Country* presents a viewer
with a great deal of artificial space mixed with outdoor locations. In

its elimination of some of the location work associated with westerns, *The Far Country* ranks with Lang's *Rancho Notorious* and Ray's *Johnny Guitar* as a directorial exercise in abstraction of his own familiar territory. Just as Hitchock elected to use painted backdrops and rear projection in *Marnie*, Mann elected to use similar devices here. The mining town of Skagway looks like a representational "western town" set. The shack in which Stewart and Brennan live, the porch of Ruth Roman's saloon (which seems too big for the rest of the building), the bar which is turned into a courtroom, are all designed with a look that says, "I am a western set—do you know which one I am?" The interior spaces of these settings are false and often not matched to their exteriors. A steamboat tied up to a dock presents such an alienating sense of space and dimension that it would be laughable were it not so skillfully, deliberately used by Mann. As the steamboat pulls away from the dock, Stewart is seen to be escaping. The area that is supposed to be the boat deck is arbitrarily shortened and narrowed to accommodate the narrative needs as Stewart flees in the restricted space from the steamboat officers. The deliberate use of a falsified reality in films that present themselves as real is a justifiable artistic decision, but one that Mann seldom opted for in the westerns. In *The Far Country*, he not only proves that he could do it, but, by doing it, offers proof that he thoroughly understood his own work, that it was not intuitive.

This awareness is announced with the very first image of the film, in which the credits are presented against a picture that is meant to represent "the far country." This image, static and unchanged, is seen repeatedly in the film, most notably when the hero first moves out into the landscape. It is an icy image of a distant space, set against a hard blue sky. It is an unreachable distance, not a place, but a concept. As they gaze at it together, Jay C. Flippen remarks to James Stewart, "The constable up there has a hard job. Sometimes he doesn't get home for two or three months . . . ridin' up in that far country." By using this single image to represent the physical and emotional setting of the film, and by repeating it often, Mann sets the tone of the film. From that moment on, the use of backdrops, mattes, rear projection, and day-for-night shooting carries out this idea. Although the sight of these devices in the middle of an outdoor western film disconcerts many viewers, it is consistent to the intent of the film.

Dialogue is also often unrealistic, almost satiric. Certainly it is

The Naked Spur final confrontation between Robert Ryan (atop cliff) and James Stewart (making the torturous climb, chipping his way with his boot spur).

self-conscious. "I'm gonna like you. I'm gonna hang you, but I'm gonna like you," says a judge to Stewart who just seconds after decides, "Have a drink, you're acquitted." Corinne Calvet, one of the two leading ladies, constantly insists, "Don't call me freckle face. I'm a woman." The self-conscious, artificial quality of the sets and storyline is carried out through this *mysterioso* dialogue, which has a muted humor. "Alaska is most difficult for the medical profession," a doctor tells Stewart. "Then why did you come here?" he replies. "Because I'm going to Vienna," comes back the nonsequitur worthy of the "I came to take the waters" discussion between Bogart and Rains in *Casablanca*. (Conversations like that are what Godard is talking about when he refers to the power and mystery of the American film!)

Largely because of the dialogue, *The Far Country* has more consistent humor than the other Mann westerns. Like its opening image, however, it is a hard, cold, icy humor—distant and representational. Where *Bend of the River* began with humor and warmth, and changed direction, totally abandoning its laughter, *The Far Country* carries from beginning to end a deeply veined, ironic sense of humor, designed not to make an audience laugh, but to make them think about the proceedings. Thus, the humor, too, is artificial, calling attention to the idea of the film as a film. It is a laughter that laces the violence like an ice cube in a glass of bootleg whiskey—welcome relief, but not able to overpower its surroundings. "Me dance?" asks Walter Brennan, when a saloon girl takes him onto the floor. "Why, this is ridiculous." And it is.

The plot of *The Far Country* tells how James Stewart is cheated out of his cattle by a corrupt judge (John McIntyre) in Oregon Territory. Stewart is then forced to earn money by hiring out to Ruth Roman, a saloon owner who is taking some wagons up into the gold-mining camps. Stewart goes with Roman (who is attracted to him), but later resteals his own cattle, sells them, and becomes a miner himself. Roman and McIntyre bring corruption to the mining camps, but Stewart refuses to join the community in fighting them until the very end of the film.

Stewart's character is a loner, by conscious choice an outsider. The opening "far country" image represents his internal state—an isolated, cold, unchanging image. With the exception of his faithful companion (Walter Brennan, the old-man comic relief), he allows no

one to be really near him. He refuses relationships with others,
even when help is offered. Desperate, he may take a favor, as when
he allows Roman to hide him in her stateroom, but he is always
suspicious. "I don't need help. . .I take care of me. . .that's the only
way."

His relationship to his world is one of observer. He sees the world
he lives in, but he is not a part of it. He himself is unconnected to his
space—a two-dimensional figure. Mentally and emotionally, he always lives in the far country, that far, distant world that is as cold
and remote as he is. Even in love and sex, he never compromises.
When Roman demands a thank you for her having saved his life, he
tells her, "That's a term I seldom use." His motto is, "Nobody does a
favor for nothin'."

Stewart does, however, make an exception of the Brennan character, his living and traveling companion. He wears a tiny bell on his
saddle horn, a gift from Brennan, who says it will be for their house,
which will be built in Utah. When the house is finished, the bell will
be put out front to announce the arrival of friends, so they'll know
"when to put the coffee pot on." Their present reality, however, is
quite different. The shack they live in at their mining claim is at the
farthest point of the settlement. Like the "far country" image, their
shack, both interior and exterior, is obviously not a real place. Its
artificiality is representative of their situation (and of the look of the
entire film).

Brennan loves and understands Stewart. He himself has all the
honest social instincts that Stewart lacks. In fact, it is those instincts
which bring about his death. When he goes into town to buy extra
coffee for their secret departure with their gold, he can't resist
talking to others, and thus alerts the villains to their plans.

In *The Far Country,* the link between villain and hero is not
clearly defined. The hero is not a bad man, struggling with his own
violence. He is just by choice a person who will not help others or
become committed. In this regard, the "old man" character, becomes his better self, and represents his more social instincts. The
traditional link that is usually between hero and villain is between
the hero and the old man in *The Far Country,* but it is not the main
link for the hero. The central conflict is that of Stewart's linking
himself to a community. The community—with its love and
friendship—is what Stewart lacks. It is his missing third dimension.
Composition stresses this artificial relationship between him and his

(Top) *The Far Country* image of ice and distant snow. (Bottom) Stewart defends his isolated shack in *The Far Country*.

environment, by way of artificial devices. Stewart is never fully a part of any group or of the situation, and he is not always seen fully in the frame. Although Stewart is often seen in the frame with Brennan, he is more usually seen alone or in opposition to others in the frame.

Just as Stewart is not really present in the film, living as he does symbolically in the far country, his secret is never really explained. "I trusted a man once," says Roman to him. "Quite a coincidence," he replies. "I trusted a woman." This cryptic sentence plus a nightmare in which he cries out, "Mary! Mary!" is the only real explanation (except for a few words from Brennan) the audience has to go on. No more is really needed. Motivations are as abstracted as the far-country image itself. (Besides, Mann had already explained it in *The Naked Spur!*)

Stewart has a choice of two women in *The Far Country*, one like himself and one different. Or, more specifically, one like the self he has become, and one like the possible better self. These two women are the saloon owner (Ruth Roman) and the doctor's daughter (Corinne Calvet).

Like Stewart, Roman had chosen to remain aloof from "good" society. But Calvet is completely different. She is a part of the positive community of miners who eat together, sing and dance together, and support one another in times of stress. Their attempts to band together to stamp out McIntyre and his kind are a major source of plot development.

The death of Walter Brennan marks the changing point in Stewart's life. The death occurs under typical Mann formal conditions. As Brennan gabs in center-left frame about how he'll have coffee every day when they get their ranch in Utah, the killers appear behind him and above on a cliff overlooking the sight. Within the unit of the frame, the situation is redefined through the arrival of danger. Brennan is shot and killed, and Stewart is knocked into the water by gunfire and left for dead. The friendly cliffs become menacing, and the beautiful river, their avenue of escape, is redefined as the wounded Stewart's trap.

Brennan's death is the ultimate motivation for Stewart's change. It was Brennan who loved and understood him. Brennan would complain, "You always get the hankerin' for the far country," accepting it one moment, and another time, bursting out, "Always

movin', movin', movin'. Where's it all gonna end, boy? Are we just
goin' on and on?" Stewart, wounded and alone, rides into the mining camp, the bell Brennan gave him symbolically ringing for help.
Stewart is nursed back to health by Corinne Calvet, who says,
"You've got to help people when they need help. What kind of a
world would it be if everyone were like—" "Like me?" replies
Stewart.

During Stewart's recovery, one image makes a simple statement
of his quandary. As he sits with his arm in a sling, feeling his in-
jured, painful hand, trying to move it, his gun in its holster hangs on
a peg frame left. Whether he will take hold of the gun, take up the
violence and thus his community responsibility, is the question of
the remainder of the film. The position of the gun in the frame is a
constant reminder both to him and to the audience.

The final shoot-out of *The Far Country* preshadows the one in *The
Man of the West*. It is played on horizontal levels, underneath a
porch. Stewart has sent word to McIntyre that he is coming, and his
horse rides into town with Brennan's bell ringing. Stewart has, of
course, used the bell to trick the villains. Roman runs out to protect
him and is shot and killed. Her death represents the death of
Stewart's non-social self, the self she represented in opposition to
Calvet. The final image is a close-up of Brennan's bell, symbol of
civilization and Stewart's acceptance of society.

Seen alone without an understanding of the rest of Mann's work,
The Far Country functions well as a piece of western entertainment.
However, viewers often remark on how odd it is, pointing out its
backdrops and weird dialogue. Although it tells a clear story, its
meaning is best understood by thinking of it as an abstraction of the
basic Mann pattern. The audience is never given the whole story,
just pieces of it. Similarly, they are never given the entire realistic
picture of the settings, just strangely shaped, artificial pieces of
them. The film *refers*. Its sets refer directly to other western film
sets, and thus indirectly to reality. Its characters and their dilemmas
refer to other western characters (particularly other Mann western
characters). Walter Brennan plays Walter Brennan, and James
Stewart plays James Stewart in the iconographic sense, and
Stewart's secret remains his secret. *The Far Country* appears to be a
step forward for Mann in which, having established once and for all
his themes and methods, he experimented with them. If his hero

must be allied with the landscape, could the film still work if he presented only part of the total landscape—or a false, two-dimensional landscape?

It could and did. It is the core film in which he experimented with the abstraction he would pursue further in *The Tin Star*.

The Man from Laramie

I wanted to recapitulate, somehow, my five years of collaboration with Jimmy Stewart: that work distilled our relationship. I reprised themes and situations by pushing them to their paroxysm.

—ANTHONY MANN[11]

Filmed in New Mexico on location, *The Man from Laramie* is the only one of the four core films to be shot in CinemaScope. The 'scope image provided the viewer with a greater sense of continuous space. Thus, it was not only ideal for the western genre, but practically perfect for the Mann western. The expanded frame gave Mann the chance to increase the complexity of his compositions. In particular, he used its wider space and potential for greater depth to strengthen his theme of duality, or the link between hero and villain. Of course, he had always set up complex relationships between two such characters inside his frames. *Bend of the River* abounds with masterful examples. But, with CinemaScope, he could present the two equal, but opposing, forces in one shot with even greater space and depth. Furthermore, huge close-ups inside the wide space provided a striking intensity perfect for his violent stories. Not only could he link the two characters as equals, but he could also employ the new shape to divide them. One framed composition, carefully done, could show the landscape divided between the two opposing forces. Mann developed a pattern of exploring all the possibilities inside the frame for the two opposing characters, and then, as narrative tension reached a breaking point, of making an abrupt cut. The cut seemed to explode the area inside the frame (and thus the situation), and the initial cut was often followed by a series of rapid, alienating cuts as violence erupted between the two men. The formal demonstration of long take abruptly cut, followed by a series of rapid cuts, was the equivalent of the eruption of violence in the narrative line. The effect on a viewer was obviously one which matched story action.

"I always tried to build my films on oppositions of characters,"

Mann said. "Putting the accent on common points of two characters then making them collide, the story acquires more strength and you obtain a greater intensity."[12] CinemaScope lent itself perfectly to this concept.

The Man from Laramie follows the basic pattern of the core Mann western, but it is also closely related to the earlier films *Winchester '73* and *The Furies*. Its narrative seems to present the prehistory of *Winchester '73* in that it tells a story of an old man with two "sons." One is good, one bad, and the bad one ultimately shoots him. In *The Man from Laramie*, however, one son is *not* a blood relation, but a ranch foreman, and the old man survives the bullet.

Like *The Furies*, *The Man from Laramie* concerns complicated familial relationships. Stewart is out to avenge his dead brother. Donald Crisp is the patriarchal figure with one real son (Alex Nichol) and one "son" by instinct (Arthur Kennedy). Nichol has no real love for his father, but Kennedy desperately wants the old man's love and respect. Cathy O'Donnell, the love interest, hates Crisp because he was her father's brother and cheated him out of his land. The matriarchal figure, Aline MacMahon, loves Crisp, but he jilted her in their youth to marry "a little piece of fluff from the East." As in Greek drama, a great deal of the motivation has taken place prior to the action, off-screen.

This sense of Greek tragedy the film carries is conveyed through the figure of the old patriarch, Donald Crisp. Once strong and powerful, he is now losing his eyesight and becoming helpless. "I own land," he says pathetically, "but I can't see it." The theme of blindness applies also to his character. He can't "see" what his real son is. He can't "see" what Arthur Kennedy feels about him. His lack of vision is compensated for with dreams, in which he "sees" events that are to come. He tells Stewart of his most frequent nightmare, in which a stranger, tall and lean, comes into his home with a gun, coming to "kill my boy, my Dave." When the son is killed, the old man believes Stewart ("tall and lean") to have been the killer.

In a scene of epic tragedy, Crisp rides alone to avenge his son's death. Unable to see at all by then, he rides blindly toward Stewart, shooting wildly, but determined to carry out the rules of the western code by which he has lived. Finally, Stewart says simply, "I am not the man in your dream," and the old man gives up, riding off into the landscape. It is a scene of uncommon poetry and madness, with no physical resolution in violence whatsoever. Rather, it illustrates the futility of violence, and draws a fine line between insanity and the code of the western.

The sense of Greek tragedy is visually portrayed when Kennedy carries home Nichol's dead body. Kennedy is really the killer himself, but he carries the body as if he were only the messenger of death, not the agent. The use of twilight, mournful music, and silhouettes creates a powerful emotional effect.

The Man from Laramie has two strong female figures, both defined by their own landscape, or environment. Cathy O'Donnell lives in a cozy home, with a teapot, furniture from Connecticut, and apples laid out invitingly in a wooden bowl. She is a domestic woman, not a wanderer. Sure of who she is and what she wants, she attempts to learn the same about Stewart by asking him where his home is. (By his landscape she will know him!). He replies, "I always feel I belong where I am."

Aline MacMahon, the other woman in the picture, is the matriarchal counterpart of Donald Crisp. Like him, she lives on a wealthy, successful ranch. Her world, however, is incomplete. As she tells Stewart, she needs a man there. She awaits the man to complete her environment, and finally receives him in the form of the blind, wounded old Crisp. He is her true love, who, by way of his helplessness, can now be both her man and her child.

Stewart plays a more balanced human being than in the other three core films. He is capable of love, humor, and warmth. His seeking of revenge for his brother's death is not presented as an act of madness of which he must cleanse himself. The unbalanced emotional nature is this time placed more fully onto the second villain, Arthur Kennedy. Nevertheless, Stewart's character is capable of rage, and Stewart's ability to portray intense pain is well used. In a confrontation between Nichol and Stewart, the former pulls off Stewart's glove and shoots his hand, to punish him. "Why, you scum," spits Stewart, in an agony of pain which is graphically portrayed in intense close-up. The use of 'scope has Stewart's hand filling the entire frame, naked and vulnerable, without its glove. Nichol's gun arrives in the frame from the opposite side and fills the space, literally driving the hand out of the frame, destroying it.

The moral link between the hero (Stewart) and the villain (Kennedy) is not clearly defined in the narrative of *The Man from Laramie*. They might be said to be linked by their capabilities, in that both are more than able to deal with whatever dangers they encounter. Or they are linked by their desires for revenge for personal hurts, in that Stewart seeks his brother's killer and Kennedy is motivated by his rage at what he considers unfair treatment from Crisp. They are also linked by their mutual love for Cathy O'Donnell. They are not, however, blood relations, nor have they shared a mutual past. They are not emotional counterparts. In fact, *The Man from Laramie* might be said to be an exercise in aloneness. Each individual is alone within the frame with his own personal problem. This idea is carried out visually by use of intense close-ups, effectively photographed in CinemaScope against the wide, flat, arid space. As tensions mount, these spaces grow more spare, unfertile, suggesting the barren relationships of the people in the film, who live either alone (like Stewart and O'Donnell) or in emotional isolation (like Crisp, Kennedy, and Nichol).

The hot, dry landscape, photographed in 'scope, is used effectively in a dramatic scene in the salt flats, in which Stewart is lassoed by Nichol and tied onto a horse. The sight of his shackled body being dragged through the burning sands in the glaring sun is a widescreen glimpse of hell. Later, a second violent fight between Nichol and Stewart erupts in the streets of the town. Punching and gouging amidst the frightened townspeople, rolling among a herd of milling cattle, the two men become layered with the powdery white dust of the southwest. The 'scope compositions enhance the brutality of the fight, which is one of the most vicious in Mann's western work.

The Man from Laramie is resolved in the classic Mann pattern. Since the hero's problem must always be worked out in physical, geographical terms, the hero and villain ride out into the landscape, over rocky trails, and up into the high trees. "I came 1,000 miles to kill you," Stewart says, catching Kennedy with the guns for the Indians. Yet when the two men face each other for the final showdown, Stewart cannot bring himself to kill. He leaves it to the Indians to do the job. In the end, he is the hero, true to the better side of himself.

The Man from Laramie has a short coda in the tradition of an older western film. The old couple have decided to marry at last. The patriarch is blind, but the matriarch still loves him. "I've never left you, Alec," she says. Stewart says good-bye to O'Donnell, preparing to ride off into the sunset like the footloose western hero of old. "If you go east, you'll pass through Laramie," he tells her. "Ask anyone for Captain Lockhart."

"I'll remember that," is her cryptic reply, as the title song comes on the sound track. "Oh, he was friendly and kind to everyone he met . . . everyone admired the man from Laramie . . . but danger was this man's specialty." The man from Laramie may be less psychotic than others but the words of the song remind an audience that, in a Mann western, even the most balanced of the heroes has a dual nature.

Inversion and Abstraction: *The Last Frontier* and *The Tin Star*

The Last Frontier and *The Tin Star* represent variations on the basic Mann pattern. *The Last Frontier*'s villain is the man with a guilty secret and the hero behaves animalistically, by killer's instincts, without moral consideration. *The Tin Star* has two leading men, one a hero and one not a hero, and allows the hero to teach the nonhero how to take over his role through the method of learning formal control.

The Last Frontier

The Last Frontier represents a total inversion of the basic Mann situation. In the core films, the need for the hero to be integrated (or reintegrated) into a group, or civilization, is firmly established. The need for human relationships—both platonic and romantic—is demonstrated. In *The Last Frontier*, civilization is seen as a restrictive force, one which will undo the hero and lose him his freedom and sense of self. "They'll snare ya," says the older trapper (James Whitmore) to the hero (Victor Mature), speaking about the soldiers in the fort. "They speak with forked tongues." Despite an ending which puts the smiling hero in an army uniform, the film reinforces and demonstrates this meaning. ("That ending was forced on me," says Mann.[13])

As is true of so many Mann films, the opening image of *The Last Frontier* illustrates the theme. In a typical movement, Mann lowers the camera from the top of the frame. Where first the audience has seen a beautiful, unspoiled western landscape (trees, mountains, sky), the lowering movement reveals the fort, sturdy and solid at the bottom of the frame. The wilderness has already been invaded by civilization—one camera movement tells the whole story.

The conflict internal to the hero in *Last Frontier* is illustrated by two dominant spatial areas: the fort representing civilization and the

(Top) James Stewart, *The Man from Laramie,* trapped and tortured, and (Bottom) stalking the villain across the western landscape.

approaching end of the frontier; and the great out of doors, representing the old, unrestricted West and its semilawless heroes. The film takes place "back when the law was the law of the open spaces."

The area of the fort is spatially complicated. It is a maze of stairs, posts, walkways, porches, levels, interiors, catwalks, corners, windows, and pits. The viewer is never clear what the topographical layout really is.

The out of doors, on the other hand, is open and free. Although it is a space that can become instantly treacherous in the Mann tradition (as when Indians materialize mysteriously from the bottom of the frame, their feathers coming first to announce the arrival and impending dominance from an alien source), it is for the hero a safe place which he readily dominates. He is a trapper and early settler, at home with the environment. Mature is often photographed from a low angle against the hard blue sky, so that he looks enormous, equal to the space of all outdoors which is seen behind his head. These shots both equate him with the outdoor landscape, and indicate his mastery of that space. Even the swish pan, the traditional device by which Mann introduces the forces of danger, is here inverted. Where before it revealed an alien force, potentially treacherous to the hero, *The Last Frontier* presents a scene in which a rapid swish pan to the left reveals—the hero, casually observing the Indians from high above, in control of his space.

Victor Mature is clearly allied with the landscape. He is presented as if he were literally a part of it, wearing a natural camouflage of animal skins and forest colors. In the opening scene of the film, he and his two companions sit calmly in the underbrush, surrounded by Indians. They are more a part of the landscape than the natives. Similarly, the climax of the film finds him calmly atop a tree, watching the Indians below him (also in tree tops), who are watching the cavalry, out in the dangerous open spaces below them. (This ability to contain a complicated series of story levels in one frame is characteristic of Mann.) It is only in the fort that Mature seems ill at ease, particularly when drunk. Usually he drinks with his companions, and can roll through open spaces, shouting at the moon and making the noise that will prove him a human being alive in the wilderness. In the fort, the camera follows him as he reels through the confusing space, falling down, bumping into people and objects, proving himself only a fallible man, crude by civilized standards.

A significant spatial conflict takes place between Mature and a demented army colonel who is his rival (Robert Preston). By not heeding the more experienced trapper's warnings, Preston has fallen into a bear pit the Indians have set. He falls into the darkened, deep interior space while Mature stands above him against the sky. Background illustrates their respective roles—Preston inside in darkness and cramped space, trapped . . . Mature outside, free and in control. As Preston tumbles into the pit, a swish pan to left brings the viewer to a head shot of Mature, in smiling profile against the sky.

The link between hero and villain is established by way of the desire for a "blue coat"—or enlistment in the army. The blue coat, like the rifle in *Winchester '73*, functions as an externalization of character conflict. Preston wears the blue coat and discusses its significance with his wife (Anne Bancroft), telling her that without it he's not a man: "I married a man, not a uniform," she says. "Then I deceived you. I am not a man without this," he replies. Mature *is* a man without the coat, but he wants one, as he feels that with it he will be acceptable to Bancroft. "I guess you have to have a fancy uniform like this to get a woman like you," he says when he sees her husband's photograph. Later, Mature steals a blue coat from a dead Indian and begins wearing it.

The crisis point for Mature comes when his blue coat, symbol of civilization, is taken from him. "You're not fit to wear a uniform and you never will be," says Guy Madison. Mature becomes very drunk, and reels into the frame, laughing. "I need room," he says, "Lots of it." He opens the gates of the fort and runs out into the night, releasing himself from the entrapping space of the fort.

Victor Mature is a character worthy of Zola's naturalism. He looks and acts like a huge bear. The idea of him as a bear, like the use of bear pits and lairs, is paramount in the organization of the film. "You're a drunken, filthy animal," Bancroft says to Mature the first time they meet. "I'm not an animal," he replies, and his civilizing process begins. Mature discusses the issue of civilization vs. frontier in personal terms several times in the film. In a conversation with the sympathetic officer played by Guy Madison, he asks, "What's wrong with me?" Madison replies, "You're just not civilized."

MATURE: "What does it mean?"
MADISON: "Even I don't always understand it. You have to belong."

The Mann hero insecure in his landscape, dragged across the burning salt flats, surrounded by uncaring cowboys. James Stewart in *The Man from Laramie*.

The Mann hero secure in his landscape, Victor Mature, free and open against the western sky in *The Last Frontier*.

MATURE: "To what?"
MADISON: "To other people."

Mature's trapper friend, James Whitmore, tells him, "You and I are two of the most ignorant men alive." Mature tells Whitmore that Bancroft looks at him "as if I were a bear."

"There's some comfort in bein' a bear in bear country," replies Whitmore.

"But I don't want to be a bear," stubbornly insists Mature.

Gently, like a father, Whitmore tries to warn Mature about Bancroft: "She's a fancy lady, and she needs a fancy gent."

A key fight scene clearly equates Mature with a bear in his pit, or lair. It is also a return to the *film noir* sense of tight, cramped space. (The fort, oddly enough, is urban in its relationship to the wilderness. This use of *noir* space is thus totally appropriate!) As Sgt. Dekker (Peter Whitney) climbs to Mature's room, an overhead shot shows Mature below, crouched like a wary animal in his den, ready to pounce, craftily letting the enemy be lured into his own space. When the sergeant opens the door, Mature pulls his animal-skin rug out from under him, and they engage in a brutal and vicious fight. Broken light peeks through the cracks between the logs of the walls as they struggle—a traditional *noir* lighting pattern. Intense close-ups emphasize the desperation of the struggle. Finally, they burst open the door, and fall out into the sunlight (the larger, more out-of-door space) and Mature wins the fight. He is seen atop the lookout bridge of the fort, defiant, big in space. "I would have died for this," he says of his blue coat, taking it off. "It's nothing but a filthy blue rag."

Mature's character attempts to understand civilization and its rules. Knowing Bancroft and everyone else wants to get rid of the demented colonel, Mature leaves him in the bear pit and returns to the fort. When his friend Madison as well as Bancroft reject him for what he has done, he cannot understand: "I did what they all wanted. It was what you wanted, wasn't it?"

"Yes," she replies, "but not this way."

"There's no other way," he tells her, with his primitive logic. "You can't kill a man by wishing him dead."

He has straightforwardly left his rival to die, knowing that she, too, wants it that way. But she can't face the implications of her feelings. Frustrated and angry, he bursts out at her, "I did it for you . . . and the captain . . . and the rest of them. And now I'm not clean enough to touch you." He slaps her, realizing only dimly that civilization often doesn't understand its own motivations.

In *Last Frontier* Mann gives an inordinate amount of attention to the woman's character. Bancroft knows she is attracted to Mature, but asserts herself to resist the attraction. "I don't want to be saved by you or any other man," she tells him. "First it was Colonel Marsden, saving me from being a spinster. Now it's you, wanting to save me from being a squaw. I'm different now."

Mature's relationship to her is one that seems to suggest he is her own less repressed nature. In a key scene, he leaps out of the darkness to grab her, taking possession of her as if he were a part of her inner self, as demonstrated by his lurking in the space of her shadows. Inside her rooms, they are seen together in profile, with her in the light and him in darkness. He speaks simply to her: "I care for you. I need you," a primitive language that speaks about basic sexual needs. The two profiles melt toward each other, finally merging in darkness as they kiss. The striking portrayal of light (Bancroft) and dark (Mature) meeting and fusing effectively presents not only their love, but the sense of Bancroft coming to terms with forces inside herself that she has long repressed.

The rest of the film brings about the ultimate civilization of Mature. Mature and Mongo, his Indian friend, have one last conversation, set against a distant mountain (the far country). In a simple and meaningful gesture, Mongo hands Mature his gun, saying, "You'll need it."

"But I'm going with you," protests Mature.

"You can't no more," replies Mongo. "You don't belong up there."

"Why are you going?" asks Mature.

"I belong there," replies Mongo, with simple dignity. The final image of the film is unconvincing to most critics, and was forced on Mann. Mature, in the blue uniform, is saluting the flag with Bancroft waiting for him on the stairs above. A soft snow falls. Although it is certainly true the scene is unsatisfying, the audience has been prepared for Mature's acceptance into the forces of civilization by the entire film. (The fact that we don't like it when we see it is quite another matter.) In particular, the climax of the film indicates the direction things will go. As Whitmore and Mature see the rout of the cavalry by the Indians, they try to salvage the forces. Running into the battle, Whitmore yells, with the instinct of the old trapper,

"Back to the trees! To the trees!" He seeks the wilderness for his protection, to save his life as he has lived it. Mature, however, prophetically calls out, "Back to the fort! To the fort!"

The Tin Star

It's quite a simple story, a lesson in apprenticeship.

—ANTHONY MANN[14]

Andrew Sarris called *The Tin Star* Mann's most didactic film. Few *more* didactic films exist. An older man, a former sheriff, teaches a young man, an inexperienced sheriff, how to do his job well, with the apprenticeship presented entirely in formal terms. The film is almost totally an exercise in style.

In its time, *The Tin Star* was seen by most critics as a pale imitation of *High Noon*. (It seemed to be Mann's fate to have his films juxtaposed with others that had similar plot structures. *Devil's Doorway* suffered because of *Broken Arrow*'s popularity, and *The Tin Star*, although released later, is almost always compared to *High Noon*.) On the surface level, both films are stories about sheriffs that are let down by their communities. In a sense, the character played by Henry Fonda is a refugee from a "high noon" that went wrong. He gave up being a sheriff because of what happened with the township he thought he could rely on. Anthony Perkins, the young sheriff, is let down by his town in the course of the film, but accepts the renewed love of the community when he triumphs.

Although plot similarities exist, *The Tin Star* is not like *High Noon*. The lack of formal coherence in Zinnemann's film separates it completely from the cohesive, highly formal tension of *The Tin Star*. *High Noon*'s success lay in its presentation of a strong star in a strong story, and its pretentions to moral and social comment. While it contains formal elements in abundance (use of time, in particular), it contains them in no consistent pattern. There is no equivalent in Zinnemann's form for an emotional behavior in the characters, although there is ample manipulation of form.

It is significant that *High Noon,* one of Hollywood's most respected and famous westerns, has very little action. It is a *talk* drama of the sort that those who feel superior to westerns find uplifting. "Now the western gets serious," critics say when watching it, a reflection of the snobbery that surrounds Hollywood genre films, as well as an indication of the lack of sophistication most critics have about what film really is. The remarkable formal achievement of *The Tin Star* is overlooked, while critics find it "empty" because its characters are not enacting a metaphor for the McCarthy era.

As Perkins learns how to be a sheriff from Fonda, his lessons become lessons for the audience in cinematic technique:

—The exact moment at which to draw the gun is a lesson in editing.
—How and when to approach an armed man is a lesson in camera movement.
—Target-shooting is a lesson in camera placement, angles, composition, and point of view for the audience.
—The complex rules of gunfighting are a lesson in using the far and the near in photography.
—Keeping an eye on an impending gunfight in a bar is achieved through watching that space by way of a mirrored reflection—a very complicated lesson in composition and internal editing within the frame.

The Tin Star makes the basic assumption that if Perkins learns Fonda's knowledge of form, he can then take over the role Fonda plays within that form. If he can possess and dominate space the way Fonda does, he will then, of course, become the hero, for the hero in an Anthony Mann film is always the man who controls the space. Thus, as the film unfolds, the audience first sees Fonda exert control over the image, and then Perkins exert that control.

This change-over takes place subtly in the story. At first, it is Fonda who is clearly aligned with the landscape. In addition he moves inside the frame with grace and ease, particularly in comparison with the awkward, coltish Perkins. By the end of the film, Perkins's movements smooth out, become more fluid, as he becomes a man, and thus a hero.

Fonda is the man of the West, the hero with the guilty secret. He is a bounty hunter—a despised character in western terms—but once he was a respected sheriff. He refuses to talk about himself, but finally tells Perkins his story. He gave up his own tin star in bitterness and anger when his wife and son died as a result of his town's apathy. He chose his present occupation because polite society rejects a bounty hunter, and Fonda rejects polite society.

Perkins does not quite have a guilty secret, but he has a problem. He doesn't know how to be a sheriff. Since he lives in a small town, he can't really keep this information secret, but it becomes a source of worry (guilt) for him.

There is no link between hero and villain in *The Tin Star*. The "link" (or presentation of the hero's opposite self) is between the father figure (Fonda) and the "son" (Perkins). They are the dual sides of the same nature, one rejecting community and one embracing it . . . one skilled, one unskilled . . . one alone in life, one loved by his fiancée. They both recognize themselves in each other, but reject that idea. "Is it true that you used to be a sheriff like me?" Perkins asks the older man. "Not like you," is his grim reply. Mann places the audience in the same position as the hero. As the hero learns where he is in relation to events, the audience also learns where they are. The audience is taken through the same emotions as the hero.

In *The Tin Star*, Mann works a variation on his usual pattern. Since he has two heroes, he has to choose which one will embody meaning. At first he uses Fonda, who is equated with the landscape in the opening scene. But he varies this alliance by having the viewer learn the same lessons as Perkins. As the film plays out, the emphasis is shifted from Fonda to Perkins, which is appropriate to the story of apprenticeship.

Thus, Fonda and Perkins change places. Perkins learns to dominate his town and become a successful sheriff. He moves outdoors and captures the secondary villains in their lair. Fonda, on the other hand, is integrated back into society by his regard for Perkins and also by his relationship with the young widow (Betsy Palmer) and her son. Both men have their space altered. Perkins moves out of his office and dominates the landscape. Fonda moves in from the landscape and takes up residence in Palmer's home. Yet each retains his mastery of the other space, too. Where both have had weaknesses, they gain strength from their association. Each has something the other needs, and both end up equally comfortable indoors or out. *The Tin Star* illustrates the typical Mann hero and his opposite-self pattern by presenting two incomplete heroes who become whole. It is as if the duality inherent in the Mann hero had actually split into two separate people.

Two confrontations show the before and after of Perkins, when he conflicts with the major villain (Neville Brand) in the streets of the town. In both cases, the space utilized is exactly the same, and events unfold similarly. In the first scene, set in daylight, Fonda must rescue Perkins, who does not yet understand the role of hero. But, in the final confrontation, Perkins steps out into the streets at night confident of his role. He has learned to control his space by altering its composition. In the conflict he seems to be literally dictating what the camera does. It MUST follow him. It MUST take a vantage point that suits his needs. In addition, he manipulates the angry crowd in the same way that the image is manipulated by the director. Because of this close alliance among story, image, and form, Perkins's lessons in formal control are learned equally well by the audience.

The tin star itself is a symbol of force in both their lives. Just as Perkins must learn how to be worthy of the star, Fonda must learn to reaccept the responsibility it carries with it for other people. Fonda's picking up the star to wear it again is his reentry into organized society. This is borne out by his finding a new family, a wife (Betsy Palmer) and a son, to replace those he has lost. By putting on the star, he finds what he has lost. Or, as Perkins says, "Once a man pins it on, he can't take it off." Perkins teaches Fonda that the star was always a part of him.

The Tin Star opens with an image of hills, and a lone rider moving down them, leading a second horse. As credits unfold, he rides toward a destination, into a more settled and inhabited-looking landscape. The rider is seen to be Henry Fonda, who is clearly equated with the landscape in this opening (and thus established as the hero). With ominous music on the track, a remarkably fluid scene unfolds in which Fonda rides into town, down the streets past the onlooking townspeople, while the camera follows the action. Through windows, the audience can see into interiors in which townsfolk are pointing at the dead body Fonda brings with him. Fonda rides into the frame from far back, on a diagonal line to right of frame, growing larger as he advances into town.

The opening sequence is as follows:

IMAGE: Fonda rides in the distance atop hill, riding across and down the hill.

CUT TO: Fonda riding down the hill and into a valley.

CUT TO: Fonda's horse in water, walking down stream.

CUT TO: The street of a western town, with Fonda entering far back, at
          distant point, with the camera moving toward him to the right
          and forward.
CUT TO: Townspeople coming out of their shops and moving forward as he
          rides by the general store.
CUT TO: A view of the dead body across Fonda's extra horse, with people
          following. As the horse moves by, the body is clearly seen hanging
          over the side of the horse, its dead hand dangling.
CUT TO: A close-up of the dead hand.
CUT TO: Townspeople watching, one group on porch playing checkers.
CUT TO: Another group of townspeople watching.
CUT TO: Fonda moving on into town, across town square, out of the
          frame, to the right, down the street.
CUT TO: Fonda by a tree in the town square. He dominates space as he is seen
          full in frame, riding across frame to right, no longer on the diagonal,
          as he ties up his horse outside the sheriff's office. Behind him, in
          depth of field, townspeople have flowed out into the streets and are
          running across frame behind him, watching.
CUT TO: Fonda entering sheriff's office, as townspeople, all outside, are
          seen. Fonda looks around office and enters a back room, an
          interior space from which townspeople can be seen through win-
          dows. Fonda sees Perkins practicing with his guns. Sees him
          drop a gun, facing forward to audience, Fonda behind him in
          frame.
CUT TO: Perkins, who turns to see Fonda.

This wordless opening sequence establishes the space of the town,
plus the mood of the townspeople, the two heroes, and their relationships to one another and to the town. All the oppositions of the
narrative are clearly established through the spatial area of the
town. The town is the landscape of *The Tin Star*. People and stores
replace rocks and cacti.

Actually, the entire story is told formally in the opening five
minutes. A man comes across the landscape into town. As he advances into the space of the streets, he slowly and deliberately fills
and dominates that space. He creates an uncomprehending stir
amidst the townspeople who watch him, an unmistakably hostile
stir. The townspeople who watch his invasion of their space gather
together and form into a unit, watching. As they pour out into the
streets when he rides by—reclaiming their space and establishing
their right to it—he enters the sheriff's office. This entry into interior space separates him from the townspeople, cuts him off from
them. Fonda aligns himself with the interior space of the sheriff's

office, his safe haven within the town, as only the sheriff accepts him.

The Tin Star moves back and forth between interior space and exterior space. It combines the artificiality found in *The Far Country* (with its extensive use of interiors) with the more realistic location westerns, such as *The Naked Spur* and *Bend of the River*. An inside/outside relationship exists both physically, by way of the landscape, and narratively, by virtue of Fonda's being a loner who has rejected society and Perkins's being at odds with his township.

Perkins is first seen inside, allied with interior space. His office defines him. He is often seen inside it, almost trapped, as he is stuck in the role of sheriff despite his inadequacy for the job. Outside, through his windows, he can see the townspeople. He is distanced from them, alienated from them by his job. They are outside in the streets, standing almost like statues. They hold their space, the town, by occupying it physically. Perkins is one of them, having been born and raised in the little community. He is not a loner like Fonda, but the tin star has temporarily separated him from his group.

A dramatic scene points up this indoor-outdoor dichotomy. When Perkins is holding two stagecoach robbers inside his jail, he pulls down the blinds on the windows of his office, shutting out the town and its menacing forces. Suddenly, someone from outside shoots the blind. It flies up, revealing the streets of the town (danger) outside. This piece of action occurs within the frame—no cuts—and it readjusts the entire composition of the scene. At the same time, the narrative situation is shifted. As is typical of Mann, formal and dramatic events are made equivalent, this time by way of an internalized piece of action which is almost a type of editing.

The concern with integration into a community that is expressed in Mann's films finds its ultimate expression in *Tin Star*, which is a film about a community. The primary landscape is a township, and "You can't run away from responsibility" is the main theme.

The final moments of *The Tin Star* show a repeat of the original camera movement that brought Fonda into the streets of the town. As he leaves town with his new family, the camera moves back, recreating the original pattern in reverse. *The Tin Star* traces a perfect formal pattern from beginning to end.

The Last Frontier and *The Tin Star* vary the basic Mann narrative of the core films. However, they also maintain it as follows:

(Top) A compositional lesson. Anthony Perkins (right) faces down villain Neville Brand (left) while Henry Fonda stands deep center, teaching Perkins how to control his space in *The Tin Star*. (Bottom) Two halves of the Mann hero healed. Perkins shakes Fonda's hand in *The Tin Star*, against the inside/outside relationship of sheriff's office to the landscape of the town.

The Last Frontier	*The Tin Star*
HERO(ES)	
A straightforward, uneducated, animalistic trapper (Victor Mature), *and* a fair-minded, straightforward army officer who represents the good in civilization (Guy Madison).	A bounty hunter, once a respected sheriff, who has turned against the society he blames for the death of his wife and son (Henry Fonda), *and* a young sheriff with a problem he can't keep secret, his lack of ability (Anthony Perkins).
VILLAIN	
An army officer with a guilty secret (Robert Preston). He is called the Butcher of Shiloh, because he led inexperienced troops into certain death for his own glory.	A town bully, who is deeply prejudiced against Indians (Neville Brand).
OLD MAN	
The hero's trapper friend (James Whitmore), who has been like his father.	The kindly and beloved doctor of the town (John McIntyre).
WOMAN	
The cavalry officer's wife (Anne Bancroft), who hates yet pities her husband and falls in love with the hero.	A widow, once the wife of an Indian, who lives outside town as a social outcast—a good woman who will help the hero (Betsy Palmer).
SECOND VILLAIN	
A brutal army man who hates the hero (Peter Whitney).	Two men who rob a stagecoach and kill the kindly doctor.

The journeys of the two films are personal. In *The Tin Star,* the journey represents a reconciliation with the community, as the landscape crossed is primarily a township. The Mann hero heals himself, and his duality is resolved. In *The Last Frontier* also, the hero's journey is personal, and the resolution of his problem lies in his acceptance of a community. But the personal journeys are set against a microcosm and macrocosm of the old West. *The Tin Star* is a highly personal story set in a representational township, for the resolution of a private problem. *The Last Frontier* is a highly personal story set against a representational background for the resolution of an historical problem, the closing of the frontier. With *El Cid,* Mann would mesh the personal (microcosm) against the historical (macrocosm) for the ultimate resolution of the Mann hero and his journey. His next film, his final western, was the last rehearsal for the epic films.

Culmination: *Man of the West*

I said to myself, why not accentuate the hieratic aspects of the group? You know . . . like on a medallion.

—ANTHONY MANN, speaking of *Man of the West*[15]

After naming *Man of the West* one of the ten best films of 1958, Jean-Luc Godard went on to explain:

I have seen nothing so completely new since—why not?—Griffith. Just as the director of *Birth of a Nation* gave one the impression that he was inventing the cinema with every shot, each shot of *Man of the West* gives one the impression that Anthony Mann is redefining the Western. It is, moreover, more than an impression. *He does re-invent.*[16]

As Godard observes, *Man of the West* is "both course and discourse." It is Mann's final statement in the genre in which he found his fullest creative flowering. The film not only was his last real western, but it was also his crowning achievement, one of the greatest westerns ever made. In it, all he had done previously culminated in one final, epic story.

As has already been established, the Mann westerns concern a journey in which the landscape and the sets closely reflect the dramatic development. *Man of the West* maintains this pattern. In addition, the basic set of Mann characters is present:

THE HERO:	A man with a guilty secret. He was once an evil outlaw, a member of the notorious Dock Tobin gang. He was responsible for robberies, raids, and the murders of innocent victims (Gary Cooper).
THE VILLAIN:	A blood-relation, his cousin, with whom he shared an evil childhood and membership in the gang (John Dehner).
THE OLD MAN:	An evil patriarch, Dock Tobin, the leader of the gang. A foul father figure to the two cousins (Lee J. Cobb). A second "old man" is a gambler who sacrifices his life so that Cooper may live. Somewhat of a comic relief related to the Millard

	Mitchell and Walter Brennan characters, he is a con artist (Arthur O'Connell).
THE WOMAN:	A saloon singer in the tradition of Shelley Winters in *Winchester '73*. Basically a good woman who would be willing to help and sustain the hero (Julie London). Offstage, there is a second woman, who is never seen: the loving and beloved wife of Cooper.
SECOND VILLAINS:	The remainder of the Dock Tobin gang (primarily Jack Lord, an evil thug, and Royal Dano, a deaf man). Their purpose is to define the lowest animal instincts of the hero and villain through their behavior.

As in the core westerns, these characters embark on a journey through a terrain which is used to signify the psychological journey of the hero. The hero of *Man of the West* typically confronts his own internal "geography" and its implications. The film, however, is something more than the usual matching of landscape, narrative, and character development. It incorporates the mythology of the western genre itself, and, ultimately, the mythology of the hero. As if he were the hero of a Greek myth, Cooper makes a symbolic journey into self. He leaves the real world he inhabits and enters the evil underworld to confront the forces which would destroy him, forces which are clearly of and within him. He makes a journey with ghosts back into things buried and dead in his past, from civilization to noncivilization and back to redemption. Mann did indeed "accentuate the hieratic aspects."

The credits sequence of *Man of the West* establishes the hero and his equation with the landscape. As the title words are seen, Gary Cooper, a readily identifiable star, and one known to be "of the West," rides against a rocky landscape. The visual statement is made about the hero and his identity. He is *a man*. Of *the West*. From that moment on, the film unfolds as a near perfect expression of the final epic vision of Mann's work in the western. Scene by scene, it can be examined to reveal his mastery of form and narrative.

The town: Three of the main characters meet and are established in the introductory section, which takes place in a small western town called Crosscut: the hero (Gary Cooper), the leading lady (Julie London), and the conman/gambler/comic relief, (Arthur O'Connell). Their three paths cross literally in Crosscut.

During the action of this section of the film, Cooper is established as a man of mystery. He tells people two different versions of his name and home town. He changes his clothes, taking off the traditional western garb and putting on the more civilized outfit of a suit jacket. He shaves to change his identity, and secretly stashes his money and his gun inside a carpetbag. Although this action is straightforwardly performed, the effect on the audience is one of watching a man don a disguise. In this case, it is the guise of a civilized man. Later, the audience learns that this costume change is symbolic of Cooper's character, a reformed outlaw.

Crosscut is seen as a bustling western town, rowdy and busy, fairly well settled. The music on the soundtrack is light, buoyant, even slightly humorous. In fact, this portion of the movie is almost a comedy. Not since *Bend of the River* had Mann set up such a purposely lighthearted opening section.

As Cooper boards the train to leave town, however, the threat of the law is established. The sheriff questions him, and once again he gives a false name. This threat is established visually by composition within the frame. As Cooper moves to board the train, the lower torso of the sheriff, his gun on his hip, fills the forward portion of the wide-screen frame, dominating the space. The sheriff's gun looms large over Cooper's image, as Cooper's space within the frame is menaced by the law.

The first journey—the train: Cooper, London, and O'Connell all board the train and embark on a journey. Both London and O'Connell are dressed in the traditional clothes associated in the genre with their standard character types of saloon singer and con artist. They settle into their seats with relative ease. Cooper, on the other hand, seems too big for the seats, uncomfortable in the surroundings, and somewhat unsettled by the jerking motion as the train pulls out. Since the train is a basic unit of civilization (an enclosed, protected space), Cooper appears to be ill-at-ease, or alienated, from order and civilization.

Mann uses the space inside the train to reflect levels of meaning: literally the interior of the train is a train interior; but symbolically, it represents a basic unit of civilization, and thus a safe interior.

Finally, generically, the interior of the train is a basic unit of the western film. Trains are held up, and they carry such stock characters as outlaws, saloon girls, sheriffs, gambling men, etc. Thus, Mann's use of the train speaks to the viewing audience on three levels. The characters are enclosed within the story (they are taking a train trip), within civilization (they are in a safe place), and within the genre (they are on a western train which is likely to be held up).

The landscape is seen outside the train windows by way of a complicated wide-screen composition. A diagonal visual line allows the viewer to see the interior of the train and its passengers, as well as the world the train is passing through outside the windows. The world outside is a civilized world, verdant, settled, with houses, gardens, fences, grazing cattle, and telegraph poles.

When the train stops to refuel, the expected generic action occurs. The train is attacked and robbed by outlaws. The lawmen on board order the train started up immediately, and it pulls out. The three main characters, all of whom have been out stretching their legs, are suddenly left behind. Civilization and order desert them.

The second journey–the walk: The second journey extends the first journey across a landscape, outside a unit of civilization. The three characters must walk on foot to shelter. As they walk, their characters are developed further with dialogue. London's character is tough, jaunty, cheerful under duress. The gambler is weak, gabby. Cooper is taciturn and practical. Their walk takes them across a basically verdant terrain, with softly rolling hills on which occasionally cattle are observed grazing. A few isolated small rocks are seen, like tiny visual warning notes. During this hiatus, which is used primarily for character development, they are within a sane world and maintain the roles that were established in the opening section of the film. This journey ends abruptly as they approach a shack located in a hollow of the landscape. Surrounded with a few small gnarled trees (the first such seen in the film), the shack seems to sit waiting for their approach. Cooper speaks to London: "I used to live here once."

"When you were a boy?" she questions.

"I don't know what I was," he replies. Thus the shack, the outlaw's hide-out, is established as a link (the Cooper character's name is Link) to his secret past. The shack is an objective correlative, a physical indication of another self.

As Cooper walks toward the hide-out, he removes his suit jacket, the civilized garb he donned in Crosscut. He hands it to London, as if it were a shield. It is his promise of protection for her, a pledge of civilized behavior for her to hold on to in the coming events. Without this jacket, Cooper wears a leather vest which marks him once again as the Man of the West.

As Cooper moves toward the shack, London and O'Connell hide in the barn to await his signal. The music marks the narrative change in which people seek shelter and hiding places. A solemn warning note is heard played on a xylophone. Using the instrument, the score sounds more and more menacing and heavy as Cooper approaches the door of the shack. Cooper walks to the door in the sunlight, and is seen knocking on the door. An abrupt cut transfers the viewer inside to the darkened shack. The switch from bright sunlight to extreme interior darkness has the unsettling effect of plunging the viewer into the waiting chaos, a perfect narrative equivalent.

The shack: from the moment the door is opened and Cooper enters the outlaw's hideout, the film is never again the same. Totally gone is any humor or lightness. The roles the three characters have been playing are stripped away from them, and, indeed, a protective layer of decency is stripped away from the film itself. The violence and cruelty many westerns are really about is revealed to the viewer for what it is. *Man of the West* is a film with a secret. It has deceived the audience with its lighthearted opening section. Its inner truth is now revealed.

A long, extended scene takes place within the hideout. Nearly a third of the running time of the film is played inside that interior. When Cooper steps inside from the sunlight, he enters darkness. His entry is seen from within the shack, where an unidentified hand, large and menacing, enters the wide-screen from frame left, holding a gun. The gun moves into the frame and dominates the space. The inside of the shack is thus identified as a violent space, potentially dangerous for the hero, and, by extension, the audience.

The space inside the shack is presented as small, cramped, dark. The evil of the underworld is visualized. Intense close-ups of the three train robbers inside indicate tension of the highest order. As Cooper enters, he is asked where he comes from, and he instinctively gives a lying answer.

The shack sequence introduces new characters, but primarily introduces the main tensions and conflicts of the narrative. Inside the shack, the audience learns what Cooper's secrets are. And they are ugly. It is made patently clear that he was at one time in his life not only a member of this gang, but that he participated fully in ugly, brutal murders and robberies.

The character of Dock Tobin is introduced (Lee J. Cobb). He is Cooper's uncle, the leader of the gang. When Cobb enters the frame, and the narrative establishes that Cooper is at least temporarily safe, the space of the cabin is redefined. It is seen to be larger than originally indicated, and lamps are lit which provide a sense of safety through their warm color. A breathing space for the hero is provided both in the narrative and in his physical surroundings through Mann's method of redefinition of space.

Cobb/Tobin moves restlessly around in the frame, a treacherous figure, shifting his alliance by way of composition from Cooper to various members of his gang. The framing and composition perfectly present the narrative relationships. Cooper is first seen alone in the frame, as an outsider. When Cobb enters, he is allied with Cobb in the frame. Cobb establishes mastery over the scene. Cooper is seen alone in the frame, followed by an image which contains the three outlaws as a group. Cobb is clearly the master of both groups' fate. As Cobb describes Cooper's former exploits as an outlaw, Cooper is for the first time united in the frame with the outlaws, as if he were one of them, even though he stands slightly apart. The pace of the scene follows Cobb's movements. It is stately, deliberate, slow. Prior to the shack sequence, the film was leisurely. Now it is deliberate. When Cooper realizes he is trapped and must rejoin his old gang if he hopes to live, he says, "I'm back," and the entire group is seen together in the wide-screen frame: Cooper, Cobb, and the three outlaws, united in evil in the dark shack.

During this sequence Cooper has been stripped bare for the audience of the heroic associations of the genre. He is *not* the traditional hero. He truly is no more than a brutal outlaw. He is a Man of the West, but not the one usually associated with the western genre. In the same regard, when London and O'Connell are brought into the shack, the stripping of her traditional role will occur. (O'Connell's turn will come later.)

In London's case, the stripping is quite literal. Cobb removes the pins from her hair, so that it falls loose, indicating her vulnerability as a woman in the situation. After Cooper and O'Connell are sent outside, the outlaws force her to undress. In one of the most vicious scenes in American film, sex and violence are clearly linked with a solemn, almost polite and respectful pace which makes the action all the more horrible to watch. London is stripped of the traditional saloon-girl-with-heart-of-gold-and-strength-to-match role. She loses all her defenses and flippancy. This stripping will also take place in the storyline, in which she will fall in love for the first time in her life.

Later, Cooper explains to London how he was raised by Cobb and taught to be a killer. Because he spends the night with her, he feels compelled to tell her that he has lived down his past and is now a happily married man, the father of two children. "There's a point where you either grow up and become a human being or you rot, like that bunch." In speaking to London, Cooper faces the truth about himself. "I want to kill every last one of those Tobins. And that makes me just like they are."

O'Connell observes the change in Cooper: "You've changed. Since the moment you walked into that shack, you changed. You're a different man. You act as if you belong to these people." London tells Cooper, "You're not like them at all." But he replies, knowing the truth, "I was. There wasn't any difference at all."

In the sequence in the darkened shack, secrets are revealed, and sex and violence rise to the surface. There is no way back to civilization except out through destruction and violence.

The third journey: The morning is introduced to the viewer by the camera's tracking forward into the sunshine. In the scenes which follow, the violence in Cooper will burst out in a similar fashion, in a relentless, unstoppable forward movement. The matching of his interior to the landscape will be complete. Cooper has been reunited with his past in the darkness of the shack and the night. From this scene on, he begins to behave like the other outlaws.

This journey also introduces the primary villain, Cooper's blood-relation, his cousin Claude (John Dehner). Although Cobb is the evil patriarch, he remains separate from the action of the film, particularly the shoot-out. He is a villain, but not *the* villain linked to the hero. That figure, Dehner, joins the gang in the morning light, so that the evil family is reunited to make an evil journey. This uncivilized journey (to rob the town of Lassoo) is in direct opposition to the earlier journey on the train. It represents the inner journey in terms of Cooper's character.

As the group leaves the shack behind, the score reflects the increased drama by becoming heavier, more menacing. The land-scape is spare, but still contains some greenery. As the journey progresses, the green will gradually disappear, along with all marks of civilization and order. The terrain will undergo a complete change to a dry, rocky, barren soil, representing the undisciplined, lawless world into which they are moving.

Cooper's first physical battle takes place on this journey. Until this conflict, he has behaved like a civilized man, trying to out-think his captors, playing along with them until he can overcome them. But when the train of wagons stops in an open clearing, violence erupts. It is significant that this violence is instigated by Cooper himself. In the first narrative indication that he has begun to behave like the outlaws, he goads one of them (Jack Lord) into a fight.

The two men struggle. On the distant horizon, giant rocks can be seen. The two adversaries are photographed in intense close-ups. As Cobb watches, he is shown framed against these big rough rocks, equating him with them and defining his uncivilized nature. As the fight grows increasingly violent and brutal, Cooper becomes more animalistic and brutal. He, too, is then seen framed against those rocks, indicating his blood-relationship to Cobb as well as his shared evil. The landscape itself is brought into the struggle. The two fighters use tree branches and rocks in the attempt to annihilate each other. They are trapped beneath the stomping hooves of horses, and Cooper finally overcomes Lord.

In a key character shift, he does not accept the victory as being enough. He proves visually to the audience that what they heard told about his past is clearly true. In an act from his degraded past, he forces Lord to undress, as Lord had helped to force London to strip the night before.

When Lord tries to shoot Cooper, the stripping-down of O'Con-nell takes place. Like the characters played by James Stewart in *The Naked Spur* and *The Man from Laramie*, Cooper has hesitated, unable to go through with the ultimate violence of killing Lord. Lord uses the advantage, and O'Connell takes the bullet. Unable to bear the violence, he sacrifices himself for Cooper's safety. His role of illegal gambler who cheats society is stripped off. He has lived the life of a minor outlaw, but, faced with what that life truly is, he rejects it. Underneath, he is a civilized man.

As the journey progresses toward rougher, drier country, the link

between Cooper and Dehner is fully expressed. Side by side they
ride on a wagon seat, equals in the frame. They address one another
ironically by their blood-relationship, calling each other "cousin" in
mocking voices.

"We used to talk when we were kids," says Dehner, explaining
that Cobb is a bit soft in the head now, but that no one is allowed to
say that except him. He defines his loyalty to Cobb. "I watch out for
that old man. I love him." Dehner tells how Cobb cried when
Cooper left him, and he warns him that if Cobb had not grown old
and soft, he would already have killed Cooper.

The two men understand each other. Dehner does not have to
have explained what Cooper's motivations are. He *knows* that
Cooper has not really rejoined the gang, and that he plans to kill
them all. "But you're not gonna make it, Link," he warns. "You're
not gonna make it."

Dehner's speech is representative of the complexity of the Mann
villain/hero relationship. Dehner's description of love and loyalty to
the old man is the most noble speech in the entire film. Although
Dehner lacks their charm, he is kin to the characters played by
Arthur Kennedy and Robert Ryan in *Bend of the River* and *The
Naked Spur*.

Dehner *is* like Cooper. He has his own code of honor. Although it
is an outlaw code, he is seen to have loyalty and purpose. Dehner is
a bad man, with a kind of good that makes him stick by the man who
cared for him when he was a child. Cooper is a good man, with a
kind of cruelty that makes him want to kill his former father. Or,
more specifically, both are part bad, part good, in different balance.
The tendency to good in Dehner makes him remain loyal, no matter
what. The tendency to good in Cooper has forced him to leave the
outlaw life behind, and thus come into opposition to his former
family.

During the journey, the terrain has grown increasingly dry and
barren. Majestic, menacing rocks loom over the wagons. The rocks
seem to hang over them physically and psychologically, threatening
their very existence.

A short interlude before an eruption of extreme violence takes
place. The group of outlaws, including Cooper and London, is seen
around a campfire the night before the bank robbery in Lassoo is to
take place. It is decided that Cooper and the deaf man (Royal Dano)
will ride ahead into Lassoo alone. The darkness of the night represents both a respite before violence, and the total evil that Cooper

Courtesy of the Museum of Modern Art/Film Stills Archive

The stripping down of characters from *Man of the West:* Gary Cooper proves he "was just like them" by stripping Jack Lord after the vicious fight, and (Bottom) Julie London, stripped and vulnerable before the outlaw gang.

Credit: The Museum of Modern Art/Film Stills Archive

has fallen into. He is seen isolated from the others (excepting London). He is alone in the evil, awaiting his fate.

The ghost town: As Cooper and Dano ride toward Lassoo, it is seen nestled amidst dry rocks, in contrast to the earlier town, Crosscut, with its verdant surroundings. As the two outlaws ride into the streets, they discover the ironic truth. Lassoo is a ghost town. Cooper has ridden into his own dead past and is totally cut off from any civilized world. He is in his own private hell.

The events which take place in Lassoo unleash the violence that has been building. Within a few seconds, Dano has killed an innocent Mexican woman, and Cooper has shot Dano. The mute man runs down the abandoned streets of Lassoo, the camera following in reckless, useless pursuit. Suddenly, he finds his voice and dies screaming in the dusty streets. This sound is like the xylophone notes before the entry into the shack—a warning knell of the violence and danger to come.

Dano's death sets the stage for the final shoot-out. Dehner and another outlaw ride into Lassoo out of the rocks, like insects or scorpions. Finding Dano dead, they are alerted to Cooper's treachery. Dehner is prepared. "I want to see you, cousin," he calls to Cooper. "Over here, cousin," Cooper calls back.

In the ultimate of western rituals, Cooper and Dehner begin their dance of death. It is no ordinary shoot-out. The space of the frame is cut apart, sliced by fences, abandoned buildings, and various levels to be found in the ghost town: rooftops, porches. Like the narrative situation itself, the physical space presented in the shoot-out is complex and stylized. There is no real geographical clarity. Each man scuttles through the area he occupies at that moment, seeking shelter and seeking his enemy simultaneously. At one moment, Cooper, Dehner, and the third outlaw are all seen in the frame in different spatial areas and levels, until the third outlaw is killed.

After a certain point in the ritual attempt to dominate the space of the ghost-town streets, Cooper and Dehner are both seen within the frame. Both hunter and hunted are kept together in one shot. The space of the frame is divided horizontally between the two men, as if they were two halves of the same man, which, in fact, they are. Cooper makes a self-conscious ritual announcement: "All alone now, Claude. You've been plannin' for it all your life. Now it is finally here. Just like you know it always would be."

The moment is here for the audience, too, just as they knew it

Pursuer and Pursued in one frame. Gary Cooper and John Dehner, the cousins of *Man of the West* in their final shoot-out.

always would be. Every audience for a western film knows this moment must sooner or later appear, the ritual confrontation between the bad and good man. As the two men have moved through space, it has been sometimes impossible to tell where they are in relationship to one another. Other times, they are linked so closely that they appear in the same frame. Finally, they lie horizontally in the frame, Cooper flat on the porch floor above, and Dehner flat underneath the porch in a scene reminiscent of the final confrontation in *The Far Country*. Cooper kills Dehner, his evil self. Before leaving him, he folds the hands of the dead body.

Finale: The scene in Lassoo resolved the dramatic tension of the film. The finale resolves the psychological tension. Returning alone to the campsite, Cooper finds the abandoned London, raped and beaten by Cobb. In his final ritual, Cooper sets out to kill the evil patriarch.

High atop a rocky terrain, in long shot, Cobb is discovered. He is totally identified with the rocky landscape, the unsettled, uncivilized outlaw world. He is like a figure from some distant past, an apparition out of mythology. Cobb even looks like a ghost, white-haired and pale-eyed.

"I'm comin' to get you, Dock," shouts Cooper. "I'm comin' to take you in. Lassoo's a ghost town and that's what you are. A ghost. You've outlived your kind and your time."

The old man accepts the challenge. "Shoot! Have you lost your taste for it?"

Cooper finally shoots to kill, and the old man falls down from his high perch. He tumbles down through the rocks, a lifeless rag doll. It is the death of the outlaw world and the outlaw psychology, the closing of the frontier, and the end of the western genre, at least for Mann. His final evil character rains down on the hero just as the landscape itself has so many times in the prior westerns. But it is the final attack. It's over this time, really over.

From the beginning *Man of the West* has set itself a deliberate pace. It does not betray that pace with its violent ending. It concludes with a scene in which London and Cooper ride back toward civilization. As their wagon bounces along, the terrain begins to even out and look green again—the return to normalcy. Cooper asks London what she will do with herself now. "Sing," she replies, and thus their roles are restored. She's once again a saloon singer, and Cooper is inarguably *the* Man of the West.

Man of the West strikes such a slow, stately pace that it might appropriately be seen as a dream, or a nightmare. Not only is it an allegorical film, it is a downright spook story. Through it, Mann translated the genre into an epic, mythological tale. There was no point in his making another western. What more could he do with the form? The next step was logically into an epic itself, in which the total use of the width and depth of frame could serve his ends in a mythical way.

Anthony Mann had made his final journey with a western hero.

5

The Epic Mann

BEGINNING IN 1960, Mann turned his attention to a type of film that was becoming popular: the international all-star blockbuster. In a last-ditch effort to stem the tide of television, films decided to blow the budget and give the public what TV couldn't: size, spectacle. Casts of thousands thundered over the tundra toward the box office, and Mann was afforded the opportunity to work on the grandest scale imaginable.

Mann's first project of such scope was *Cimarron*, a remake of a 1931 film that had enjoyed both critical and commercial success (a box-office hit, it was also voted best picture of the year by the Motion Picture Academy). Although *Cimarron* has been defined as a western by some critics, it is not a traditional genre film but an historical drama about the settling of the West, with a primary focus on the woman's role. It is based on a book by Edna Ferber which tells the story of a well-to-do eastern girl, Sabra, who goes west with her glamorous husband, Yancey Cravat. Sabra was meant to represent the force of civilization, and Yancey the old, untamed West. The plot depicts their early days wildcatting in Oklahoma, including the great land rush and the ultimate discovery of oil. When the West becomes too settled, Yancey disappears, leaving Sabra to become a successful newspaperwoman, and ultimately a politician. Yancey is later found as a down-and-outer working in the oil fields as a driller. In a last act of heroism, he is killed saving the lives of coworkers. Sabra arrives in time to embrace him before he dies, smothering him with her furs and orchids and weeping onto his oil-drenched chest. "Oh, mother of Earth," he says, "peerless woman, clasp me to thy bosom."

It's not exactly Anthony Mann material. Predictably, Mann wanted to shift character emphasis onto the male role[1] and to stress

Charlton Heston, the epic hero El Cid, confronts the King's Champion for family honor.

159

the changing landscape as the old West becomes settled and civilized: "I wanted to retrace the history of the U.S.A. A remake didn't interest me . . . the virgin land and the cordons of troops, the pioneers who set out and put down their stakes . . . the houses spring up one by one, the streets, the school, railroads . . . but Yancey couldn't integrate. He missed the open spaces. He was dying."[2] In other words, he needed the landscape. Directed totally by Mann on his own terms, *Cimarron* might have been a great film, but Mann quarreled with producer Edmund Grainger and quit in the midst of shooting. Mann wanted to film entirely on location, and Grainger wanted the majority of scenes to be shot in the studio. The result is a weak film, unfortunately bearing Mann's name. It was a box-office flop.

Cimarron contains, however, many examples of the typical Mann style. A graceful movement of the camera opens the film, taking the viewer into the well-appointed home the young girl is leaving behind. After a touching farewell to her family, the newlyweds are beautifully established in the landscape by way of their two wagons, his leading, hers following trustingly along behind.

The high point of the film, which comes very early, is the Oklahoma land-rush scene of April 22, 1889. The huge wide-screen image is able to show simultaneously stretches of open space on one side and the waiting line-up of wagons on the other . . . the two sides of the screen marked off by a line-up of cavalry officers—an unforgettable image. The rush itself is a whirling mass of speed and involvement, with death and danger illustrated over and over again through smash-up after smash-up. One of the chief problems for *Cimarron* is that it never regains this sense of energy and pace.

The story of *Cimarron* held little appeal in the emerging decade of the 1960s. Essentially a soap opera, the story is also optimistic and vigorous, celebrating the American spirit and the American way of life. It was out of step with the downbeat decade that questioned all American values. What *Cimarron* did have to offer—a spirited heroine who, despite a coddled life, learned to care for herself and make her own way—was destroyed in the Mann remake. Sabra was turned into a a sweetly smiling creature who cries when the going gets rough. As played by Maria Schell, she is little more than decorative, and hardly that. The film is stolen by Anne Baxter, playing a bordello owner who loves Yancey. "Don't confuse me with one of those in the storybooks," she warns Sabra, in an offbeat gesture of sisterhood that is the only good dramatic scene in the film. "You know, with a heart of gold. If I had a heart of gold I'd have sold it for twice its worth."

From time to time Mann asserts his style, and the film that might have been is glimpsed, as when a group of outlaws hold up a bank and Yancey captures them. In watching such scenes, it is possible to imagine Mann creating a great epic in which, as the landscape is tamed from wilderness to civilization, the characters' lives—and the entire American world—are changed accordingly. But *Cimarron* is not it. Mann's next epic, however, was quite another matter.

El Cid

El Cid represents the ultimate journey for a hero a la Anthony Mann. An ordinary man, Rodrigo Diaz de Bivar, begins a journey to his bride on his wedding day. It ends only years later after he has become the mythical liberator of his people, El Cid. The film is an extended journey through Rodrigo's life. It shows his transformation from an ordinary man into a hero, from a hero into a legend, and from a legend into a myth.

The film may be seen as a series of eight movements around a recurring pattern of Action, Decision, Ordeal, and Heroic Reward. As the plot unfolds, the pattern is stretched out, so that the initial episodes come rapidly upon one another, and the latter ones more slowly. The earlier episodes rely more upon dialogue than the latter, because the transformation of Rodrigo to El Cid is not a political or moral event, but a visual one. Thus, as he moves forward in his destiny, his story becomes increasingly visual. This stripping-out of dialogue carries a larger meaning in that it also represents an exaltation, a cutting-away of humanity and a lifting-up into a godlike status.

The pattern of Action, Decision, Ordeal, and Heroic Reward may be charted in the plot as follows:

162

Action	Decision
1. Rodrigo Diaz journeys to his bride on his wedding day.	He decides to take the shortest way. The shortcut takes him through a village being sacked by Moors.
2. Rodrigo resumes his journey, taking along two Moorish commanders he has captured.	He decides to set his captives free because it is his wedding day.
3. Rodrigo is brought to trial, and when his father speaks on his behalf, the father is insulted by the king's champion.	Rodrigo decides to defend his father's honor against the champion.
4. Rodrigo is brought to trial before the king.	He decides to prove his innocence by taking the place of the dead champion in the battle for the city of Calaharra.
5. Rodrigo acts as the king's champion in all battles with the Moors.	He decides to dedicate his life to the honor of the throne of Spain.
6. The king dies, and his three children fight for the throne. The elder son is treacherously murdered under the daughter's orders.	Rodrigo forces the new king, the younger son, to swear publicly that he had nothing to do with the murder.
7. The people of Spain ask El Cid to be their leader.	He accepts the responsibility.
8. El Cid spends his life defending Spain. He is summoned by the king to come out of exile to defend Valencia from the Moors.	El Cid accepts the challenge.

Ordeal	*Heroic Reward*
He fights the Moors.	He wins the battle, earning the gratitude of the village.
He is branded a traitor to Spain for having released the enemy.	One of the released Moors names him "El Cid" in gratitude. "El Cid" means "A warrior with the wisdom to be judge and the courage to be merciful."
He fights the champion, his intended father-in-law; wins the battles but loses his bride.	His family honor is restored.
Rodrigo jousts for the honor of Spain.	He wins and, cleared of treason, is named the king's champion.
He suffers physically in battle and emotionally in a marriage in name only with Chimene.	As the years pass, he becomes the national hero of Spain.
Rodrigo is exiled.	Chimene's love is restored to him, and they become husband and wife.
He loses the normal life he could have led with Chimene.	He becomes the legendary hero of Spain.
El Cid loses his life in the final battle, although the battle is won as a result of his sacrifice.	The legendary hero becomes a myth as his dead body rides into battle at the head of his troops.

Epic action: (Top) The Oklahoma land rush from *Cimarron* and (Bottom) The entry of El Cid "the purest knight of all," into Valencia.

The Museum of Modern Art Film Stills Archive.

The implications of this plot lie in understanding the character of El Cid, who is Mann's last real hero, as the film itself is his last really great work. The Mann hero who evolved out of *film noir* through the westerns and into El Cid was initially a hero with a problem/secret who carried within himself the seeds of his own destruction because he was obsessive, unbalanced, or nearly psychotic. The link between hero and villain made this defect of the hero's clear, and the action of the films resolved his internal tension.

El Cid is not such a hero, but he is the logical culmination of the evolution of such a figure. Inside himself he carries not a *guilty* secret, but a *great* one—a manifest destiny. El Cid, "the purest knight of all," is the Mann hero raised to the loftiest heights. By beginning the story as an ordinary person and journeying toward his destiny, he represents all the Mann heroes rolled into one, purified and simplified, and set against an epic landscape.

Thus it becomes unnecessary to discuss *El Cid* in terms of the link to a villain, or a conflict with the community, or the resolution of psychotic tension. He is linked to his destiny, not to another character, except possibly to Chimene, his female counterpart.[3] He represents all conflicts, all mankind, and the father-son, hero-old man relationships are either dropped or merely touched on, since El Cid and his legend incorporate primary meaning. El Cid is the ultimate Mann hero. The man with a secret becomes the man with a destiny, and the depth of characterization and complexity of moral struggle of the earlier films are stripped down and channeled into the legendary story of his transformation.

El Cid incorporates and summarizes the characteristics of the heroes of both *film noir* and the westerns. Rodrigo Diaz de Bivar, an ordinary man, meets his destiny through an accident of fate, like the heroes of *film noir*. By fighting in a battle that he happened across, he receives a *label*—that of El Cid. By undergoing two trials of combat—killing the king's champion and jousting for the honor of Spain—he accepts the burden of his heroism, like the western heroes. Although "El Cid" has been only a label he acquired by accident, he earns the right to the label through two personal trials. The killing of the king's champion is undertaken because the champion has insulted Rodrigo's father. The fact that the champion is also his bride's father complicates the issue, but does not change the inevitability of the situation. The jousting for Spain is a voluntary act. Rodrigo offers to take up the cause because he has himself killed the champion. Therefore, it is his duty, as well as his honor, to prove his loyalty and purity in the eyes of his countrymen and of God.

During the years which follow, the label becomes meaningful not just to him (as it has through his first two ordeals), but also to all of Spain—and thus, by extension, to the audience. Through his years of heroism and service, he becomes El Cid. He is a national hero, but he is still a mortal hero. After his exile, however, the heroic title becomes a legendary one. By offering up his life for his country, the legend becomes myth, as he rides out after death to insure the winning of the battle.

El Cid opens with a familiar Mann device—a narration which sets the events to come in their proper time (A.D. 1080) and place— "This is Spain, half Christian, half Moor." The voice is not the voice from the Mann documentaries, but a voice for all ages—that of a storyteller, the right man to repeat the legend of El Cid.

The first sight of the man who is to become El Cid establishes him as the hero, not through the traditional use of the landscape associated with the westerns, but through a more suitable device for an epic film. He is preceded into the frame by the bloody tip of his sword, the blade moving across the wide space of the frame and dominating the body of a praying priest. With simple dignity, he sweeps a collection of enemy arrows from off a wooden cross, and lifts the cross to carry it back into the church. The hero takes up his burden, one he will not be able to put down even after death. The use of costume, decor, and a symbol associated with sacrifice to introduce the hero is appropriate to an epic film, where much of the depth and meaning is naturally dictated by such symbols. It has been the fate of the bridegroom Rodrigo Diaz to pass through this small village at the moment the Moors attacked it. He was there only because "I thought it was the shortest road to my bride." It was, instead, as the priest tells him, "the shortest road to your destiny."

From the beginning, Rodrigo shares with the heroes from Mann's *noir* films the inevitable burden of his fate. (His taking up the cross is an obvious visual symbol.) The sense of fate entrapping Rodrigo is furthered by the fact that the audience does not see the original battle with the Moors (at least not in the prints available for viewing today). The issue is already determined when the audience first meets Rodrigo. His decision is made, the two Moors are captured, and he is already involved in a situation beyond his control. The audience is placed in this same position. The viewer does not see the battle, but is involved in its aftermath, the predetermined victim of its meaning.

The first villain to be seen in the film is a traditional Mann villain in that he dominates his space, or landscape, with ease. Dressed totally in black, in sharp contrast to the colorful costumes of those he seeks to incite, a Moorish chieftain reaches out his hand across the frame as he speaks. "Burn your books . . . make warriors of your poets . . . the Prophet has commanded us to rule the world." His hand begins to look like a claw as it fills the wide-screen, moving forward in an almost three-dimensional effect. "First Spain—then the world." With his twisted hand outstretched, his demented words echoing in the minds of the viewer, and his dark-robed body ominous in the frame, he is a perfect image of madness. A freeze-frame holds him suspended for the viewer, so that this image can be retained throughout the film as the thing that menaces the hero.

The scene in which Rodrigo is first labeled "El Cid" takes place out of doors more against a landscape than in it. The characters are framed by a blue, blue sky. In the distance can be seen an extensive landscape, marked with barren trees, snow-tipped because of the winter season. Fluttering banners, colorful standards, and long lines of warriors mounted on their horses contribute to the look of an ancient tapestry come to life on the screen. Thus, the use of the landscape is less a direct alignment with characters than it is a setting for them—a setting which suggests the legendary status of El Cid.

The initial scene which introduces Rodrigo's bride, Chimene (Sophia Loren), furthers this sense of pageantry and tapestry. It takes place in a vast space within the castle, dominated by a skylight which allows a pool of warm yellow sunlight to fall into the center of the room. Below this sanctuary can be heard the angry shouts and quarrels of El Cid's trial for treason. The shock of these sounds reverberates and echoes upwards toward where El Cid is listening, awaiting Chimene. Across the wide space of the huge screen, he stands at frame left as she enters at frame right. Between them in the center is the pool of warm light. Each character is shown in intense close-up, looking toward the other. Slowly they move toward each other, with stately grace, their hands outstretched. A close-up of their hands touching in the light, while they each remain at the far edge of the screen in darkness, is followed by their loving embrace as they enter into the light. They move across space, to be joined in an exalted state, emerging from darkness and distance into light and love. This movement is the total story of their relationship in the film, beautifully realized in the first scene in which they are seen together. The angry sounds from below engulf them. The anger is outside their world, but penetrating it and changing their relationship within their private space.

Two major events begin the internal change of El Cid from an ordinary man into a hero . . . the fight with Chimene's father, and the joust for the honor of Spain. El Cid's father, once the King's Champion, speaks up in defense of his son's honor at the treason trial. The current Champion, Chimene's father, refuses to give him combat, insulting him by saying "I don't want to stain my sword with the blood of an old man." El Cid is forced to seek out Chimene's father to recover the family honor. As the two men talk, the editing presents them by cross-cutting. They are seen in matching medium shots, indicating they are equal in combat, but separate in purpose and attitude. El Cid crosses the large space between them, and they are seen in the frame together as El Cid begs:

CID:	I beg you. Two words are all I ask. Can't you just say "forgive me."?
CHAMPION:	I cannot.
CID, DRAWING HIS SWORD:	I will ask you.
CHAMPION:	I see that courage and honor are not dead. Go home. No one will blame you for not going against the King's Champion.
CID UNSHEATHS HIS SWORD:	Can a man live without honor?

As El Cid draws his sword, it cuts across the image of Chimene's father in the huge frame, slicing him in half visually. Before the fight begins, the tip of the sword is caught in the glow of the candles on the wall, and it seems to glow in the flames. The sword is illuminated, and transformed into a holy instrument, indicating the status of El Cid. The fight which follows is an intense matter of close-ups, punctuated by the hard, clanging sounds of their heavy swords.

Chimene proves herself the equal of El Cid when she accepts the burden of her own cross. She rejects her father's killer—as her father requested—even though he is the man she loves. Just as El Cid has asked whether a man can live without honor, Chimene says the same is true for a woman. She is heroine to his hero. When El Cid comes in to see her after the funeral, she is wearing black. They speak:

CHIMENE: You were prepared to kill him. You bought your honor with my sorrow.
CID: There was no other way. The man you chose to love could do only what I did.
CHIMENE: Did you think the woman you chose to love could do less?
CID: I told my love it had no right to live. But my love will not die.
CHIMENE: Kill it.
CID: You kill it. Tell me you don't love me.
CHIMENE: I cannot. Not yet. But I will make myself worthy of you, Rodrigo. I will learn to hate you.

El Cid and Chimene are seen in a gigantic room during this speech. The space seems too big for them, and throughout the film, until the final scenes, they are often placed inside gigantic rooms and spaces which seem too large. In fact, the largeness represents the space of history, and his legend. Their space IS too big, and does not allow them the privacy and intimacy they desire. They are small individuals caught up in a larger destiny. Loren and Heston are often linked together via matching intense close-ups, which suggests that their love binds them nevertheless, overcoming space and destiny, uniting them across history and legend, into love.

The joust is the traditional trial for a knight. In this case, El Cid undertakes the trial because he killed the King's Champion. "If I am guilty, God will direct a lance to my heart. If I am innocent, he will be my shield."

The jousting scene is set in the most tranquil of landscapes, with blooming trees and green grass. Since a joust is carried out strictly by the rules, the formal structure of the scene respects that integrity, establishing for the audience the exact space of the area via long shot. All the major characters are placed specifically and clearly in the space, as if they were chess pieces. The joust itself is played out with an established rhythm in which cuts are matched to sounds and strokes of the sword, and shots of the watching crowd are intercut

with the violence of the fight in a beautifully cadenced pattern. An
elaborate visual ballet is worked out that suggests a staged pageant
without sacrificing the excitement of the joust.

Much of the length of the film is necessarily given over to action
which establishes the increasing heroism of El Cid. Scenes in which
El Cid rides out amidst the Spanish landscape and is attacked by
Moors are photographed in a typical Mann format. The rocky landscape is presented so that the audience feels secure that it knows the
terrain well. Then a sudden redefinition through swish pan reveals
that the rocks harbor Moors in colorful garb. These scenes contribute to the sense of El Cid's earning the right to his title, just as his
painful relationship with Chimene establishes the price he must pay
for this heroism.

El Cid and Chimene marry only because he claims the right to
her by ancient custom in which a lord who deprives a lady of her
support must himself provide that support. (Since El Cid has killed
Chimene's father, he claims his right, and the king grants his wish.)
The marriage ceremony is interrupted by the intrusion of the people
of Spain from outside the large doors of the cathedral. As El Cid and
Chimene kneel for their vows, the huge cathedral doors swing open,
the sound of an ominous wind is heard, and the common people
pour in, both sound and image invading their space. It is a simple
but effective redefinition of a narrative situation in the tradition of
Anthony Mann. It also is a metaphor for the love and marriage of El
Cid and Chimene, whose relationship is constantly altered by
events outside themselves, events which concern the people of
Spain and are larger than their private feelings.

The couple's wedding night is one of the most emotional scenes of
the film. In terms of lighting and pace, it is more a funeral scene
than a wedding night, appropriate to the events which occur. At the
wedding-night supper in El Cid's chambers, he sits at one end of a
long table, and she sits at the other. They are separated physically in
space as they are separated by their political situation. Yet their love
is obvious, and they are linked for the viewer by intense close-ups
which deny the space between them just as their hearts wish to love
and deny the roles they must play to avenge their family honor.
They are united across space by their love in spite of themselves.
Yet it is still Chimene's fate to carry her cross. She must reject her
husband on his wedding night.

Chimene and El Cid are finally united through his suffering exile.

This sorrow cleanses them of their family responsibilities. It is in this sequence that the legend of El Cid emerges. As they seek shelter, the Christlike imagery that was established at the beginning of the film, when El Cid carries the cross, is reestablished. The two lovers meet beside three roadside crosses, and a leper offers El Cid water. As they join together and walk across the sparse Spanish landscape, Chimene rides a donkey, and El Cid walks beside her. The entire tone of the film makes a sudden shift to that sense of unreality and poetry that Mann could evoke when appropriate (as in the final battle of *Men in War*).

A small girl runs toward the couple. The sound of a wind is heard, not unlike that which interrupted their marriage ceremony. The little girl speaks, "Are you the one they call The Cid? . . . and you must be the beautiful Chimene . . . do you not hate him anymore? . . . my father says they will cut off our hands if we help you. . . my father says they have eyes everywhere . . . my father also says if you walk very slowly, it will soon be dark and no one will see you if you go into our barn."

The little girl's awed and haunting speech makes clear that the story of El Cid and Chimene has already become a legend to the common people. Up until this time, the story has been a personal story in which a man did brave deeds. After this, he is no longer an ordinary man, but a legendary figure.

El Cid and Chimene spend the night together in the barn. It is a typical medieval pastoral. Their happiness and laughter are the first the audience has seen in the film. They are together in a small private space, enclosed and sheltered from the world. The larger world is seen outside, through a small, open window. But here, in this quiet place, they are two normal human beings, unburdened by history and destiny. "We'll have a new life now," they say, pledging their love and devotion, but the sound of the familiar wind is heard outside their shelter.

As the lovers arise and plan to go forward to their new life, the camera tracks forward and they pull open the doors of the barn. Outside, an army awaits him. He is surrounded by the people of Spain, who await his leadership and who have gathered in the night to await his awakening. In terms of the viewing audience, it is the ultimate example of Mann's ability to redefine the narrative situation through compositions. The tender intimacy of the love scene just played by Chimene and El Cid has seemed to resolve for all time their separation by events larger than themselves. Their world inside the sheltering barn has seemed to be the entire world. The opening of the doors and the outward camera track that reveals the masses of warriors outside are physical shocks to a viewer.

As the people close in around him, El Cid protests, but they overcome him. Chimene begs them to let him alone, begs him not to accept. "You have no right to ask him. He has done enough." But he accepts, and she weeps. "Why? Why?" she asks him over and over again. "For Spain. . . . For Spain," he replies. He is seen riding at the head of their columns as the intermission occurs.

El Cid lives out his destiny as the legendary hero of Spain. He is, however, still seen as a human being by the audience. This is established by two major sub-plots: one in which the Moorish commander who originally labelled him El Cid becomes his devoted friend; and one in which Chimene and his children are taken prisoner by the King to influence El Cid's actions. Both these subplots are important in that they humanize El Cid, and remind the viewer that he began his ordeal as an ordinary man. In particular, the subplot involving his family supplies this definition.

Although he has planned to advance his troops without the King's permission—his first act of disloyalty to the Crown—he wants to abandon the plan and rescue his family. He rides in a circle inside a ring of his soldiers, crying out, "Am I not a man, too? May I not sometimes think of my wife? My children? What am I to do? What am I to do?" As he rides in a helpless circle, he remains surrounded by his obedient troops, trapped not only by what they symbolize, but also by their physical presence. The answers to his questions are clearly that he *cannot* be a man because he is a legend. He must act out his destiny, which will finally lift him out of the ordinary.

The final ordeal of the film elevates El Cid to the status of myth. The amassing of Moorish troops to attempt to take Valencia is the final big movement of the film. The Moors are dressed in black, their faces half-covered, and they advance in seemingly endless barbarian waves. The sounds of their drums establish them as a pagan, primitive force, an almost primeval enemy. In the first confrontation, El Cid is wounded. When he is taken inside and the battle is temporarily abandoned, it becomes clear he will not live until morning.

El Cid understands his responsibility. He has never stooped to desiring the throne for himself, and is, in fact, seen refusing the crown when it is offered to him after his first fight to enter Valencia. He knows he must not allow himself to heal from this wound, but must press on while he has the advantage. "You must not be frightened. I promise you, tomorrow morning I will ride with you." He tells Chimene that he *must* lead the attack tomorrow, because his men have made him their heart. When she weeps, he tells her, "You can't save my life. You must help me give it up."

As she was worthy of the burden placed upon her by her father's pledge, Chimene is also worthy of her husband's last burden. She promises to do what he asks of her. "I want you and my children to remember me riding with my king," he says. "Tomorrow. . . . " He dies.

In an incredible silence, the dead body of El Cid rides down from atop the fortress among his troops the next morning. Dressed in the purest white, with gray armor, and atop a white horse, he rides among his men, the only sound the clop, clopping of his horse's hooves. Chimene stands on the parapets with her two daughters. As the gates of Valencia swing open, El Cid rides out. As the sunlight catches his armor, he shines as if he had been touched by the hand of God. A magnificent burst of organ music swells up, and the narrator says, "And thus the Cid rode out of the gates of history and into legend."

The frightened Moors fall back at the sight of him, abandoning their battle. Victory for Spain is secure. Earlier, the villain said, "He is a man like other men. He will die, because I will kill him." And the villain is told, "He will never die." The ending of the film proves this visually, in one of the most powerful moments in any film.

The moment when the sunlight glints off El Cid's armor was a happy accident of location filmmaking. Mann described how it occurred:

It was around eleven o'clock in the morning. This white mist was all over the town. You could just see the outline of the walled city. And I yelled at Heston: "Look, I'll never capture this again. Put on the armor and ride with a white horse across the sands and across the ocean right across this scene." And in ten minutes we got it. I'd never have done it except that I saw it. It was there. *You see it.* For instance, the moment when El Cid came out strapped on his horse with his shining armor and his white horse, I was lying on the sand and looking up at the big arch and the mosque. I was looking up, and a rider passed. It wasn't even Heston. It was no one, just an extra. Well, he passed in his armor and as he came out of the shadow into the light his armor shone. I yelled to Bob Krasker [the cinematographer], "Look at it, that's what we want, that's God, that's the sun, we've got to get the sun on us." And we let him ride out, and by God that was how he shone and there was no spotlight or anything. It just happened to be the moment when the sun hit it and it was so white it was electrifying.[4]

Formally, *El Cid* holds no surprises for the Mann scholar. It reflects the patterns he has established from the beginning of his career. Scene after scene provides examples of his customary use of composition, his arhythmic editing, his definition/redefinition of space. The pace is stately, ritualistic, suitable to the material. The requirements of the epic film dictate that a larger meaning be placed upon decor and costume than in earlier films. The fluid, gracefully moving camera is more generously employed than in many earlier films, but that, too, suits the epic needs of the genre in which enormous sets are used. Initially, the landscape is treated largely as a background setting for events of epic scope. Since the Mann hero is always allied with the landscape, much of the background of the film is used to reflect, as Mann might say, "the hieratic" aspects of the story. As said earlier, the background is a tapestry, representing the legendary status of the hero and the overall pageantry of knights and their ladies. As El Cid lives out his destiny, the background shifts from being seen as a two-dimensional piece of tapestry into a world of depth and loneliness. As El Cid becomes the hero of Spain, his landscape seems to become all of Spain: vast and empty. He is seen wandering through enormous spaces which represent his loneliness and isolation in his role of hero. These barren spaces also represent his loveless life.

The major achievement of *El Cid* is in its ability to balance the intimate, human story of El Cid and Chimene against the larger historical context without sacrificing either portion. The entire narrative shifts with ease and grace from "close-up" (the personal story of Rodrigo) to "long shot" (the legend of El Cid). In a sense, the landscape of *El Cid*, to compare it to the western films, is that of history itself, or, in the larger context, that of legend or myth. The transformation of Rodrigo to El Cid, and the transformation of El Cid into a myth, is not done through dialogue. The audience is not

Epic landscapes: (Top) The scene of El Cid's jousting for the city of Calaharra and (Bottom) The magnificent set for the city of Rome in *Fall of the Roman Empire*.

told, it is shown. In this regard, *El Cid* is unique among films, and many seasoned viewers consider watching it to be almost akin to a religious experience. Because the human, intimate portion of El Cid's story is so well developed and believable, the audience accepts Rodrigo as a human being who actually *is* transformed into a legend. This gives the ending of the film its power. The sacrifice of Chimene's love is felt, and the greatness of the man who served his country has been demonstrated, not just on the epic level of battles and politics, but also on the smaller, more human level.

Most epic films fail because, although they provide spectacle, they lose the human story set against the spectacle. The triumph of *El Cid* is that the human story is preserved in the tapestry. Intimacy is achieved through editing and through the use of close-ups. No attempt was made, however, to "humanize" the dialogue to make the film seem more intimate.

One of the major difficulties of an epic film always seems to be, "How did they talk in ancient China?" In Samuel Goldwyn's *Adventures of Marco Polo*, Basil Rathbone sets out to prepare a banquet for his bride-to-be that will be more elaborate than anything previously seen in the Chinese court. "I want plenty of birds' nests in the soup," he cries out, and the audience inevitably laughs. This problem with dialogue is a no-win situation for the screenwriter and the director. If the film opts for simplicity and modernity, the critics point out that it was hardly likely anyone talked that way in those days. Audiences, too, feel endistanced and cheated, thinking they ought to have a few "thees" and "thous" for their money. On the other hand, attempting to recreate a sense of biblical or ancient conversation seems to be an even greater pitfall. It results in the "Oh, Moses, you adorable fool" syndrome which also sends audiences into gales of laughter.

El Cid is successful for many reasons, but one of its main achievements is in its having avoided the dialogue trap. Its script is simple, well written, and, in the tradition of Anthony Mann, stresses the pictorial value of the story over the political and moral.

Fall of the Roman Empire

Mann moved on to another epic, but he was not to repeat the success of *El Cid*. Unlike that film, *Fall of the Roman Empire* was not a critical and commercial success. Although it was among the top grossing films for 1963–64, its prohibitive production costs made it less profitable than its predecessor. Similarly, it is not as coherent artistically, despite many obvious assets, such as the beautiful opening sequence in which a wintry landscape represents the northern border of the Roman Empire in A.D. 180. A large fort is seen, dark against the sky. It appears to be a powerful and menacing force. Yet it also looks old and decayed. It thus is a perfect visual equivalent of Rome at that time, representing both the power and decadence of the Empire.

The camera explores the space surrounding the fort and moves inward. No sound is heard except the whistling of a harsh, cruel wind. As the camera moves, a torchlight is seen, red and hot against the cold gray of the predawn time. This light is then picked up by the rising sun as light dawns over the fort. As troops appear, arriving out of the barbarian forests, the two questions behind the film are established by a narrator's voice. "The greatest questions of history" are stated—how to account for Rome, and how to account for her fall.

Two visually powerful sequences in *Fall of the Roman Empire* take place early—the arrival of the foreign chieftains and a chariot race across the landscape. In the first, color and pageantry abound, establishing the almost unparalleled splendor of the costumes and sets. The chieftains, with their varying clothes, insignia, chariots, languages, and animals, are photographed with careful attention to details. The second sequence is a spectacular chariot race, obviously staged by Yakima Canutt, the great stuntman and second-unit director who directed the chariot races in *Ben Hur*. The race is the action high point of the film. The chariots fly off the road, down hills, across landscapes and past trees, water, and rocks.

Fall of the Roman Empire reflects Mann's thematic concerns. The familiar link between hero and villain is present. Stephen Boyd as Livius and Christopher Plummer as Commodus are boyhood friends. Boyd is blind to Plummer's faults, and loyally supports his ascendancy to the throne when the old emperor dies. Even though he knows it was the old man's wish that he himself be the next ruler, Boyd remains loyal to his friend when Plummer steps up to take the throne. Commodus is the traditional villain who sacrifices the good of the community (in this case, the Roman Empire) for selfish

reasons. Livius is linked in love and friendship to the old emperor
(Alec Guinness), in a typical father-son connection.

The link between hero and villain for the first time in a Mann film
causes a schism in the overall narrative focus. The audience is unable to ally with the hero. Unfortunately, this is partly the fault of
the actor playing the role, Stephen Boyd. Although he is handsome
and not without skill, he lacks the power and presence of Charlton
Heston. As a result, the film has no central dominant hero, one of
the basic requirements for the Mann story. Boyd is not present
during much of the running time of this long film, and the audience
is left adrift. (The rest of the cast is excellent, however. In smaller
supporting roles, Alec Guinness, James Mason, and Mel Ferrer
try to provide depth and coherence for roles that are not well
written.)

It is difficult, and almost meaningless, to point out coherent connections to earlier films, however, since *Fall of the Roman Empire*
suffers from an unfocused screenplay. This is particularly noticeable
in comparing it to *El Cid*. Relationships are not clearly drawn, and
motivations not always established.

In terms of style, *Fall of the Roman Empire* provides Mann an
opportunity to repeat many compositional and spatial relationships
he had explored previously in earlier, better films. The Mann
trademarks are all present: compositions to reflect relationships;
camera movements to reveal danger and redefine narrative situations; arhythmic editing patterns alternating from close-ups to long
shots. Troops ride through sunlit forests, exploring a dangerous
landscape in which the enemy awaits them. Swish pans rush a viewer's eye up to barbarians waiting in trees. Rocks rain down on hapless Romans. The first half of the film, which is about death, culmi-
nates in a funeral scene in which Mann's use of color—dark wines,
reds, coppers, and burnished gold shades—highlights the cold gray
gloom surrounding the fortress. His repeated use of softly falling
snow is a visual token of the impending death of the Empire. He is
in control formally of this vast film. Unfortunately, that control
seems more like a bag of repeated tricks than like one of the great
motion pictures he has made in the past.

The space inside the northern Roman fortress is cut and divided
by levels, stairs, and parapets, for example, in what appears to be a
massive expansion of the basic set-up for *The Last Frontier*. As

Loren and Boyd meet for the first time in the film, they are drawn across a vast space toward one another like Loren and Heston in *El Cid* (and Tina Louise and Aldo Ray in *God's Little Acre*). Alternating close-ups—first of him, then of her—grow in intensity as they move toward one another, speaking their love out loud for the first time, until they finally meet and kiss.

The problem for *Fall of the Roman Empire* is that, unlike *El Cid*, it loses its human focus against the big canvas of history. What might have been a great film becomes instead a good film. Its breadth and depth of space are beautiful, but when it opts for beauty of image it cannot match that beauty with plot and performance. The very size of the film swamps it.

The finale, however, works well. Like many other historical epics, *Fall of the Roman Empire* reflects the times in which it was made. It is not about the issues of the fall of the Roman Empire quite as much as it is about the issues of the 1960s. Thus, *Fall of the Roman Empire* speaks to Americans of 1963 by warning that an empire which has grown old begins to die if its people no longer believe in it. We must grow bigger—grow or die—says the film. "We have changed the world. Can we not change ourselves?"

This idea of death through lack of faith and decadence is well represented in the final moments. On a huge set built to represent the heart of the city of Rome, the final chaos is acted out. Amidst riotous music and flames, the people await the celebration that will dull their senses to their coming destruction by the barbarians. Boyd and Plummer fight to settle their lifelong rivalry in an arena created by the placement of soldiers' shields. This combat is photographed by alternating intense close-ups (to provide drama) and long shots (to provide a look at the total space). The switch from the small, dangerous place of the individual in the fight to a sight of the total area, sometimes from above and outside the shields in the total space of Rome, illustrates perfectly the larger historical dilemma.

When Boyd is offered the Empire, he refuses it and just walks away amidst the flames and chaos. A shout goes up, "Two million dinars for the throne of Rome!" This sound of bargaining slowly fades out as the narrator says, "This was the beginning of the fall of the Roman Empire. A great empire is not conquered from without, until it has destroyed itself from within."

The Heroes of Telemark

Mann's experience with his final epic film in many ways repeats the first. As *Cimarron* is sometimes mistakenly called a western, *Heroes of Telemark* is sometimes labeled a war film. Both films incorporate conventions of those two respective genres, but their large, sprawling stories mark them as epics. Mann's inability to unite the generic with the overall narrative line also unfortunately marks both films as failures.

"Anthony Mann's *Heroes of Telemark*," as the credits read, should have been a great film. It was based on a true-life incident which took place in German-occupied Norway during 1942. A group of Norwegian commandos broke into a factory to stop the German production of heavy water, thus slowing down Nazi research on the atom bomb. The film, an epic adventure, has moments of genuine tension but its smaller, personal stories were simply not as interesting as the events they were set against. Furthermore, its climactic high point came before it was half over.

The opening sequences are promising. At first, the cold Norwegian landscape is beautifully established in a guerrilla attack on Nazi tanks. This action is followed by a complicated shot which appears to be from inside a huge container of heavy water. Through its slow dripping, Nazis are observed demanding 10,000 pounds of heavy water from the Norwegian factory. As the question is asked—for what reason?—scenes of German firing squads executing Norwegian hostages intercut the answer.

These slow drops of the heavy water are used throughout the film to illustrate the narrative's race against time. Each drop falls like the ticking of the clock, and this "ticking" is a recurring formal motif. In addition, Mann utilizes most of his familiar stylistic devices—swish pans, elaborate compositions, etc. The cutting pattern, however, is somewhat at odds with his more classic films. The self-conscious jump cuts of the 1960s are in ample evidence. However, they do serve to illustrate the danger and potential treachery of the world the characters inhabit, and are not used gratuitously. The strength of the film lies in its visual use of the snowy landscape. Scenes of guerrilla fighters on skis, flying over snow under a blue sky, with darkening clouds threatening above, are stunning. An exciting chase takes place on skis, with the Nazis pursuing Kirk Douglas through the icy landscape.

At the center of the film is a sequence that is one of the best Mann ever put on film. Nine guerrillas start out on skis to knock out the heavy-water factory, with the camera following both their skiing and their on-foot descent down wooded mountain slopes. The soft, lush, wet snow has great beauty. Brilliantly photographed by Robert Krasker for unusual angles, the scenes involving dramatic mountain-climbing techniques are totally engrossing. As the men move toward the town, the only sound is that of their feet hitting the hard rocks as they descend down the mountains. As they disturb the landscape, giant sifts of snow fall from great heights. Tension is generated largely through this ominous and total silence. Not a single sound is heard on the track except those that would be natural to the events. Since the snow muffles most of that, there is practically no sound at all. The sound of a lock being forced cuts into the

Sophia Loren, Charlton Heston, and director Anthony Mann, on the set of El Cid (1961).

silence with the power to bring an audience out of their seats. After this long sequence, in which the guerrillas sneak up on the factory, destroy it, and depart, the film is finished. Unfortunately, it runs nearly another hour. Despite moments of excitement to follow, it never again reaches the same peak. *Heroes of Telemark* bogs down in its plot complications, particularly in a subplot involving scientist Kirk Douglas and his ex-wife.

In fairness, *Heroes of Telemark* is seldom seen today in its proper format. Prints that are available are 16mm., with faded color and scanned visuals. Nevertheless, it is not a coherent picture, and, considering its potential, it is a major disappointment from Mann.

Of the epic films directed by Mann, only *El Cid* was really successful. As the old studio system collapsed and filmmaking became an international business, Mann's films grew bigger and fewer and, unfortunately, not better. In a sense, he had pushed his private filmmaking journey to its own limits. After *Man of the West* and *El Cid*, where was he to go? This was particularly true in a shriveled market, which demanded a new, more self-conscious style of directing than Mann would ever stoop to. The end was near.

6

Two Majors: *Men in War* and *God's Little Acre*

ANTHONY MANN'S REPLY to the inevitable question, "What do you consider to be your best work?" was *"Winchester '73, El Cid, God's Little Acre, Men in War."*[1]

The first two are expected. *Winchester '73* was the film with which Mann achieved his first real success, and it began his long association with James Stewart. In it, he defined for himself the genre in which he would find his greatest artistic satisfaction. *El Cid* was, quite literally, his biggest film. It was not only commercially successful, but most critics agreed it was one of the few really satisfying epic films.

Men in War and *God's Little Acre,* however, are virtually unknown. Neither one was a box-office blockbuster, and both were greeted with general critical indifference. "Just another war picture" was the word for *Men in War,* and the usual "not as good as the book" or "just as terrible as the book" opinions greeted the Caldwell adaptation.

It might therefore seem surprising that Mann named these two pictures among his best work. However, both are prime examples of the Mann style, and neither is typical of its generic family. Made on relatively low budgets by Security Pictures, each succeeds both as entertainment and as art. Although neither one fits readily into the categories suggested by Mann's career, each is distinctly an Anthony Mann picture.

God's Little Acre (1958)

At first glance, nothing seems more unsuitable to Anthony Mann's sensibility than an adaptation of Erskine Caldwell's novel *God's Little Acre.* Caldwell's books were an amalgam of violence, sex, and humor, and of those three, only violence seemed appro-

priate for the Mann universe. Humor was always a secondary ele-
ment in any Mann film. As for sex, his films could and did portray
male-female relationships with depth and sensitivity, as he proved
with Dennis O'Keefe and Marsha Hunt in *Raw Deal*, James Stewart
and Janet Leigh in *The Naked Spur*, and James Stewart and June
Allyson in *Strategic Air Command* and *The Glenn Miller Story*. That
talent would reach its peak, as everything did with Mann, in the
Sophia Loren-Charlton Heston relationship in *El Cid*. However,
love scenes were never the central event in any Mann film, and sex
was used most effectively by him when it was linked to violence, as
in *Man of the West*. The steamy relationships and earthy humor of
God's Little Acre seem ill-suited to Mann.

However, *God's Little Acre*'s primary concern is with a father
figure, the character Ty-Ty played by Robert Ryan. Ty-Ty is involved in a deep emotional relationship with his landscape. For
years, he has been digging holes in his own property, searching for
his grandfather's gold. The one place he will not allow himself to dig
is the place he staked out as a tribute to his Almighty, the "God's
little acre" of the book's title.

Ty-Ty, the father figure digging up his landscape, is thus obviously a perfect choice to be a hero in an Anthony Mann film. Working from a complicated novelistic structure, Mann elected to stress
those aspects of the story which concern the father's relationship
with his landscape—and also with his sons and daughters. Ty-Ty
represents the force of life, as he embraces experience and talks folk
wisdom to his family. The opposite force is represented by his son,
Jim-Leslie (Lance Fuller). The two men are depicted in typical
Mann fashion through the physical worlds in which they live.
Ty-Ty's is a ramshackle house with an easy, undecorated interior,
set in a beautiful pastoral place. The house is full of love and
warmth, even though sexual tensions abound. Jim-Leslie's house,
on the other hand, contrasts violently with Ty-Ty's. The son's compulsively clean home with everything in its proper place is indica-
tive of his repressed, materialistic nature. The contrasts between
these homes demonstrate the lack of sympathy between the father
and son.

An emotional link exists between two female characters, Griselda
(Tina Louise) and Rosamund (Helen Westcott). Both women love
the same man, Will (Aldo Ray). Rosamund is Will's wife, but his
heart belongs to Griselda. The women are not overt rivals in the

film, but are instead involved in a common cause because of this
mutual love. Their concern and care for Will take precedence over
their petty jealousies. Thus, they represent a female variation on
Mann's idea of opposite characters linked by some common interest
or shared emotion.

The primitive quality of Aldo Ray as an actor suits the role of Will.
His desire to "pull the switch and light up the whole world" defines
his desire to make their small-town world active by starting the
closed-down cotton mill working again. Ryan, who is contrasted so
well with Ray in *Men in War*, seems less perfectly cast here. He was
more believable as an urban type (Nicholas Ray's *On Dangerous
Ground*) or a stark western hero (Andre DeToth's *Day of the Outlaw*) or even as a villain (Mann's *The Naked Spur*) than he is as a
lusty, rural southern patriarch.

God's Little Acre is a beautiful film to look at. Its opening image,
like so many in Mann's films, is a scene of great visual poetry. A
depth-of-field image clearly defines a figure in the distance, driving
a team of plow horses across a bridge, with the trees in the foreground perfectly reflected in the water under the bridge. As the
camera moves slowly to the right to reveal figures digging in the
earth, the dirt breaks loose and cascades down on the diggers. Once
again, it is the perfect statement of Mann's idea—a pastoral landscape erupts and attacks human beings.

God's Little Acre presents the depth-of-field and complex compositions of the *film noir* years brought out into the sunshine. Although major scenes take place at night, much of the film is photographed outdoors on location in the dazzling light of a southern
summer's day. The warmth and laziness of the Caldwell world is
captured in these sun-dappled images.

In keeping with the more joyous nature of the book, the camera
moves more freely in this film than in most Mann movies. The
moving camera explores space freely with a life of its own, rather
than just following action or one main character. The typical Mann
cutting pattern of arhythmic alteration between long shots (which
establish space and character's position in it) and intense close-ups
(that show individuals trapped inside their personal space) is present
and appropriate to a story of shifting passions.

One of the most beautiful scenes takes place when Aldo Ray and
Tina Louise meet outside the house on a dark summer night. The
sultriness of the night is well established by the music, as Ray comes

out onto the porch, unable to sleep. He watches Louise going to the pump for water, dressed only in her slip. The house, the back porch, and the area of the pump are presented in one image through a complicated composition, and a mobile camera tracks slowly through the space. The lighting illuminates Louise in the area of the kitchen, while Ray watches from the darkness, bare-chested and sweaty. Through the impact of editing which slowly cuts down and diminishes the space between them, they meet at the corner of the house, their hands grabbing for one another. They are seen as abstracted, headless bodies as they lose all reason and grope for one another, their physical needs dominating.

As she leans toward him and he embraces her, a slow dissolve occurs. The dissolve, which traditionally represents the slow passage of time in film, is used to stretch out the moment of their love, their one and only moment in the film. The desire for the moment has stretched out over the years through the agony of their longing and passion. Their past love, which has accumulated and grown, is laid down over the *now* of the image through the dissolve. They meet across both space and time, with the distance slowly broken down and dissolved as they embrace in a perfect illustration of Mann's control over form. In addition, the beauty of the photography, with Ray bare-chested and Louise's body wet from the water of the pump, provides a scene of great eloquence.

God's Little Acre was adapted for the screen partly to cater to the preoccupation with sex and explosive emotions of the audience of the 1950s. Many similar films were released at the end of the decade, *Baby Doll, East of Eden, Cat on a Hot Tin Roof, Rebel Without a Cause, Hot Spell,* and more. Several had southern settings and presented lower-class people in situations in which their emotions swept them up in a violent world. The middle-class audience apparently preferred to digest their passions as if they were something "those other people" had. The vicarious enjoyment of throwing off middle-class manners and correct behavior was best approached through a distanced setting, both geographically and socially.

Mann's presentation of *God's Little Acre* disappointed such audiences. He had far too much taste to indulge their shallow wants, and he was far too skilled a filmmaker to make a straight literary adaptation. The several plots and subplots of the book were woven by screenwriter Philip Yordan into a tightly coherent script, with Mann participating closely in the adaptation. Unlike many literary adaptations, the film does not seem to lurch from episode to episode in an attempt to recreate faithfully the book. Nor is it static or talky.

The eloquent images of *God's Little Acre* take the place of the words of the book. Instead of transferring all the novel's dialogue to the screen, Mann and Yordan stripped it down to something simpler, more pictorial, and found visual equivalents for the raw power Caldwell had put into the story. The settings—Ty-Ty's farm, Jim-Leslie's house, Will's house, and the tiny mill town itself—all speak volumes about the world the characters inhabit. Mann's experience in selecting real locations—both in his *film noir* and in his westerns—guided him to selecting actual townspeople and photographing a southern cotton mill with a poetic documentary sensibility.

The night scenes are beautifully photographed, harking back to the Alton-Mann collaborations of the late 1940s. The stark images of Pluto's truck driving out to Ty-Ty's farm, its headlights cutting a sharp path through the dark night, capture the Grapes-of-Wrath-like world of the protagonists.

The highpoint of the film, and its main success in terms of the adaptation, comes when Will sneaks into the closed mill at night, and, with Griselda's help, reactivates it. The sight of the long-unused machinery chugging slowly into life and action again is a visualization of the meaning of both film and book. The lights of the mill blaze forth in the dark night—one picture illustrating much more than 1,000 words.

Men in War (1957)

"Tell me the story of the foot soldier, and I will tell you the story of all wars." These words appear over the image at the beginning of *Men in War*, followed by a simple declaration: "Korea, September 6, 1950." The purpose of these time and place words does not lie in the old-fashioned device of locating the audience geographically and historically. Rather the purpose lies in providing the audience the last grasp it will have on reality and sanity. Although *Men in War* is shot on location in a real landscape, "Korea, September 6, 1950," is a door that opens to a house of horrors, and he who enters never again knows exactly where he is or why he's there. *Men in War* not only shows the death and destruction of war, but also the psychological horror of the foot soldier, the man at the lowest level of combat. These men, suggests the film, must fight—and fight again—and be destroyed for reasons which may or may not be clear or important.

Men in War is the story of a patrol led by Robert Ryan. At the beginning of the film, their entire division has fallen back in the great Korean retreat. The patrol is ordered to get themselves to "Hill 465" to rejoin their battalion. As the patrol wanders the earth amidst bombs and gunfire, dutifully following these orders and carrying out their daily assignments as if it all made perfect sense, the insanity behind a day-to-day life of combat is depicted in an orderly and realistic fashion. The men move forward, totally surrounded by the enemy, in a classic Mann narrative pattern. As they make their journey through the hostile landscape, they encounter a tough-minded sergeant (Aldo Ray) and his shell-shocked colonel (Robert Keith). Throughout the film, the patrol remains caught between disaster and death, but always moving onward.

As the film opens, a moving camera explores a place in which it is obvious a battle has just taken place. Moving past a wrecked jeep, through a landscape smoky with bombs and fire, the camera searches for humanity. A whispering voice is heard desperately repeating: "Red Dog 2 calling Sunrise 6, Red Dog 2 calling Sunrise 6." This careful exploration of a smoking hell establishes the isolation and chaos of war. Although the location is a natural setting, the moving camera explores it as if it were an artificial stage set. Objects seem to have been deliberately placed to *suggest* an aftermath of war, and yet they are real objects in a real setting. Thus Mann establishes his primary idea for *Men in War*. The space in which a war is fought *is* artificial. War is basically about space—the fight to occupy it, to win it, to dominate it. Thus all the space in which battles of the war occur becomes the *setting* of the war, or the artificial space selected to represent the terms of the conflict.

Men in War is presented as a story about men inside an arbitrary and dangerous space, the space of war. Their space is their story. *Men in War* is an extension of the idea Mann developed to its height in his western films carried over into a new genre, the war film. As the events of the story occur, their space shifts and their position in it is altered.

To accomplish his idea, Mann presents the characters in the film as disembodied faces in intense close-ups, looking drawn and anguished inside the frame. These close-ups sometimes present only abstractly the position of the actor—a gigantic ear beside a field telephone, or a huge mouth whispering a secret message. As the danger the men of the patrol face increases, their space decreases and seems to close in around them. They are seen cut off from one another as well as from any room in which to maneuver or escape. This use of intense close-ups increases just before moments of extreme violence which burst out into an action sequence. In matched form, the actors seem to burst out of their enclosing frames to gain space, and thus, momentarily, safety. Because the heroes are fighting to seize and occupy space, they are not equated with the landscape in *Men in War*.

Most of the time, the enemy is unseen. He is a ubiquitous enemy who owns the land, the trees, the flowers, the very air. "I can't get nothin' out of the air but Korean," complains the radio operator. The air the patrol breathes is included in the hostile landscape. It is a foreign space filled with and dominated by enemy sounds. From an image which appears to be nothing but range grass and tree branches, an enemy rifle emerges. What is established as ordinary landscape is redefined as a hidden nest of machine guns. The space before the viewer's eyes is revealed for the danger and treachery it contains.

The fatal error any one foot soldier can make is treating this landscape of war as if it were real and to be enjoyed, smelled, felt, touched, rested in. This is graphically illustrated by one of the most powerful scenes in the entire film, in which the black soldier James Edwards is assigned the task of rear guard for the patrol. It is a sunny day, and Edwards sits to rest beside the road. Behind him are the tall grass and the burgeoning wildflowers of the Korean hillsides. A typical Mann movement of the camera reveals to the audience that this is not a benign situation. The enemy is lurking in that same grass, those same wildflowers. Edwards smiles at the flowers, and picks field daisies to decorate his helmet. The camouflaged enemy—camouflaged, of course, with those same field daisies—creeps toward him, the tip of a bayonet in the same frame with Edwards in medium close-up illustrating how close they are to him physically. As he eases off his boots to cool his weary, hot feet, the enemy soldier fills the forward frame, rising in it and dominating it. His image covers that of the black soldier, blotting it out, as he literally erases him from the film. Edwards's death is illustrated by an abstract portion of his body—ironically, his foot without the boot—jerking violently as he dies.

The point is made that, during war, personal space is so limited for any one soldier that at any moment it can be seized by an alien. All any one soldier ever has is his personal space—thus the stressing of intense close-ups—but that, too, can be taken from him suddenly if he makes the mistake of relaxing and not realizing that the space around him, immediately outside his body, is full of peril.

After Edwards's death, a parallel scene in which the exact action nearly takes place further illustrates the point Mann is making. Aldo Ray sits in the same position by the side of the road as Edwards sat only moments before. Ray, however, does not decorate his hat with daisies, does not feel or enjoy the sunshine, does not relax. He sits wary and waiting, a half smile on his face. He *pretends* to trust the landscape, and thus lures the enemy out of it to kill him. "You don't have to see them to kill them," says Ray. The relationship of the patrol to their landscape reaches its peak in a long scene in which they are forced to march through a forest filled with land mines. Where they have previously been able to take refuge from danger by crawling on their bellies through the earth, they now learn that not even the earth is safe. Any movement, any contact they might have with land is potentially destructive.

When the patrol makes its last battle by attempting to take Hill 465, hand grenades roll down the hills toward them, exploding as they go, like the rocks and pebbles from *The Naked Spur*. Finally, the landscape overwhelms them and the patrol is killed.

Although *Men in War* is his only war film, it is one of Mann's most personal and typical works. It contains parallels to the basic pattern of his westerns in links between two men (the hero/villain relationship), a conflict between an individual and the community, and in the development of a father/son relationship.

Robert Ryan and Aldo Ray are the two linked characters who fulfill the hero and villain roles. Ryan is the hero, but Ray is not the traditional evil villain. However, he represents an undisciplined force in a situation that requires discipline, so his role is in direct conflict with that of the hero. He can thus be defined as the hero's opposite.

Ryan and Ray conflict throughout the film. They disagree on day-to-day procedures, but also in the larger context of the attitude to take toward the war. "You're not in my army, and I'm not in yours," Ray warns one of the patrol members. Ray is concerned with self-preservation. He is animalistic, and his closest parallel in the

western films would be Victor Mature in *The Last Frontier*. Like
Mature, he is not civilized, in that he places his personal safety
above all considerations. He, too, is attuned to the landscape, un-
threatened by its dangers because he understands them.

Ray is a perfect soldier. He trusts no one and nothing. He senses
danger like an animal, sniffing it, feeling it by instinct when it draws
near. "Someone's got the eye on me," he tells Ryan, feeling himself
watched by an enemy sniper. Ryan, on the other hand, is a civilized
man. He compulsively records the names of his dead in a little black
book, stringing their dog tags on a large safety pin he wears. He,
too, is a perfect soldier, but because civilization has taught him
bravery, honor, and methods by which to make war.

Through these two opposite heroes, Mann illustrates his traditional conflict of the individual and the community. Ray fights only
for himself and the one person he cares about, his shell-shocked
colonel. He guards the colonel with his life. In moments of extreme
danger, he literally covers the colonel with his own body as a protective shield. Ray feels the war is irrelevant. He has long since
realized it has no real meaning. For him, the only point to any day is
keeping his colonel alive.

Ryan fights for the group, his patrol. He leads his community of
loyal soldiers through the days, from place to place, assuming that
there is order somewhere and meaning somewhere if only they can
link up to it again. Like Ray, he wonders about the larger meaning
of what he does, but he makes sense out of the war by dedicating
himself to keeping his men alive. If they die, he seeks to make their
deaths meaningful—or real—by recording them in his black book.

Ironically, Ryan and Ray are trying to do the same thing. "All I'm
trying to do," says Ryan, "is keep one man alive." Ray is trying to do
that same thing by keeping his colonel alive. Ray will kill with blind
instinct, not waiting to be certain his victim is not on his own side.
"God help us if it takes your kind to win the war," says Ryan. Both
men see their duties as not to themselves, but to others, but they
are opposite sides of the same coin. Ryan watches over his group as
if they were a community united in war. Ray has run away from the
war, splitting himself apart from others, trying to save his one man
through isolation. They represent a perfect fusion of the individual
vs. community conflict from the western films.

Both Ryan and Ray survive. Eventually they are united in battle.
In the final conflict, they have only each other to try to save. As the

The Landscape of War. (Top) "It's you. It would be you." Robert Ryan and Aldo Ray, two survivors in *Men in War* (Bottom) Ryan (back to camera) confronts Robert Keith (left) and Aldo Ray (right) for possession of the jeep.

two men set out to take the hill together, a sense of total unreality permeates the film. In the first wave of the battle which has just passed, both of them appeared to have been knocked down—killed, even—yet they both rose again to carry on. In the aftermath of this fight, the two men confront each other. "It's you. It *would* be you," Ray says to Ryan. They confront each other in a cryptic and disjointed conversation.

RYAN:	"You want to kill somebody. Why don't you kill me?"
RAY:	"They can't hurt us anymore. . . . We're lucky. We're lucky. The two of us can take that hill."
RYAN:	"If you have to go, I'll go with you."

Thinking they are the only two men left alive, neither man now has any purpose left, either individual or community. As Ray says, "They can't hurt us anymore." By killing all those that were their charges, the enemy have, in fact, killed them, too. There is no reason now for the two men to do other than try to take the hill alone.

As they set out together, they seem unreal, ghostlike. Considering that the audience has watched them fall and rise again in the previous battle, there is a sense of their actually being dead. To the effect that their reasons for living have been killed, they *are* dead. The music, eerie and mysterious, reinforces this sensation.

Ryan and Ray advance on the final hill. They are no longer human beings, but part of the landscape of war. Thus, they are now equal to the enemy. During the final battle sequence, marked by the use of flame throwers creating patterns of intense light in the darkness, almost no other human beings are seen. Except for two brief shots of enemy soldiers manning the guns on the hill, there seems to be no one present in the battle but Ryan and Ray. Against the noise of the bombs, the sound of hideous screams, and the whooshing of the flame throwers, the two unreal heroes fight it out with the landscape.

The film also presents a parallel to the father-son relationship found in many of Mann's other works. Aldo Ray's first appearance in the movie is his desperate attempt to drive his shell-shocked colonel to safety. As the patrol moves out toward Hill 465, they take cover when they see a jeep coming toward them through an open field.

("What's up, Lieutenant?" asks one of the soldiers as they drop to the ground and observe the landscape through field glasses. "Indians?")

Ray careens in his jeep through the landscape, driving without reason or logic, across the roadless space. The forward movement of the small vehicle appears as an act of madness, as if it were propelled by demons. Irrational cuts are made, from long shots of the jeep, lurching through space, to intense close-ups of the watching patrol, and then to the driver of the jeep and his occupant. This sudden cutting from long shots into close-ups creates an atmosphere of tension and alienation.

Ray cares for his colonel as if the man were his father. Their relationship is reflected in a subplot involving the black soldier's mothering a coward in the patrol. Before the final battle in which the colonel is killed, Ray tells him, "We've had our share of action. . . . I miss hearing you call me son. You're the only man who ever called me that, as if you were my father." The colonel's final word—in fact, his only word in the entire film—is his dying word. "Son," he says to Ray, himself acknowledging their relationship. After the colonel's death, Ray is united with Ryan emotionally for the first time in the film. "The Colonel's dead," says Ray. "So are all my boys," replies Ryan. As the two men share a smoke, they realize what has happened. Ray has lost his father, and Ryan has lost his children. Now they need each other. "All you've got now is me," says Ryan to Ray, and Ray accepts the offer. As they move out to take the hill, Ray says, "Let's go . . . Colonel."

The possibility that the father/son relationship can be regenerated is not a basic part of the Mann canon. Usually, the father is good or bad, and the hero's relationship with him is one of working out the evil or avenging the good. In *Men in War*, the suggestion is made that, like everything else in the chaos of war, a relationship is what you say it is. When one father dies, he can be replaced with another if that other is willing, has a need himself for the relationship, and, above all, if the two individuals decide to define it that way.

Ray's relationship with his colonel (Robert Keith) is father/son, but the incapacitation of Keith suggests also that he is Ray's helpless child. In this way, he is as much Ray's boy as Ryan's patrol are his boys. When Ray and Keith are first stopped by Ryan's patrol, Keith is tied down into the jeep. When Ray is asked, "What's the matter with him?" he cryptically replies, "Nothing." The answer testifies both to his loyalty to the man and to his unwillingness to deal with reality about anything related to him. In all other matters, Ray is the soul of practicality. About the colonel, his father figure, he is irrational. This extends the basic idea of the film, which is that, in war, the irrational act may be rational, or vice versa. Ray's concern for Keith, his one act of humanity and kindness, appears crazy or sane, depending on how you want to look at it.

Throughout the film, Keith as the colonel sits in a nearly comatose state, looking straight ahead and neither speaking nor acknowledging words spoken to him. Ray continues speaking to him, however, as if their relationship were perfectly normal.

Keith comes alive only twice in the film. The first time occurs when he responds to Ryan's dilemma in trying to get his men through a mined forest. In begging Ray to help him, Ryan says, "I'm only one man. I need help. I can't help everyone. I can only get to four or five if something goes wrong. I need you." Hearing these words and recognizing the burden of leadership they represent, the colonel appears agitated, the first sign of real life he has shown. Ray understands that he is under orders to help Ryan.

When the loud noises of the big battle for Hill 465 begin, the colonel literally comes alive before the audience's eyes. It is as if he is a killing machine that is set in operation only by certain sounds. Slowly, the staring-eyed, tied-down, nearly dead man turns into a human being, alert, bristling with awareness and ready for battle. He unties his own hands and lights a cigarette, his dulled eyes now sparkling with perception. He moves out into battle at the side of Ray, and it is clear they are a team. As they bravely and efficiently begin to climb the hill, their past is effectively demonstrated for the audience. Prior to the action of the film, they have spent days, months, years, in such action. They understand all too well the requirements of war.

When the colonel is hit, he speaks his only word to Ray, "Son," as he hands him a fistful of Silver Stars he has been carrying on his person. His death unites Ray and Ryan, and those two men fight the final encounter together in the frame as equals. Their walk up the hill is a slow dance of death.

Men in War is not a traditional genre picture. There is a notable absence of the types usually associated with the war film—no intellectual with glasses who carries his books along, no innocent young boy who will be killed, no old veteran with a family back home.

None of these characters exists in *Men in War*. Similarly, the types of situations and dialogue patterns associated with the genre are not present. There are no reminiscences about Mom's apple pie or plans to retire on a little chicken farm back home. On the contrary, *Men in War* is a spare, purely personal film which defines the concept of war visually rather than making an attempt to propagandize or re-create the experience.

Men in War is based on a pattern of tension-and-release. The compositions and camera movements repeatedly reveal danger in the landscape in the typical Mann style. The audience seldom has a view of the larger landscape, but, like the soldiers themselves, is kept close in the immediate space of the conflict without knowing what—other than danger—is really out there. The film establishes a realistic sense of the ordinary man's war. He never has the big picture.

Long, tense waits occur between episodes of violence and danger. No narrative logic connects these episodes. Jump cuts are used frequently, dislocating the audience and the patrol across time and space as the war has dislocated them. This use of jump cuts to consciously enhance the sense of dislocation for both viewer and characters is three years ahead of Godard's *Breathless*. (Godard saw and admired *Men in War*.)

One of the reasons for Mann's success in his epic films was his ability to present simple, cryptic dialogue. Without intending to devalue the contributions of his script writers, it seems clear that this type of conversation appears from film to film despite different writers. *The Far Country*, *Men in War*, and *El Cid* all share a simplicity of script which can be interpreted at the symbolic level without losing narrative strength. Yet the three films were written by, respectively, Borden Chase, Philip Yordan, and Yordan and Frederic M. Frank. Certainly Mann's influence must have been felt.

In *Men in War*, the dialogue has an eerie quality. When Aldo Ray is stopped by Ryan's patrol, the two strong men engage in a battle over his jeep. Ray explains his need to continue his journey in the jeep: "I've got to get myself out of here. They're trying to kill me." When asked if he has become lost from his outfit, he replies, "I'm not lost. They're lost." Ryan describes the situation the patrol is in. "Regiment doesn't exist. Battalion doesn't exist. The U.S.A. doesn't exist. They don't *exist*. We're the only ones left to fight this war."

Men in War is considerably ahead of its time in presenting clearly a conflict between two soldiers who are ostensibly on the same side. This conflict is not one of personality or training or background, as such conflicts *had* appeared previously. It was one of basic attitude toward the war. Ryan is the dutiful soldier, involved in keeping himself and his men alive. There is no other issue. Unlike the films of World War II (and some other Korean War films), *Men in War* does not delineate a political issue. There *is* no political issue in this film's war. It is a game, a conflict over space. Ray sees the madness of the game, and feels the war is lost. Ryan sees both points as irrelevant—keeping going, keeping to the rules of the game, is his motivation. "You and the colonel took yourselves out of the war. You're expendable. Me and my men aren't," he tells Ray.

After they take the hill, Ryan says it was not worth it, since they did not save even one of his patrol. Suddenly, a man emerges from amidst the dead bodies. "Who are you?" asks Ryan, unable to believe that one of the men he presumed dead had, in fact, been left alive after all. They *have* saved one man, making the war worthwhile on the human scale, if not in its overall pattern of logic. The soldier emerges from the smoking hillside as a reason for fighting, an issue personified.

In one of the most stunning finales to any film, Ryan and Ray award the Silver Stars entrusted to Ray by the colonel before his death. As the names of the dead are read aloud from Ryan's black book, the Silver Stars are tossed out into the landscape, where they belong, where the war was fought, and where the dead bodies lie untended. In a war film by Anthony Mann, it is inevitable that the landscape will be the winner.

In an ironic voice, Ryan says, "Make a note of these awards." The eloquence of the gesture—tossing the coveted medals into the earth—illustrates the futility of war better than 400 speeches in the United Nations. A theme song swells up as the image fades down. "I'll remember men I knew . . . men in war," say the lyrics. Mann only made one war film, but it was all he needed. *Men in War* is not only a tribute to Mann's artistry, it is one of the greatest war films ever made.

The last Anthony Mann hero, attempting to make his final journey. Still trapped and
desperate inside a carefully composed frame. Laurence Harvey in *A Dandy in Aspic*.

7

Mann's Journey

ANTHONY MANN'S FILMS are about journeys undertaken by a hero in which he crosses a landscape and emerges with a new understanding of himself. Similarly, Mann's career is a journey he undertook in which he explored all the possibilities of cinema and emerged with a complete understanding of film. Because of the nature of commercial filmmaking, it is unusual for any career to have such a coherent, forward-march thrust to it. It makes Mann an ideal candidate for film study. Before his final, weak films, he seemed to understand himself as a great storyteller/myth-maker. Accordingly, his heroes became mythical, but they were never mythical like John Ford's. Where Ford responded to history, someone has said, Mann responded to archetype. His heroes are like the heroes of the old Greek myths. Although they undertake different tasks—and have different names and different faces—they all represent man himself. Thus, Mann's films will stand the test of time not only because they are great examples of a particular art form, but because they speak to the essential concerns of life. In Mann, form and content are beautifully wedded into entertainment that is also art.

Furs and flowers for the perfect epic heroine. Sophia Loren as Lucilla In Fall of the Roman Empire.

203

The Museum of Modern Art Film Stills Archive

Notes and References

Chapter One

1. Andrew Sarris, *The American Cinema, Directors and Directions, 1929–1968.* (New York, 1968), pp. 98–99.

2. The musicals were *Moonlight in Havana, Nobody's Darling, My Best Gal, Sing Your Way Home,* and *Bamboo Blonde.* The atmospheric thrillers were *Strangers in the Night, The Great Flamarion, Two O'Clock Courage,* and *Strange Impersonation. Dr. Broadway,* the first film, was an atmospheric thriller mixed with tough comedy.

3. Mann in an interview with J. H. Fenwick and Jonathon Green-Armytage, "Now You See It: Landscape and Anthony Mann," *Sight and Sound,* 34 (Autumn 1965), p. 186.

4. Jean-Claud Missiaen, "A Lesson in Cinema" etc., p. 48.

5. Ibid., p. 50.

Chapter Two

1. Jean-Claude Missiaen, "A Lesson in Cinema," *Cahiers du Cinema in English,* No. 12 (December 1967), p. 46.

2. A swish pan is a rapid panning shot, done at the highest possible speed. It was traditionally used as a transition device in Hollywood films, but Mann employed it for a specific emotional effect on the viewer as well as to reflect a sudden narrative shift.

3. Robert Smith, "Mann in the Dark," *Bright Lights,* 2,i (Fall 1976), pp. 11–12. Additional quotations from this article have been incorporated into the text.

Chapter Three

1. *Cahiers du Cinema in English, op. cit.*

2. *Film Noir's* roots have been identified as German expressionism, Hollywood Depression films, and French films of the 1930s.

3. Michael Stern, "Widescreen," *Bright Lights,* 2,i (Fall 1976), p. 28.

4. Don Miller, "The American B Film: A Fond Appreciation," *Focus on Film*, 1, V. (Winter 1970), p. 45.

Chapter Four

1. This film was *Border Incident*.
2. *Cahiers du Cinema in English*, No. 12 (December 1967), p. 46.
3. For purposes of this book, *Cimarron* is not counted as a western, but as an epic. See Chapter Five on epics.
4. Jean-Luc Godard, *Godard on Godard* (New York, 1972), p. 117.
5. Jim Kitses, *Horizons West* (Bloomington, Ind., 1970), p. 31.
6. Godard, p. 116.
7. *Cahiers du Cinema in English*, *op. cit.*
8. Steve Handzo, "Through the Devil's Doorway: The Early Westerns of Anthony Mann," *Bright Lights*, I (Summer 1976), p. 14.
9. *Cahiers du Cinema in English*, *op. cit.*
10. Godard, p. 119.
11. *Cahiers du Cinema in English*, *op. cit.* p. 48.
12. *Ibid.*, p. 46.
13. *Ibid.*
14. *Ibid.*
15. *Ibid.*, p. 48.
16. Godard, p. 117.

Chapter Five

1. The Glenn Ford character does not die broke in the oil fields, but nobly, fighting in World War I. It is much more his story than hers in the remake.
2. *Cahiers du Cinema in English*, *op. cit.*, p. 50.
3. There is a secondary male character, played by Raf Vallone, who figures largely in a subplot involving Chimene's attempts to kill Rodrigo to avenge her father's honor. Because he loves Chimene and wishes to marry her himself, this character helps her plot an ambush on Rodrigo, which is aborted. Later, he sees the nobility of El Cid and, with Chimene's blessing, joins her husband in his battles. It is the Vallone character who warns the Muslim villain that "El Cid will never die."
4. J. H. Fenwick and Jonathan Green-Armytage, "Now You See It: Landscape and Anthony Mann," *Sight and Sound*, 34 (Autumn 1965), pp. 187–88.

Chapter Six

1. *Cahiers du Cinema in English*, *op. cit.*, p. 50.

Selected Bibliography

ELLEY, DEREK. "The Film Composer—Miklos Rozsa, Part Two." *Films and Filming*, 23:ix (June 1977), 30–31. A fine interview with the famed film composer Miklos Rozsa, in which he discusses his work on *El Cid* in depth.

FENWICK, J. H., and GREEN-ARMYTAGE, JONATHAN. "Now You See It: Landscape and Anthony Mann." *Sight and Sound*, 34:iv (Autumn 1965), 186–89. A brief but informative interview with Mann, as well as a short critical analysis of his use of landscape. One of the first essays to identify Mann's use of the landscape and characters within it as a primary motif of his work.

GODARD, JEAN-LUC. *Godard on Godard.* New York: Viking Press, 1972. Translation and commentary by Tom Milne, pp. 116–20. An outstanding film critic as well as director, Godard wrote perceptive reviews of Mann's films which were a primary influence on this book.

HANDZO, STEPHEN. "Through the Devil's Doorway: The Early Westerns of Anthony Mann." *Bright Lights*, 1:iv (Summer 1976), 4–15. A thorough discussion of the thematic and stylistic characteristics of Mann's lesser known, early westerns, with a primary focus on *Devil's Doorway.*

KITSES, JIM. *Horizons West.* Bloomington: Indiana University Press, 1970, pp. 7–87. One of the first and most influential writings on Mann, Kitses's analysis identifies the recurrent themes of individual vs. community, the morally complex hero, and the dominance of the villain, as well as discussing his use of the landscape. His discussion also contains interesting comparisons to other *auteur* directors.

MANN, ANTHONY. "Empire Demolition." In *Hollywood Directors 1941–1976*, edited by Richard Koszarski. New York: Oxford University Press, 1977 (originally printed in *Films and Filming*, March 1964). While directing *Fall of the Roman Empire*, Mann wrote this thoughtful essay about how the past reflects the present, and how the factors which made Rome fall are present today. An intelligent short essay on his epic films and the practical problems they presented him, as well as some of the ideas behind the plots.

207

MILLER, DON. "The American B Film: A Fond Appreciation." *Focus on Film*, 1:v (Winter 1970), 31–48. A list of outstanding B films, including Mann's *Desperate*.

———. "Eagle-Lion: The Violent Years," *Focus on Film*, No. 31 (November 1978), 27–39. An excellent description of Eagle-Lion and its contribution to *film noir* and the American crime film, with particular focus on Mann, including his uncredited film *(He Walked by Night)* and his screenplay which he did not direct *(Follow Me Quietly)*.

MISSIAEN, JEAN-CLAUDE. "A Lesson in Cinema." *Cahiers du Cinema in English*, 12 (December 1967), 44–51. A perceptive interview with Mann about his work, followed by a nearly complete filmography.

MOVIETONE NEWS, Nos. 60–61 (Fall 1978). A special double issue devoted to Anthony Mann. It contains articles on *Devil's Doorway*, *The Far Country*, *Men in War*, *Raw Deal*, and *Reign of Terror*, and, most important, the first English translation by Lindsay Michimoto of an interview with Mann conducted by Charles Bitsch and Claude Chabrol that appeared in French in *Cahiers du Cinema* in 1957.

REID, H. "Mann and His Environment." *Films and Filming*, 8:iv (January 1962), 11–12. A short essay on Mann's work prior to the epic films of the last years.

SARRIS, ANDREW. *The American Cinema, Directors and Directions 1929–1968*. New York: Dutton, 1968, pp. 98–99. One of the most important books on the American cinema, in which Sarris states his auteurist theories and ranks Mann in his second level of importance, "The Far Side of Paradise," along with Ray, Sirk, Preminger, Vidor, and Walsh.

SMITH, ROBERT. "Mann in the Dark." *Bright Lights*, 1 (Fall 1976), 8–15. Detailed analysis of all of Mann's early, unknown films, written with feeling and depth by Smith, who has seen all of Mann's works and understands his development thoroughly.

STERN, MICHAEL. "Widescreen." *Bright Lights*, 2:i (Fall 1976), 26–31. Stern advances an interesting theory about the experimental use of widescreen by key American directors such as Mann, Preminger, Minnelli, and Ray. A perceptive discussion of Mann's use of wide-angle lenses in his *film noir* period as a forerunner to the compositional elements of the CinemaScope frame.

WICKING, CHRISTOPHER, and PATTISON, BARRIE. "Interview with Anthony Mann." *Screen*, 10:iv (July–October 1969), 32–54. Mann's last recorded interview, published in an influential British film magazine.

WRIGHT, WILL. *Sixguns and Society: A Structural Study of the Western*. Berkeley: University of California Press, 1975. A structuralist study of key Mann films, particularly those which were successful at the box office, such as *Winchester '73* and *The Naked Spur*.

Filmography

DR. BROADWAY (Paramount, 1942)
Producers: Sol C. Siegel, E. D. Leshin
Screenplay: Art Arthur, from a story by Borden Chase
Cinematographer: Theodor Sparkuhl
Sets: Hans Dreier, Earl Hedrick
Music: Irvin Talbot
Editor: Arthur Schmidt
Cast: MacDonald Carey (Dr. Timothy Kane), Jean Phillips (Connie Madigan), J. Carrol Naish (Jack Venner), Eduardo Ciannelli (Vic Telli), Richard Lane (Patrick Doyle), Joan Woodbury (Margie Dove), Warren Hymer (Maxie the Goat)
Running Time: 67 minutes
16mm. rental: Universal 16, 445 Park Avenue, New York, NY 10022
New York Premiere: June 24, 1942

MOONLIGHT IN HAVANA (Universal-International, 1942)
Producer: Bernard Burton
Screenplay: Oscar Brodney
Cinematographer: Charles van Enger
Sets: Jack Otterson
Music: Charles Previn
Editor: Russell Schoengarth
Choreography: Eddie Prinz
Cast: Allan Jones (Whizzer Norton), Jane Frazee (Gloria Jackson), William Frawley (Barney Crane), Marjorie Lord (Patsy Clark), Wade Boteler (Joe Clark), Don Terry (Daniels), Sergio Orta (Martinez), Hugh O'Connor (Charles), Gus Schilling, Jack Norton, Grace and Nicco, and Aaron Gonzalez's Orchestra
Running Time: 63 minutes
16mm. rental: Universal/16
Note: Nine of Mann's early B pictures did not enjoy first runs in Broad-

way theaters, but were introduced without fanfare as parts of double features at neighborhood houses during the years of World War II.

NOBODY'S DARLING (Republic, 1943)
Producer: Harry Grey (for Herbert J. Yates)
Screenwriter: Olive Cooper, from an idea by F. Hugh Herbert
Cinematographer: Jack Marta
Sets: Russell Kimball, Otto Siegel
Music: Walter Scharf
Editor: Ernest Nims
Choreography: Nick Castle, assisted by George Blair
Cast: Mary Lee (Janie Farnsworth), Louis Calhern (Curtis Farnsworth), Gladys George (Eve Hawthorne), Jackie Moran (Chuck Grant), Lee Patrick (Miss Pennington)
Running Time: 71 minutes
16mm. rental: Ivy Films, 165 West 46th Street, New York, NY 10036

MY BEST GAL (Republic, 1944)
Producers: Herbert J. Yates, Harry Grey
Screenplay: Olive Cooper and Earl Felton, from a story by Richard Brooks
Photography: Jack Marta
Sets: Russell Kimball, Gand Chittenden, Earl Woodin
Music: Morton Scott
Editor: Ralph Dixon
Choreography: Dave Gould
Costumes: Adele, assisted by Art Siteman
Cast: Jane Withers (Kitty O'Hara), Jimmy Lydon (Johnny McCloud), Frank Craven (Danny O'Hara), Fortunio Bonanova (Charlie), George Cleveland (Ralph Hodges), Franklin Pangborn (Mr. Porter)
Running Time: 67 minutes
16mm. rental: Ivy Films

STRANGERS IN THE NIGHT (Republic, 1944)
Producer: Rudolph E. Abel, for Herbert J. Yates
Screenplay: Bryant Ford and Paul Gangelin, from a story by Philip MacDonald
Photography: Reggie Lanning
Sets: Gand Chittenden, Perry Murdock
Music: Morton Scott, assisted by Joseph Dill
Editor: Arthur Roberts
Cast: William Terry (Marine Sergeant Johnny Meadows), Virginia Grey (Dr. Leslie Ross), Helene Thimig (Mrs. Hilda Blake), Edith Barrett (Ivy Miller), Anne O'Neal (Nurse Thompson), George E. Stone

Running Time: 56 minutes
16mm. rental: Ivy Films

THE GREAT FLAMARION (Republic, 1945)

Producer: William Lee Wilder
Screenplay: Heinz Herald, Richard Weil, Anne Wigton, inspired by a
    character in Vicki Baum's *Big Shot*, which appeared in *Collier's.*
Photography: James Spencer Brown, Jr.
Sets: F. Paul Sylos, Glenn P. Thompson
Music: Alexander Laszlo, David Chudnow, assisted by Raoul Pagel
Editor: John F. Link
Cast: Erich von Stroheim (The Great Flamarion), Mary Beth Hughes (Con-
    nie Wallace), Dan Duryea (Al Wallace), Lester Allen (Tony)
Running Time: 78 minutes
New York Premiere: January 14, 1945
16mm. rental: Ivy Films

TWO O'CLOCK COURAGE (RKO, 1945)

Producer: Ben Stoloff
Screenplay: Robert E. Kent, from the novel by Gelett Burgess, *Two in the
    Dark*
Photography: Jack MacKenzie
Sets: Albert S. D'Agostino, Lucius O. Croxton, Darrell Silvera, William
    Stevens
Music: Roy Webb
Editor: Philip Martin, Jr.
Dialogue: Gordon Kahn
Special Effects: Vernon L. Walker, assisted by Clem Beauchamp
Cast: Tom Conway (The Man), Ann Rutherford (Patty), Richard Lane
    (Haley), Lester Matthews (Mark Evans), Roland Drew (Maitland)
Running Time: 66 minutes
New York Premiere: April 13, 1945.

SING YOUR WAY HOME (RKO, 1945)

Producer: Bert Granet, for Sid Rogell
Screenplay: William Bowers, from a story by Edmund Joseph and Bart
    Lytton
Photography: Frank Redman
Sets: Albert S. D'Agostino, Al Herman, Darrell Silvera, Harley Miller
Music: Constantin Bakaleinikoff
Editor: Harry Marker
Dialogue Director: Leslie Urbach
Cast: Jack Haley (Steve), Marcy McGuire (Bridget), Glenn Vernon (Jimmy),

Anne Jeffreys (Kay), Donna Lee (Terry), Patti Brill (Dottie), Grady Sutton
Running Time: 72 minutes

STRANGE IMPERSONATION (Republic, 1946)
Producer: William Wilder
Screenplay: Mindret Lord, from a story by Anne Wigton and Louis Herman
Photography: Robert W. Pittack
Sets: Sydney Moore
Music: Anthony Laszlo, assisted by George Lopez
Editor: John F. Link
Prod. Manager: Bartlett A. Carre
Cast: Brenda Marshall (Nora Goodrich), William Gargan (Stephen Lindstrom), Hillary Brooke (Arline Cole), George Chandler (J. W. Rinse), Ruth Ford (Jane Karaski), H. B. Warner (Dr. Mansfield), Lyle Talbot (Inspector Mallory)
Running Time: 68 minutes
16mm. rental: Ivy Films

THE BAMBOO BLONDE (RKO, 1946)
Producer: Herman Schlom for Sid Rogell
Screenplay: Olive Cooper, Lawrence Kimble, from a story by Wayne Whittaker, *Chicago Lulu*
Photography: Frank Redman
Sets: Albert S. D'Agostino, Lucius O. Croxton, Darrell Silvera
Music: Constantin Bakaleinikoff
Editor: Les Milbrook
Choreography: Charles O'Curran
Special Effects: Vernon L. Walker
Cast: Frances Langford (Louise Anderson), Ralph Edwards (Eddie Clark), Jason Robards (American Officer), Russell Wade (Patrick Ransom, Jr.), Iris Adrian (Montana), Jane Greer (Eileen Sawyer), Glenn Vernon (Shorty Parker).
Running Time: 68 minutes
16mm. rental: Films, Inc.

DESPERATE (RKO-Radio, 1947)
Producer: Michel Kraike
Screenplay: Harry Essex, with additional dialogue by Martin Rackin, original story by Dorothy Atlas and Anthony Mann
Cinematographer: George E. Diskant
Art Director: Albert D'Agostino, Walter E. Keller
Music: Paul Sawtell
Editor: Marston Fay
Cast: Steve Brodie, Audrey Long, Raymond Burr, Douglas Fowley, Wil-

liam Challee, Jason Robards, Freddie Steele, Lee Frederick, Paul E. Burns, Ilka Gruning
Running Time: 72 minutes

RAILROADED (Producers Releasing Corporation, 1947)
Producer: Charles F. Reisner, for Ben Stoloff
Screenplay: John C. Higgins, from a story by Gertrude Walker
Photography: Guy Roe
Sets: Perry Smith, Armor Marlowe, Robert P. Fox
Music: Alvin Levin, Irving Friedman
Editor: Louis Sackin, Alfred de Gaetano
Special Effects: George J. Teague, assisted by Ridgeway Callow
Cast: Sheila Ryan (Rose Ryan), Hugh Beaumont (Mickey Ferguson), John Ireland (Duke Martin), Ed Kelly (Steve Ryan), Jane Randolph (Clara Calhoun), Keefe Brasselle (Cowie), Charles D. Brown (Captain McTaggart)
Running Time: 72 minutes

T-MEN (Eagle-Lion, 1947)
Producers: Aubrey Schenck and Turner Shelton, for Edward Small
Screenplay: John C. Higgins, Anthony Mann (uncredited) from a story by Virginia Kellogg
Photography: John Alton
Sets: Edward C. Jewell, Armor Marlowe
Music: Paul Sawtelle, Irving Friedman, assisted by Howard W. Koch
Editor: Fred Allen, Alfred de Gaetano
Costumes: Frances Ehren
Cast: Dennis O'Keefe (Dennis O'Brien), Mary Meade (Evangeline), Alfred Ryder (Anthony Gennaro), Wallace Ford (Schemer), June Lockhart (Mary Gennaro), Elmer Lincoln Irey (Himself)
Running Time: 92 minutes
New York Premiere: January 22, 1948
16mm. rental: Kit Parker Films, Carmel Valley, California 93924

RAW DEAL (Reliance Pictures-Eagle-Lion, 1947)
Producer: Edward Small
Screenplay: Leopold Atlas and John C. Higgins, from a story by Arnold B. Armstrong and Audrey Ashley, *Corkscrew Alley*
Photography: John Alton
Sets: Edward Hou, Armor Marlowe, Clarence Steensen
Music: Paul Sawtelle, Irving Friedman
Editor: Alfred de Gaetano
Special Effects: George J. Teague, Jack R. Rabin (Art) assisted by Ridgeway Callow
Production Manager: James T. Vaughn

Cast: Dennis O'Keefe (Joe Sullivan), Claire Trevor (Pat), Marsha Hunt (Ann Martin), John Ireland (Fantail), Raymond Burr (Ricky Coyle), Curt Conway (Spider), Chili Williams (Marcy)
Running Time: 78 minutes
New York Premiere: July 8, 1948
16mm. rental: Budget Films, 4590 Santa Monica Boulevard, Los Angeles, California 90029

REIGN OF TERROR (Walter Wanger-Eagle-Lion, 1949—original release title: **THE BLACK BOOK**)
Producer: William Cameron Menzies, for Walter Wanger
Asst. Producer: Edward Lasker
Screenplay: Philip Yordan, Aeneas MacKenzie
Photography: John Alton
Sets: Edward Hou, Armor Marlowe, Al Orenbach
Music: Sol Kaplan, Irving Friedman
Editor: Fred Allen
Special Effects: Jack R. Rabin and Roy W. Seabright, assisted by Ridgeway Callow
Production Manager: James T. Vaughn
Costumes: Jay Morley
Cast: Robert Cummings (Charles D'Aubigny), Arlene Dahl (Madelon), Richard Basehart (Robespierre), Richard Hart (Francois Barras), Arnold Moss (Fouche), Jess Barker (Saint Just), Norman Lloyd (Tallien), Charles McGraw (Sergt.), Beulah Bondi (Farm Wife)
Running Time: 89 minutes
New York Premiere: October 15, 1949 (then titled *The Black Book*)

BORDER INCIDENT (MGM, 1949)
Producer: Nicholas Nayfack
Screenplay: John C. Higgins, from a story by John C. Higgins and George Zuckerman
Photography: John Alton
Music: Andre Previn
Editor: Conrad A. Nervig
Art: Cedric Gibbons, Hans Peters, Edwin B. Willis, Ralph S. Hurst
Production Manager: William Kaplan
Cast: Ricardo Montalban (Pablo Rodriguez), George Murphy (Jack Bearnes), Howard DaSilva (Owen Parkson), James Mitchell (Juan Garcia), Arnold Moss (Zopilote), Alfonso Bedoya (Cuchillo), Teresa Celli (Maria), Charles McGraw (Jeff Amboy), Jose Torvay (Pocoloco), John Ridgely (Mr. Neley), Arthur Hunnicutt (Clayton Nordell), Sig Rumann (Hugo Wolfgang Ulrich), Otto Waldis (Fritz), Anthony Bart
Running Time: 92 minutes

New York Premiere: November 20, 1949
16mm. rental: Films, Inc.

SIDE STREET (MGM, 1949)
Producer: Sam Zimbalist
Screenplay: Sidney Boehm
Photography: Joseph Ruttenberg
Sets: Cedric Gibbons, Daniel B. Cathcart, Edwin B. Willis, Charles De-
    Crof
Music: Lennie Hayton
Editor: Conrad A. Nervig
Special Effects: A. Arnold Gillespie
Production Manager: Charles Hunt
Cast: Farley Granger (Joe Norson), Cathy O'Donnell (Ellen Norson), James
    Craig (Georgie Garsell), Paul Kelly (Captain Walter Anderson), Jean
    Hagen (Harriet Sinton), Paul Harvey (Emil Lorrison)
Running Time: 84 minutes
New York Premiere: March 23, 1950
16mm. rental: Films, Inc.

DEVIL'S DOORWAY (MGM, 1950)
Producer: Nicholas Nayfack
Screenplay: Guy Trosper
Photography: John Alton
Sets: Cedric Gibbons, Leonid Vasian, Edwin B. Willis, Alfred E. Spencer
Music: Daniele Amfitheatrof
Editor: Conrad A. Nervig
Special Effects: A. Arnold Gillespie, assisted by Reggie Callow
Costumes: Walter Plunkett
Production Manager: Jay Marchant
Cast: Robert Taylor (Lance Poole), Paula Raymond (Orrie Masters), Louis
    Calhern (Verne Coolan), Edgar Buchanan (Zeke Carmody), James
    Mitchell (Redrock), Spring Byington (Mrs. Masters), Bruce Cowling
    (Lieut. Grimes), Marshall Thompson (Rod MacDougall), Rhys Williams
    (Scottie MacDougall), James Millican (Ike Stapleton), Fritz Leiber (Mr.
    Poole), Harry Antrim (Dr. C.O. MacQuillan), Chief John Big Tree
    (Thundercloud)
Running Time: 84 minutes
New York Premiere: November 9, 1950
16mm. rental: Films, Inc.

THE FURIES (Paramount, 1950)
Producer: Hal B. Wallis
Assistant to Producer: Jack Saper

Screenplay: Charles Schnee, from a novel by Niven Busch inspired by Dostoyevsky's novel *The Idiot*
Photography: Victor Milner
Sets: Hans Dreier, Henry Bumstead, Sam Comer, Bertram Granger
Music: Franz Waxman
Editor: Archie Marshek
Special Effects: Gordon Jennings and Farciot Edouart, assisted by Chico Day
Costumes: Edith Head
Production Manager: C. K. Deland, Herbert Coleman
Cast: Barbara Stanwyck (Vance Jeffords), Wendell Corey (Rip Darrow), Walter Huston (T. C. Jeffords), Judith Anderson (Flo Burnett), Gilbert Roland (Juan Herrera), Thomas Gomez (El Tigre), Beulah Bondi (Mrs. Anaheim), Albert Dekker (Mr. Reynolds), John Bromfield (Clay Jeffords), Wallace Ford (Scotty Haislip), Blanche Yurka (Herrera's Mother)
Running Time: 109 minutes
New York Premiere: August 16, 1950
16mm. rental: Films, Inc.

WINCHESTER '73 (Universal-International, 1950)
Producer: Aaron Rosenberg
Screenplay: Borden Chase, Robert L. Richards, from a story by Stuart N. Lake
Photography: William Daniels
Sets: Nathan Juran, Bernard Herzbrun, Russell A. Gausman, A. Roland Fields
Music: Joseph Gershenson, assisted by Jesse Hibbs
Editor: Edward Curtiss
Costumes: Yvonne Wood
Production Manager: Dewey Starkey
Cast: James Stewart (Lin McAdam), Shelley Winters (Lola Manners), Dan Duryea (Waco Johnny Dean), Stephen McNally (Dutch Henry Brown), Millard Mitchell (High Spade), Charles Drake (Steve Miller), John McIntyre (Joe Lamont), Jay C. Flippen (Sergeant Wilkes), Rock Hudson (Young Bull), Will Geer (Wyatt Earp), Abner Biberman (Latigo Means), Anthony [Tony] Curtis (Doan)
Running Time: 92 minutes
New York Premiere: June 7, 1950
16mm. rental: Universal/16

THE TALL TARGET (MGM, 1951)
Producer: Richard Goldstone
Screenplay: George Worthing Yates, Art Cohn, Joseph Losey (uncredited), from a story by George Worthing Yates and Geoffrey Homes

Photography: Paul C. Vogel
Sets: Cedric Gibbons, Eddie Imazu, Edwin B. Willis, Ralph S. Hurst
Editor: Newell P. Kimlin
Special Effects: A. Arnold Gillespie and Warren Newcombe, assisted by
  Joel Freeman
Cast: Dick Powell (John Kennedy), Paula Raymond (Ginny Beaufort),
  Adolphe Menjou (Caleb Jeffers), Marshall Thompson (Lance Beaufort),
  Ruby Dee (Rachel), Richard Rober (Lieut. Coulter), Will Geer (Homer
  Crowley), Florence Bates (Mrs. Charlotte Alsop), Leslie Kimmell (Ab-
  raham Lincoln)
Running Time: 78 minutes
New York Premiere: September 27, 1951
16mm. rental: Films, Inc.
Note: The plot concerns an alleged attempt on Abraham Lincoln's life just
  before his inauguration as president. The action takes place aboard a night
  train from New York to Washington—a tour de force in limited space.

BEND OF THE RIVER (Universal-International, 1952)
Producer: Aaron Rosenberg
Screenplay: Borden Chase, from Bill Gulick's novel *The Bend of the Snake*
Photography: Irving Glassberg (Technicolor)
Sets: Bernard Herzbrun, Nathan Juran, Russell A. Gausman, Oliver Emert
Music: Hans J. Salter, assisted by John Sherwood, Marshall Green, Ronnie
  Rondell, Dick Moder
Editor: Russell Shoengarth
Costumes: Rosemary Odell
Production Manager: Lew Leary
Cast: James Stewart (Glyn McLintock), Arthur Kennedy (Emerson Cole),
  Julia Adams (Laura Baile), Rock Hudson (Troy Wilson), Lori Nelson
  (Margie Baile), Jay C. Flippen (Jeremy Baile), Chubby Johnson (Captain
  Mello), Howard Petrie (Tom Hendricks), Stepin Fetchit (Adam), Henry
  Morgan (Shorty), Frances Bavier (Mrs. Prentiss), Royal Dano (Long Tom)
Running Time: 91 minutes
New York Premiere: April 9, 1952
16mm. rental: Universal/16

THE NAKED SPUR (MGM, 1953)
Producer: William Wright
Screenplay: Sam Rolfe and Harold Jack Bloom
Photography: William Mellor (Technicolor)
Sets: Cedric Gibbons, Malcolm Browne, Edwin B. Willis
Music: Bronislau Kaper
Editor: George White

Special Effects: Warren Newcombe

Cast: James Stewart (Howard Kemp), Janet Leigh (Lena Patch), Robert Ryan (Ben Vandergroat), Ralph Meeker (Roy Anderson), Millard Mitchell (Jesse Tate)

Running Time: 94 minutes

New York Premiere: March 25, 1953

16mm. rental: Films, Inc.

THUNDER BAY (Universal-International, 1953)

Producer: Aaron Rosenberg

Screenplay: Gil Doud and John Michael Hayes, from a story by John Michael Hayes, inspired by an idea of George W. George and George F. Slavin

Photography: William Daniels (Technicolor)

Sets: Alexander Golitzen, Richard H. Reidel, Russell A. Gausman, Oliver Emert

Music: Frank Skinner, assisted by John Sherwood

Editor: Russell Schoengarth

Costumes: Rosemary Odell

Cast: James Stewart (Steve Martin), Joanne Dru (Stella Rigaud), Gilbert Roland (Teche Bossier), Dan Duryea (Johnny Gambi), Jay C. Flippen (Kermit MacDonald), Antonio Moreno (Dominique Rigaud)

Running Time: 103 minutes

New York Premiere: May 20, 1953

16mm. rental: Universal/16

THE GLENN MILLER STORY (Universal-International, 1954)

Producer: Aaron Rosenberg

Screenplay: Valentine Davies, Oscar Brodney

Photography: William Daniels (Technicolor)

Sets: Bernard Herzbrun, Alexander Golitzen, Russell A. Gausman, Julia Herron

Music: Joseph Gershenson, Henry Mancini

Editor: Russell Schoengarth

Costumes: Jay A. Morley, Jr.

Technical Cons.: Chummy MacGregor

Choreography: Kenny Williams

Cast: James Stewart (Glenn Miller), June Allyson (Helen Miller), Charles Drake (Don Haynes), George Tobias (Si Schribman), Henry Morgan (Chummy MacGregor), Kathleen Lockhart (Mrs. Miller), Barton Mac-Lane (Gen. "Hap" Arnold), Sig Rumann (Mr. Krantz), Irving Bacon (Mr. Miller); and, as themselves, Louis Armstrong, Gene Krupa, Frances Langford, Ben Pollack, The Modernaires, The Archie Savage Dancers,

Trummy Young (Trombone), Barney Bigard (Clarinet), Cozy Cole
(Drums), Arvell Shaw (Bass), Marty Napoleon (Piano)
Running Time: 116 minutes
New York Premiere: February 10, 1954
16mm. rental: Universal/16

Note: This is the most important and best of Mann's films not discussed in
detail in the text. The untimely death at the very end of World War II of
band leader Glenn Miller saddened a nation, and a musical biography based
on his life seemed an appropriate box-office bet during the big-band revival
of the 1950s. James Stewart, the all-American movie star, was an ideal
choice to play Glenn Miller, the all-American musician. For Mrs. Miller,
Mann cast June Allyson (who would also play Stewart's wife in *Strategic Air
Command* and *The Stratton Story*). The resulting film was not only a
box-office success, but it is one of the better musical biographies ever made.
Credit has to go to Anthony Mann.

The problem of the musical biography is how to integrate the numbers
into the plot line without the "and then I wrote" syndrome. *The Glenn
Miller Story* makes no attempt to hide this problem. It's almost as if the
script-writers decided to get it out in the open and let everyone see it for
what it was. Stewart telephones Allyson long-distance and gives his number
as Pennsylvania 6-five-thousand and later gives her a "string of pearls" (the
names of two of Miller's biggest hits). The film manages to trick the audience with this device, however, by constantly bringing on references to
little brown jugs and never delivering the famous Miller arrangement. This
teaser pays off effectively at the end, when Miller's final Christmas present
to his wife is played for her on the transatlantic radio after his death. Her
favorite song, "Little Brown Jug," which Miller has always refused to play
for her, fills the room in the classic Miller arrangement. Allyson's tear-
stained face slowly fades into the same fog that claimed Stewart's life in an
air crash. Prior to this, Mann wisely avoided a big scene in which Allyson
learns of Stewart's death. The emotion the audience will feel is thus not
wasted, but saved for the music of "Little Brown Jug" at the end.

For once, Anthony Mann had a chance to use the side of Stewart's per-
sona that most people associate with him—the nice-guy side. After directing Stewart as a series of near-psychopaths in the western films, he allowed
the charming, relaxed side to take front and center. The result is a
thoroughly likable characterization in which the audience really believes
Stewart *is* Miller. This sensation is heightened by the light, improvisational
quality to the scenes between Stewart and Allyson. The two stars are totally
believable as a couple in love.

Mann's direction is sure-handed. In a sense, the "landscape" of *The
Glenn Miller Story* is the music itself. Mann knew what to stress, and all his

stylistic touches go to support the main thesis of an ordinary guy who makes an extraordinary success. Although *The Glenn Miller Story* is not a typical Mann film, it would be impossible to define it as directed by anyone else.

THE FAR COUNTRY (Universal-International, 1955)
Producer: Aaron Rosenberg
Screenplay: Borden Chase, from the novel by Ernest Haycox
Photography: William Daniels (Technicolor)
Sets: Alexander Golitzen, Bernard Herzbrun, Russell A. Gausman, Oliver Emert
Music: Joseph Gershenson, assisted by John Sherwood, Ronnie Rondell, Terry Nelson
Editor: Russell Schoengarth
Costumes: Jay A. Morley, Jr.
Cast: James Stewart (Jeff Webster), Corinne Calvet (Renee Vallon), Walter Brennan (Ben Tatem), Ruth Roman (Ronda Castle), John McIntire (Mr. Gannon), Jay C. Flippen (Rube), Henry Morgan (Ketchum), Steve Brodie (Ives), Royal Dano (Luke), Gregg Barton (Rounds)
Running Time: 97 minutes
New York Premiere: February 13, 1955
16 mm. rental: Universal/ 16

STRATEGIC AIR COMMAND (Paramount, 1955)
Producer: Samuel J. Briskin
Screenplay: Valentine Davies, Beirne Lay, Jr., from a story by Beirne Lay, Jr.
Photography: William Daniels, Thomas Tutwiler (Aerial Phot.) (Technicolor-Vista-Vision)
Sets: Hal Pereira, Earl Hedrick, Sam Comer, Frank McElvy
Music: Victor Young
Editor: Eda Warren
Special Effects: Farciot Edouart, John P. Fulton, assisted by John Coonan
Costumes: Edith Head
Technical Consultant: Colonel O. S. Lassiter (U.S.A.F.)
Supervisor for Aerial Sequences: Paul Mantz
Cast: James Stewart (Robert "Dutch" Holland). June Allyson (Sally Holland), Frank Lovejoy (Gen. Ennis C. Hawkes), Barry Sullivan (Lieut. Col. Rocky Samford), Alex Nicol (Cap. Ike Knowland), James Millican (Major-Gen. "Rusty" Castle), Bruce Bennett (Col. Joe Espy), Jay C. Flippen (Tom Doyle), James Bell (Rev. Thorne), Rosemary DeCamp (Mrs. Thorne), Enos Slaughter, Stan Musial, Red Schoendienst, "Peanuts" Lowrey, Memo Luna (five ballplayers)
Running Time: 114 minutes

New York Premiere: April 20, 1955
16 mm. rental: Paramount

THE MAN FROM LARAMIE (Columbia, 1955)

Producer: William Goetz
Screenplay: Philip Yordan, Frank Burt, from a story by Thomas T. Flynn, which appeared in *Saturday Evening Post*
Photography: Charles Lang (Technicolor-CinemaScope)
Sets: Cary Odell, James Crowe
Music: George Duning, Morris Stoloff, assisted by William Holland
Editor: William Lyon
Cast: James Stewart (Will Lockhart), Arthur Kennedy (Vic Hansbro), Donald Crisp (Alec Waggoman), Cathy O'Donnell (Barbara Waggoman), Alex Nicol (Dave Waggoman), Aline MacMahon (Kate Cannaday), Wallace Ford (Charles O'Leary), Jack Elam (Chris Boldt), John War Eagle (Frank Darrah), James Millican (Tom Quigby), Gregg Barton (Fritz), Boyd Stockman (Spud Oxton), Frank DeKova (Padre)
Running Time: 104 minutes
New York Premiere: August 31, 1955
16 mm. rental: CinemaScope: Corinth Films, 410 East 62nd Street, New York, N.Y. 10021

THE LAST FRONTIER (Columbia, 1955)

Producer: William Fadiman
Screenplay: Philip Yordan, Russell S. Hughes, Ben Maddow (not credited), from Richard Emery Roberts's novel *The Gilded Rooster*
Photography: William Mellor (CinemaScope-Technicolor)
Sets: Robert Peterson, James Crowe
Music: Leigh Harline, Morris Stoloff, assisted by Sam Nelson
Editor: Al Clark
Cast: Victor Mature (Jed Cooper), Guy Madison (Capt. Glenn Riordan), Robert Preston (Col. Frank Marston), Anne Bancroft (Corinna Marston), James Whitmore (Gus Rideout), Russell Collins (Capt. Clarke), Peter Whitney (Sergt-Major Decker), Pat Hogan (Mungo), Manuel Donde (Red Cloud), Mickey Kuhn (Luke), Guy Williams (Lieut. Benton), William Calles (Spotted Elk)
Running Time: 98 minutes
New York Premiere: December 7, 1955
16 mm. rental: Corinth Films (in CinemaScope)

SERENADE (Warner Bros., 1956)

Producer: Henry Blanke
Screenplay: Ivan Goff, Ben Roberts, John Twist, from the novel with the same title by James M. Cain (1938)

Photography: J. Peverell Marley (WarnerColor)
Sets: Edward Carrere, William Wallace
Lyrics: "Serenade" and "My Destiny," by Nicholas Brodszky and Sammy
    Cahn; "Back to Sorrento," "La Daniz," "Ave Maria," and extracts from
    Tosca, *La Bohème*, *Otello*, *Turandot*, *Il Trovatore*, and *Fedora*
Editor: William Ziegler
Costumes: Howard Shoup, assisted by Charles Hansen, Dick Moder
Supervisor for Opera Sequences: Giacomo Spadoni
Musical Technical Consultant: Walter Ducloux
Cast: Mario Lanza (Damon Vincenti), Joan Fontaine (Kendall Hale), Sarita
    Montiel (Juana Montez), Vincent Price (Charles Winthrop), Joseph Calleia
    (Prof. Marcatello), Licia Albanese and Jean Fenn (singers), Antonio
    Triana (dancer)
Running Time: 121 minutes
New York Premiere: March 23, 1956

MEN IN WAR (Security Pictures, United Artists, 1957)
Producer: Sidney Harmon
Screenplay: Philip Yordan, Ben Maddow (not credited), from the story *Day
    Without End (Combat)* by Van Van Praag
Photography: Ernest Haller
Production Designer: Frank Sylos
Music: Elmer Bernstein
Lyrics: Alan Alch
Editor: Richard Meyer
Special Effects: Jack Erickson, Lee Zavitz, assisted by Leon Chooluck
Costumes: Norman Martien
Production Manager: Elmer Stock
Technical Supervisor: Irving Lerner
Cast: Robert Ryan (Lieut. Mark Benson), Aldo Ray (Sergt. Joseph (Mon-
    tana) Williamette), Robert Keith (Colonel), Philip Pine (Capt. Riordan),
    Vic Morrow (Zwickley), Nehemiah Persoff (Sergt. Nat Lewis), James
    Edwards (Serg. Killian), L. Q. Jones (Sam Davis), Adam Kennedy (Mas-
    low), Scott Marlowe (Meredith), Walter Kelley (Ackerman), Race Gentry
    (Haines), Robert Normand (Christensen), Anthony Ray (Penelli),
    Michael Miller (Lynch), Victor Sen-Yung (Korean sniper)
Running Time: 104 minutes
New York Premiere: March 19, 1957
16mm. rental: Kit Parker Films

THE TIN STAR (Paramount, 1957)
Producers: William Perlberg and George Seaton
Screenplay: Dudley Nichols, from a story by Barner Slater and Joel Kane
Photography: Loyal Griggs (Vista-Vision)

Sets: Hal Pereira, Joseph MacMillian Johnson, Sam Comer, Frank McElvy
Music: Elmer Bernstein, assisted by Michael Moone
Editor: Alma Macrorie
Costumes: Edith Head
Cast: Henry Fonda (Morgan Hickman), Anthony Perkins (Ben Owens), Betsy Palmer (Nora Mayfield), Michael Ray (Jim Mayfield), Neville Brand (Bart Bogardus), John McIntire (Dr. McCord), Mary Webster (Millie)
Running Time: 93 minutes
New York Premiere: October 23, 1957
16mm. rental: Paramount, 5451 Marathon Street, Hollywood, California 90038

GOD'S LITTLE ACRE (Security Pictures–United Artists, 1958)
Producer: Sidney Harmon
Screenplay: Philip Yordan, from the novel by Erskine Caldwell
Photography: Ernest Haller
Production Designer: John S. Poplin, Jr.
Music: Elmer Bernstein
Editor: Richard C. Meyer
Speical Effects: Jack Rabin, Louis DeWitt, assisted by Louis Brandt
Costumes: Sophia Stutz
Cast: Robert Ryan (Ty Ty Walden), Aldo Ray (Will Thompson), Tina Louise (Griselda), Buddy Hackett (Pluto Swint), Jack Lord (Buck Walden), Fay Spain (Darlin' Jill), Vic Morrow (Shaw Walden), Helen Westcott (Rosamund), Lance Fuller (Jim Leslie), Rex Ingram (Uncle Felix), Michael Landon (Dave Lawson), Russell Collins (Claude), Davis Roberts
Running Time: 110 minutes
New York Premiere: August 13, 1958
16mm. rental: Kit Parker Films

MAN OF THE WEST (United Artists–An Ashton Production, 1958)
Producer: Walter M. Mirisch
Screenplay: Reginald Rose, from William C. Brown's novel *The Border Jumpers*
Photography: Ernest Haller (DeLuxe Color–CinemaScope)
Sets: Hilyard Brown, Edward Boyle
Music: Leigh Harline
Editor: Richard Heermance
Special Effects: Jack Erickson, assisted by Richard Moder
Costumes: Yvonne Wood, Bert Henrikson
Cast: Gary Cooper (Link Jones), Julie London (Billie Ellis), Lee J. Cobb (Dock Tobin), Arthur O'Connell (Sam Beasley), Jack Lord (Coaley), John Dehner (Claude Tobin), Royal Dano (Trout)

Running Time: 100 minutes
New York Premiere: October 1, 1958
16mm. rental: United Artists, 729 Seventh Avenue, New York, NY 10019
  (in CinemaScope)

CIMARRON (MGM, 1960)
Producer: Edmund Grainger
Screenplay: Arnold Schulman, from the novel by Edna Ferber
Photography: Robert L. Surtees (CinemaScope-Metrocolor)
Sets: George W. Davis, Addison Hehr, Henry Grace, Hugh Hunt, Otto
  Siegel
Music: Franz Waxman, title song sung by the Robert Wagner Chorale
Lyrics: Paul Francis Webster, Franz Waxman
Editor: John Dunning
Special Effects: A. Arnold Gillespie, Lee LeBlanc, Robert R. Hoag, assisted
  by Ridgeway Callow
Costumes: Walter Plunkett
Cast: Glenn Ford (Yancey Cravet), Maria Schell (Sabra Cravet), Anne Bax-
  ter (Dixie), Arthur O'Connell (Tom Wyatt), Russ Tamblyn (The Kid),
  Mercedes McCambridge (Sarah Wyatt), Vic Morrow (Wes), Robert Keith
  (Sam Pegler), Charles McGraw (Bob Yountis), Harry Morgan (Jesse
  Rickey), David Opatoshu (Sol Levy), Aline MacMahon (Rita Pegler), Lili
  Darvas (Felicia Venable), Edgar Buchanan (Neal Hefner), Mary Wickes
  (Mrs. Hefner), Royal Dano (Ike Howes)
Running Time: 147 minutes
New York Premiere: February 16, 1961
16mm. rental: Films, Inc. (CinemaScope)

EL CID (Samuel Bronston Productions–Ear Films Productions–Allied
  Artists, 1961)
Second Unit Director: Yakima Canutt
Producers: Samuel Bronston, Michael Waszynski, Jaime Prades
Screenplay: Philip Yordan, Fredric M. Frank, Ben Barzman, Diego Fabbri,
  Basilio Franchina (the last three uncredited)
Photography: Robert Krasker, Manuel Berenguer (second unit) (Tech-
  nicolor–Super Technirama 70mm.)
Sets: Venerio Colasanti, John Moore
Music: Miklos Rozsa
Editor: Robert Lawrence
Special Effects: Alex Weldon, Jack Erickson, assisted by Luciano Sac-
  ripanti, Jose Maria Ochoa, Jose Lopez Rodero
Costumes: Gloria Mussetta (Dir.), Peruzzi, Ceratelli
Technical Consultant: Dr. Ramon Menendez Pidal
Arms: Garrido Freres (Toledo)

Cast: Charlton Heston (Rodrigo Diaz de Bivar, El Cid), Sophia Loren (Chimene), Raf Vallone (Count Ordonez), Genevieve Page (Urraca), John Fraser (King Alfonso), Gary Raymond (King Sancho), Herbert Lom (Ben Yussuf), Massimo Serato (Fanez), Hurd Hatfield (Count Arias), Douglas Wilmer (Moutamin), Frank Thring (Al Kadir), Ralph Truman (King Ferdinand), | Gerard Tichy (King Ramiro),' Andrew Cruikshank (Count Gormaz), Michael Hordern (Don Diego)

Running Time: 180 minutes

New York Premiere: December 14, 1961

16mm. rental: Audio Brandon, and others. Not available in Wide Screen.

THE FALL OF THE ROMAN EMPIRE (Samuel Bronston Productions, 1964)

Second Unit Directors: Andrew Marton, Yakima Canutt

Producers: Samuel Bronston, Michael Waszynski, Jaime Prades

Screenplay: Ben Barzman, Basilio Franchina, Philip Yordan

Photography: Robert Krasker, Cecilio Pantagua (second unit) (Technicolor–Ultra Panavision 70)

Sets: Venerio Colasanti, John Moore

Music: Dmitri Tiomkin

Editor: Robert Lawrence, Magdalena Paradell (Asst.)

Special Effects: Alex Weldon, assisted by Jose Lopez Rodero, Jose Maria Ochoa (second unit)

Costumes: Venerio Colasanti and John Moore (Sup.), Gloria Mussetta (Dir.), Ceratelli, Peruzzi

Historical Consultant: Will Durant

Frescoes: Maciek Piotrowski

Cast: Sophia Loren (Lucilla), Stephen Boyd (Livius), Alec Guinness (Marcus Aurelius), James Mason (Timonides), Christopher Plummer (Commodius), Anthony Quayle (Verulus), John Ireland (Ballomar), Mel Ferrer (Cleander), Omar Sharif (Sohamus), Eric Portman (Julianus), Douglas Wilmer (Niger), Peter Damon (Claudius)

Running Time: 185 minutes

New York Premiere: March 26, 1964

16mm. rental: Audio Brandon Films, ROA's, and others. Not available in Wide Screen except from UFSC.

THE HEROES OF TELEMARK (Benton Films–Rank and, in the U.S.A., Columbia, 1964–65)

Producer: S. Benjamin Fisz

Screenplay: Ivan Moffatt, Ben Barzman from *Skis Against the Atom,* by Knut Haukelid, *But for These Men,* by John Drummond, and certain episodes from Titus Vibe Muller and Jean Dreville's film *La Battaile de L'Eau Lourde* (1947)

Photography: Robert Krasker (Eastmancolor–Panavision 70)

Direction and Photography (Second Unit): Gil Waxholt

Sets: Tony Masters, Jack Maxsted, John Hoesli, Bob Cartwright, Ted Clements

Music: Malcolm Arnold

Editor: Bert Bates, Timothy Gee, Lindsay Hume (asst.)

Special Effects: John Fulton (phot.), Rom Ballanger, Syd Pearson, assisted by Derek Cracknell, Christopher Stamp, Jonathan Benson, Michael Douglas

Costumes: Elsa Fennell, Gloria Barnes (asst.)

Cast: Kirk Douglas (Dr. Rolf Pedersen), Richard Harris (Knut Straud), Ulla Jacobson (Anna), Michael Redgrave (Anna's Uncle), David Weston (Arne), Anton Diffring (Major Frick), Eric Porter (Terboven), Mervyn Johns (Colonel Wilkinson), Jennifer Hilary (Sigrid), Roy Dotrice (Jensen, the Mysterious Stranger)

Running Time: 131 minutes

New York Premiere: March 9, 1965

16mm. rental: Audio Brandon and others. Not available in Wide Screen.

A DANDY IN ASPIC (Columbia, 1968)

Screenplay: Derek Marlowe, from his novel

Photography: Christopher Challis (Panavision-Technicolor)

Music: Quincy Jones, ("If You Want Love" sung by Shirley Horne)

Cast: Laurence Harvey (Alexander Eberlin), Tom Courtenay (Gatiss), Mia Farrow (Caroline), Lionel Stander (Sobakevich)

16mm. rental: Select Films, 115 West 31st Street, New York, NY 10001. Not available in Wide Screen.

NOTE: Projects which Mann wrote or worked on, but did not put his name to are not included in this Filmography. These include *Follow Me Quietly* (which he co-authored but did not direct), *Quo Vadis, Night Passage, Spartacus,* and, most importantly, *He Walked By Night. He Walked By Night* was a 1948 Eagle-Lion production with Richard Basehart and Scott Brady which was largely directed by Mann, but signed by Alfred Werker. The special issue of *Movietone News* on Anthony Mann (see Selected Bibliography) contains my article on this film, attributing its style to Mann, and can be referred to for details. Mann is also rumored to have directed an unreleased episode for *It's A Big Country,* and was planning various projects at his death (such as a version of King Lear set in the old West, with John Wayne).

Index